T0000903

More Praise for
Floppy
Tales of a Genetic Freak of Na
at the End of the World

Graybeal's sharp wit and keen attention to details makes reading *Floppy* an intimate journey across the Canadian landscape to the Pacific Northwest and into a queer body with Ehlers-Danlos syndrome, a condition that wreaks havoc on connective tissue. An exemplar on how to DIY a beautiful life, despite having a body insistent on falling down and coming apart. It's both a tale of self-care and a call for change in a healthcare system that has historically gaslit people with chronic illnesses.
—Rebecca Fish Ewan, author of *By the Forces of Gravity* and *Doodling for Writers*

In a spiral through time, Graybeal knits a wise, generous story of resilience and beyond. It's about alignment and aligning—with the body, with every body. It's also a story about connection and connectivity and a larger ideal of care. With a hard won and ever-present sense of humor, this is a powerful story with a cure for the ableism that ails us all.
—Jenny Forrester, author of *Narrow River, Wide Sky* and *Soft-Hearted Stories*

Alyssa Graybeal is a genius. This coming-of-age memoir with its sick queer perspective will remind you that sensitivity is a strength. Her voice is refreshingly honest like a great weird friend; you can trust her to tell the truth even when it's painful.
—Ariel Gore, author of *We Were Witches* and *The Wayward Writer*

Graybeal, a self-labeled "genetic freak" who was diagnosed as a child with Ehlers-Danlos syndrome, pulls us into the landscape of her "floppy" body with precision and grace. Brimming with queer love, cats, and the awkwardness of being human, *Floppy* is a roadmap for how we must learn to fight for the truth of our experiences, and how we can love the broken, beautiful body-homes we all live in.

—Laraine Herring, author of *A Constellation of Ghosts*

Graybeal performs the remarkable literary feat of narrating complex childhood experiences of embodied uncertainty and suffering in a voice that is sincere—but never precious—and critical—but not jaded. For people with EDS and their loved ones, this book is a rare blessing, the first of its kind to address not the "how-tos" of living with this condition but the emotional landscape it creates. The importance of this writing for the future of this community cannot be overstated.

—Megan Moodie, Associate Professor of Anthropology, UC Santa Cruz

Floppy is an unflinching yet charmingly written memoir of one person's negotiations with love and body, family and geography, the internal and the external. I very much enjoyed it.

—Michelle Tea, author of *Against Memoir* and *Knocking Myself Up*

FLOPPY

TALES OF A GENETIC FREAK OF NATURE

AT THE END OF THE WORLD

a disjointed memoir

Alyssa Graybeal

2020
Red Hen Press
Nonfiction
Award

Red Hen Press | *Pasadena, CA*

Book design by Mark E. Cull

Library of Congress Cataloging-in-Publication Data

Names: Graybeal, Alyssa, 1982– author.
Title: Floppy : tales of a genetic freak of nature at the end of the world
   : a disjointed memoir / Alyssa Graybeal.
Description: First edition. | Pasadena, CA: Red Hen Press, [2023]
Identifiers: LCCN 2022049428 (print) | LCCN 2022049429 (ebook) | ISBN
   9781636280974 (paperback) | ISBN 9781636280981 (ebook)
Subjects: LCSH: Graybeal, Alyssa, 1982– | Graybeal, Alyssa, 1982—Health.
   | Ehlers-Danlos syndrome—Patients—United States—Biography. |
   Ehlers-Danlos syndrome—Popular works.
Classification: LCC RC580.E35 G73 2023 (print) | LCC RC580.E35 (ebook) |
   DDC 616.7/7—dc23/eng/20221202
LC record available at https://lccn.loc.gov/2022049428
LC ebook record available at https://lccn.loc.gov/2022049429

The National Endowment for the Arts, the Los Angeles County Arts Commission, the Ahmanson Foundation, the Dwight Stuart Youth Fund, the Max Factor Family Foundation, the Pasadena Tournament of Roses Foundation, the Pasadena Arts & Culture Commission and the City of Pasadena Cultural Affairs Division, the City of Los Angeles Department of Cultural Affairs, the Audrey & Sydney Irmas Charitable Foundation, the Kinder Morgan Foundation, the Meta & George Rosenberg Foundation, the Allergan Foundation, the Riordan Foundation, Amazon Literary Partnership, and the Mara W. Breech Foundation partially support Red Hen Press.

First Edition
Published by Red Hen Press
www.redhen.org

For my fellow zebras

AUTHOR'S NOTE

This is a work of creative nonfiction. The events described in this book are true, but I reconstructed details and conversations from my memories of them. Thank you to my real-life friends and family members, whose memories of the events described may be different than my own. Some identities and locations have been changed or are composites to protect privacy. Some timelines have been condensed or expanded for readability.

CONTENTS

PART I

The Shins of Shame   3
How to Dress for Montreal Winter   11
Wilting Flower Girl   20

PART II

Framed   25
Little Miss Perfect   37
Puppeteers   41
The Sugar Situation   51
Biker Chick Wedding   56
Trust Me   61
Halfway Hot Springs   69
Lucky Fall   79
Saving Ida   83
Pitchers and Belly-Itchers   87
DIY or Die   94
Spinning a Tale of Chest Pain   106
Sockie Baby   113
Hurricane Earl   118
Eye-Masked Outlaws   129
On a Mission   132
Kudos   137
Denial Bonfire   140
The Power of Now   145
Fractal   152
Swearing to the Queen   156

PART III
Genetic Freak of Nature   165
Revolving Soul Mates   173
Girls Who Wear Glasses   176
Fold Bathtub   180
Sibling Rivalry   185
Untangling   187
Waiting for the Bus in Lyon   199
The Marfan Specialist   205
Waiting for Godot   207
The Lavender Menace   216
Escape Babies   223
Reality Check   229
Unfair   239
Cauliflower Fractal   243
Beachcomber   246

Afterword   250

Acknowledgments   256

FLOPPY

LIST OF MEDICAL ACRONYMS

EDS: Ehlers-Danlos syndrome. A connective tissue disorder that affects collagen; comes in various flavors.

MCAS: Mast cell activation syndrome. An immune response that releases an overabundance of mast cell mediators into the bloodstream; allergies to everything.

ME/CFS: Myalgic encephalomyelitis/chronic fatigue syndrome; linked to mitochondrial dysfunction.

POTS: Postural orthostatic tachycardia syndrome. A type of dysautonomia that messes with blood pressure and heart rate upon standing.

Part I

THE SHINS OF SHAME

My neon green scrunchie flew out of my unkempt ponytail and landed three steps below me. I'd fallen again. My ankle twisted and knee bent, aligning my shin to knock on the edge of the treads as I slid down the polished stairs. When I closed my eyes, adult voices echoed in my head. *Be more careful, Alyssa.*

Then my own voice of frustration. *I am!*

I'd caught my weight on the banister, so my wrist stabbed too. I held it close to my chest as I sat there, running my fingers over the bumpy friendship bracelet I'd knotted myself. I held my breath and pulled up my pant leg to inspect my shin, bracing myself for exposed flesh and pooling blood. But my shin hadn't split open, only grown purple with a fast bruise.

Exhale. No stitches required.

My scrunchie glowed bright against the dark wood, rippling in my vision like glow-in-the-dark seaweed at the bottom of the ocean.

Out the transom windows on either side of the front door, the dogwood tree in the front yard bloomed pink. I wouldn't need to call my mom at work to have her take me to the emergency room. After school, I'd latch-keyed myself into the gray house with black shutters that didn't close, one block outside the old city limits of Vancouver, Washington. It was a suburban street—no sidewalks, big yards—but not a subdivision. The houses didn't match, and towering evergreens shaded the asphalt. Red rhododendrons as tall as the house sent gnarled shadows onto the living room carpet in the afternoon. In the backyard, if the wind blew just right, the smell of rotten eggs wafted down the Columbia River from the Camas paper mill. Planes flew so low on their descent into the Portland airport across the river they rattled the house.

Falling *on* the stairs beat falling *down* the stairs, which was what usually happened. The sound of my single thud reminded me of all the other times I'd actually fallen down every tread like a bag of disconnected bowling balls. By ten, I'd made half a dozen trips to emergency rooms for little black stitches on my shins, losing count after 329.

With no one in the house but me, my little brother at a friend's house, I didn't have to pick myself up off those stairs as fast as possible to prove that I wasn't too much, wasn't too sensitive, hardly felt any pain at all. Alone, I had the privacy to hurt. My wrist stabbed; my shin bloomed with a dark ache; my twisted ankle burned. I'd just been going downstairs to make myself an Eggo.

My lucky calico cat, Lucky, paused to sniff my errant scrunchie on her way up the stairs to rub against my knees. She followed me to the school bus stop in the mornings. I'd wanted the other kids to see how, even though I didn't talk much, animals gathered around me like a magnet. But stealthy Lucky; when the school bus squeaked up and flipped out its stop signs, only I knew she watched from her perch in the rhododendrons across the street.

I pet Lucky and calmed my adrenaline rush.

I was okay. No stitches required. But why me?

⸻

My hands didn't split open as easily as my shins, but my palms wrinkled like sheets of printer paper crumpled into tight balls and reopened, even more wrinkly than those of my great-grandmother. I worried that the rest of my skin would follow, possibly sooner rather than later, making me look a hundred years old before I even got to be a teenager.

⸻

I mean, I knew why me. My clumsiness was genetic.

I'd recently been examined by a room full of doctors who confirmed what I already knew: Something was seriously wrong with me. Something so wrong that even though my parents had been divorced since I was eight, they'd both accompanied me to the appointment. I'd never been in such a crowded exam room. A half dozen silent doctors in white coats formed a semicircle behind the one who asked questions.

He pulled at my skin, pushed my fingers backward, and analyzed the angles at which my knees bent, all to tell me that my fragility had a name, Ehlers-Danlos syndrome (EDS), a rare genetic collagen disorder. Turns out I wasn't just double-jointed. I had something even weirder. EDS affected more than joints and ligaments. I also had stretchy arteries that could split open, and bones and organs constructed from wobbly building blocks.

I felt crinkling hot to be stared at by all of those doctors in white coats, but the validation of their murmuring doctor talk also brought relief. Aside from my scars and densely wrinkled palms, I looked healthy to most people. Up until now, emergency room doctors hadn't quite understood why relatively small mishaps led to such serious injuries. So even though their doctor talk was mostly gibberish, I understood the gist: It was no longer my fault that I fell so often or that I had so many scars. It was genetic. I might even have a valid excuse to be tired and aching and needing to sit down way more often than other kids. Maybe I wasn't too difficult after all, with this doctor-given explanation for my falls and sensitivities.

And maybe they could fix me?

The paper on the exam room table stuck to my legs as I sat there in the paper gown, my shins exposed. The thin, crinkly scars caught the light, and I swung my legs to kick off my nervous embarrassed energy.

"Characteristic scarring," the doctor said to the others. Those behind him scratched notes on clipboards.

I tried to make light of the scars. "I've had 329 stitches," I said, proud like I might win a contest. I faked the pride though. I hated it when other kids asked about my scars, or even looked at them.

"That's a lot of stitches," he said with a quick smile before continuing the exam.

After they finished staring at me and taking notes about what they saw, the doctors talked to my parents for a very long time. They talked about when I was a baby, two months premature and having spent a full month in an incubator before they could take me home. I already knew that. I'd weighed three pounds, two ounces and had a tube coming out of my head. But my mom also described how, when I started walking, I'd walked on my ankles instead of my feet.

"We took her to a clinic in Seattle," Mom said, "and they said she'd probably grow out of it."

I'd never heard that story and couldn't picture it. Had my feet pointed in or out? I wanted to ask, but the conversation had moved on to my mom's family, many of whom had another connective tissue disorder, Marfan syndrome. A researcher in another state was studying my family's novel mutation, so they wanted to do genetic testing for my mom and brother, as well as for me. From what I understood, everyone on my mom's side who had Marfan syndrome was extra tall and thin, and they had to be careful so their hearts didn't explode. But the doctors in that room didn't think I had it. I wasn't tall, and I definitely wasn't thin, so I didn't match the Marfanoid body type. Based on the clinical exam of a dozen doctor eyes, I had EDS, a condition caused by different genes entirely.

"There's no cure," he said to my parents. "It's a degenerative condition, and treatment is mostly preventative."

The paper gown didn't protect me from the cold of the drafty room, and I looked down at my hands to see that they'd already made their chameleon shift to purple.

"The next step is to run genetic testing to rule out Marfan syndrome and also to confirm which type of EDS she has," the doctor continued. "We'll go from there."

I expected to see them again, that team of doctors in white coats.

"Be careful," he said to me, giving me a pat on the head before leading the others out the door.

Not long before my diagnosis, I had complained of fatigue to my pediatrician.

"Do you feel like you can't keep up with other kids?" he'd asked, scratching his gray-and-white beard.

I shrugged. That was one way to put it. I mean, I was a fast runner and great at sports, but it all hurt. I preferred curling up with a book. I loved naps and hot baths.

He proceeded to lecture me about healthy snacks. Apples and carrots. I'd gained weight, but I already knew about healthy foods, and I already ate them. Did he think I was stupid? I felt so offended that I stopped listening to gaze at a poster on the wall about vaccines. Three skinny kids with blond hair. My body had hurt before I'd gained weight too, and it seemed unreal that a doctor who was supposed to be helping me had missed the point entirely.

"You'll have more energy if you lose some weight," he finished, brisk and sure of himself as he wheeled back on his padded stool.

I nodded, my face still hot. So even before I slipped into that pediatric genetics clinic, I'd already begun losing trust in doctors. They could sew me up, but that was about it.

⸺⌇⌇⸺

My skin felt softer than other people's, the difference between a dry newspaper and one that's been sitting in a puddle in the driveway. If you rub too hard, it peels away right under your finger, tearing in a jagged line without a sound. Once torn, my skin pulled back onto itself like a curled flap. Doctors had to stretch it taut like elastic before sewing it back together.

⸺⌇⌇⸺

My most recent trip to the emergency room for stitches had been after an incident with a milk basket in fourth grade. I'd gashed my shin on the way out the door of the classroom to recess, where I had planned to win at tetherball.

"Are you okay, Alyssa?" Mrs. Lewis asked as I stood back up.

I nodded and righted the milk basket, then fled down the ramp of the portable. But before I reached the playground, I saw blood pouring through my tights and all the way down to my flat slip-on shoes that I'd recently been yelled at for wearing because, according to my dad, they had no ankle support. The week before, he'd crouched down and slapped his palm on grocery store tiles. "Do you want your feet to be flat like this when you grow up? Huh, do you?"

I'd shaken my head, embarrassed to be yelled at in the grocery store for wearing pretty shoes. My feet were already flat.

7

I tried to return to the classroom, ready to re-answer Mrs. Lewis's question. Actually, I wasn't quite okay. But she'd left and locked the door, so I limped to the front office where the secretary laid me down on the narrow cot in the health room, and a teacher I didn't know held a bandage firmly against my leg and waited for my mom to arrive. The stranger teacher's compression on my shin hurt, and I didn't feel like answering her questions about my favorite subjects.

Art and writing.

"Are you always so quiet?"

I nodded, my throat too itchy to speak. I wanted her to go away and let me curl up into a ball in peace. I fidgeted underneath the school blanket, and Mrs. Lewis saw me on the cot as she passed through on her way out of the teacher's lounge. "Alyssa! I thought you said you were okay."

"Well, I thought I was, but when I looked down . . ." I shrugged.

"She's bleeding a lot," the stranger teacher said.

Mrs. Lewis frowned, and I sensed her hurt feelings. I thought she'd have been pleased by my toughness, that I hadn't made a big deal about an injury even when blood poured all the way down to my slip-on shoes. Were there times when I should actually say that I hurt when I was hurting?

⎯⎯∿∿⎯⎯

The doctors described the translucent scars on my shins as like cigarette paper, which didn't make sense because they weren't white but variegated browns and pinks. The thin scar tissue folded into itself like pleats when I pinched it.

⎯⎯∿∿⎯⎯

I slumped on that slippery staircase at my mom's house for a long while, scratching Lucky behind the ears and disinclined to move. Other kids could manage walking without tears and bruises and lectures. They could manage stairs without sprains and trips to the emergency room. They yelled and ran around the playground at recess as if gravity posed no risk at all.

I ached for their obliviousness.

In that moment, I had what glowed like a neon revelation about how I might stop being so difficult: The only way to not hurt myself was to move slowly every second. What if I walked in slow motion like trying to run in the shallow end of a swimming pool? I could focus all of my attention on my purple Converse shoes, monitoring every step, watching for signs of betrayal. This idea resonated in my head like I'd been struck by the truth, as if I'd stumbled upon mindfulness as the answer well before I'd ever heard the word. I'd never fall again if all I ever focused on was my very next step.

And then my heartache redoubled at the impossibility of such caution. I knew from experience that self-protection required toughness, a numbing of all the places that hurt. I liked getting lost in my head. If I was extra sensitive every second, it would be all pain all the time. I wasn't trying to be difficult. I just wanted to be myself and not get hurt. Possible or impossible, to reconcile my fragile body and eager brain?

I told myself to wrap up my pity party before anyone saw me, so I straightened my mismatched slouchy socks—one hot pink, one orange— and scooched down the rest of the stairs, grabbing my neon green scrunchie on the way. I made myself that Eggo and took it to the living room, where I settled in front of the TV.

Lying on the carpet with a blanket over the heating vent, I watched a documentary on PBS about the Maya prediction of the end of the world. The screen flashed black and red, images of fire and chaos. The narrator's deep voice sounded like the guy from *Unsolved Mysteries*, asking question after question. Were the Maya right? Will the world really end on December 22, 2012?

I did the math.

The year I would turn thirty.

When the show ended, I brushed the Eggo crumbs off the blanket and snuck back up the treacherous hardwood stairs to do the only thing that could soothe my whole aching body at once, running myself an extra hot bath and soaking until my fingers wrinkled and the water cooled. In the tub, my limbs floated free of the relentless weight-bearing pressure of the world.

My fragility would increase as I got older, but maybe that didn't matter if the world would end the year I turned thirty. Maybe I could scrape by with only bruises and stitches until then. I sunk my head to let the hot water shiver my ears. It muffled and contained every sound, augmenting only my own heartbeat. I'd be okay after all. The apocalypse would get me before I degenerated. Lucky sat silent on the edge of the tub, standing guard with eyes closed.

My first bout of existential despair came early. I wanted to wear all black to school that year so everyone could see I was a deep thinker with awareness of the end times, but most of my clothes had big pink flowers on them and my allowance wouldn't cover a more sophisticated wardrobe.

It would be decades before I'd see sensitivity as a strength instead of a liability.

HOW TO DRESS FOR MONTREAL WINTER

My first autumn-turned-winter in Montreal, I lived in a basement studio apartment on avenue Laval, a twenty-five-minute walk east of McGill campus. It had wood-paneled walls, a built-in desk and bookshelf, and a window seat that looked out at boot level onto the patchwork of maple leaves plastering the sidewalk. I hung olive green curtains and watched the foot traffic in front of the row houses with spiraling black staircases.

I loved that apartment.

It was my second year at McGill but my first winter. The previous winter semester, I'd stayed home to grieve the death of my six-year-old half-sister, Elizabeth. So even though I wasn't totally new to the city, I'd yet to experience the eyelash-freezing cold the city was known for.

The first extracurricular activity I'd joined the year before was a student-run crisis line, where I spent five-hour shifts in a hidden room, accessed by alley and key code, with one other volunteer at a time. Pre-smartphones, students called Nightline with questions about anything from the mundane to the existential. Pizza delivery numbers, STD info, panic attacks. The walls were covered with poster board that listed phone numbers in Sharpie, large enough to be read from anywhere in the room. It turned out that spending hours locked in a room with one other person was my ideal friend-making setup. We had time to move beyond small talk, but we also had phone calls and course readings to break up any conversational pressure.

I met Daniel during one shift, a wiry linguistics major from Massachusetts who was learning Irish in his spare time. He made me laugh and had one more semester before he graduated. During another shift, I met Hope, a smartly dressed linguistics major in my own year. Hope had spent her childhood in Ontario. While both Daniel and Hope had grown up knowing the cold, they had different opinions on the coming Montreal winter.

Daniel: "It's really not that bad."

Hope: "You think this is cold? You just wait."

Hope's dire warning seemed more realistic. Even before winter had fully arrived, I had to talk strength into myself before leaving my warm apartment. As the last leaves fell from the maple trees, I already dressed in my every West Coast defense: corduroy pants, a thick cotton sweater, and a velvet blazer. I even wore the thin acrylic gloves I'd bought at the dollar store.

"How did you end up here, all the way from Portland?" Hope had asked the first time I'd met her.

I shrugged. "In high school I spent a year in France as an exchange student, so I wanted to go where they spoke French." My standard answer for how I'd landed in Quebec, at an anglophone university in the middle of a French-speaking city.

"It's a different French though, eh?"

Hope was right. My first week in Montreal had been shocking because, after considering myself fluent—at least in the speech patterns of late-nineties Lyonnais sixteen-year-olds—I could barely understand the Quebecois accent, a.k.a Laurentian French, with its vowel shifts and unfamiliar slang. It took years for my brain to adjust to the new dialect. Almost all of my new friends were English-speaking.

On my walk to school, I took a right at carré Saint-Louis onto the cobble-stoned pedestrian section of rue Prince Arthur, where restaurant tables spread into the street. I passed Café Campus, the music venue where students lined up for hours on weekends. And by "students," I don't mean me. Standing around in a crowd made me lightheaded, not that I ever gave that excuse. I just said I thought the music was lame.

When I invested my energy into a late night, it was often for a games night at Daniel's place in Pointe-Saint-Charles, where he and his room-mates hosted Nightline parties. At least there I could sit on a couch while I drank past my bedtime. Hope knew my best party trick, the one I pulled out to disprove her theory about its physical impossibility. "Alyssa can lick her elbow!" she shouted whenever a party lulled. On the spot,

I'd lick my elbow in a circle of drunken weird looks. It hurt my shoulder to stretch it from its socket, but it's not like I was turning myself into a permanent pretzel like a sideshow freak. Just a few little elbow licks.

The closer I got to campus—passing the falafel place where you could sit and study for hours, and Lola Rosa, the vegetarian café with the wall-sized portrait of Frida Kahlo—the more student commuters streamed along the sidewalk carrying bestickered travel mugs. By mid-autumn almost everyone wore a knit toque, Canadian for beanie. The wind from the Saint Lawrence River, which surrounded the island of Montreal on all sides, gave a sharp blast, reminding me to buy one for myself. When I caught a glimpse of my gait in the door of a *dépanneur*, corner store, it threw me off. I rarely saw my body move from that angle, with twisting hips and toes pointing inward. My book-filled green canvas messenger bag gave me a limp. Newly self-conscious, I paused along the sidewalk to switch the bag from one shoulder to the other, and I wondered if my gait would look less weird if I wore a skirt.

A little early for Syntax I, I sat down and shed my coat in the sauna of the classroom, my red ears tingling as they warmed back up. Hope walked in wearing business casual and draped her spotless pea coat over the back of the chair next to me, revealing a shiny black sweater I hadn't seen before. She worked a shift at the alumni center after class, and she often complained that other student staffers only wore jeans and T-shirts to work. "It's so unprofessional," she'd say.

Hope was my only friend who wore such sleek outfits. I was mostly surrounded by students who wore offbeat secondhand finds and spiky bedhead, whether genuine or affected. So I knew the importance she placed on clothing. "I like your sweater," I said. "Is it new?"

Hope spread her fingers and palmed her shoulders with both hands, grinning. "It's not a sweater," she said. "It's a down payment on my future!"

I smiled. Her running joke after every purchase.

She looked at my outfit as if searching for something to compliment in return, but she fell short. Luckily, she had more to say about her sweater. "People always say you can't wear brown and black together, but they're wrong." She waved her right hand between her brown face and black sweater. "I wear them together all the time, and I look fabulous!"

She did look fabulous. I picked at the pills on my sleeve.

The Irish linguistics professor walked in carrying a worn leather satchel and began his lecture about how different world languages stacked noun vs. noun phrases, diagramming syntax trees on the chalkboard that looked like multiple V-shaped formations of flying geese. I enjoyed his accent, but majoring in linguistics—which I'd latched onto as my plan in high school before I quite understood it—wasn't as compelling as I'd expected it to be. I'd wanted to learn actual languages, maybe even do translation. But I didn't want to be a quitter at something I'd already chosen.

After class, I noticed the hot pink mittens dangling from a crocheted cord that ran through both sleeves of Hope's wool pea coat. An ingenious technique, but I felt a little embarrassed for her. I thought mittens were for building snowmen and for keeping babies from scratching their faces.

I pointed at the thick wool. "Mittens?"

"I knit them myself," she beamed.

But how was an adult supposed to function without fingers? I looked down at my dollar store gloves. I was pretty sure gloves kept hands warmer than mittens because they had more finger coverage. Besides, who sat around knitting?

I sighed when we reached the exterior doors. "Here we go," I said. "It's only October, and I'm freezing already."

Hope looked at me with raised eyebrows. "I keep forgetting you're an American," she sighed. "You're just underdressed."

I squinted as she slipped on her second dangling mitten. I was used to being an unsatisfactory example of loud Americanness, but what the hell was "underdressed"? At home, a person could wear flip-flops and shorts and still be considered fully dressed. With goosebumps, maybe, but fully dressed.

I don't remember ever seeing a snow plow during my childhood in the Pacific Northwest, where snow was primarily removed by melting. The most important question when it snowed was whether it would stick. It only took half an inch to earn us a day off school, or at least a late start.

Magical stuff.

It softened and quieted the streets, and stopped traffic so reliably that we could take over a city street for sledding. No one drove when snow landed and stuck. On those rare snow days, I'd dig through the metal tin of my mom's dusty winter accessories, which were seen so rarely they held exotic appeal. And if I didn't feel like playing dress up in an itchy hat with a pom-pom, I could stay in bed reading all day, which was even better.

Montreal had a different rhythm.

The snow plows, an army of rumbling trucks, stood on continual standby. If a lot of snow had fallen, like, meters worth, the plows sprayed the snow into dump trucks that followed behind them, which then hauled it off to some mysterious snow graveyard. Salt and gravel trucks followed the plows and dump trucks, the sounds of which my wet toilet paper earplugs barely muffled. From my bed at 2:00 a.m., I only had to assess the city's ambient noise level to know how much snow had fallen.

In Feminist Theory, the professor wore red go-go boots and a short skirt. She gave us an assignment: for one day, dress in a way that does not broadcast your sexual orientation.

"If you're not straight," she added, "the assignment is optional."

A girl in the front raised her hand. "Why is it optional if you're not straight?"

The professor nodded. "Presumably, those who are not straight already have experience with this."

The next day, Hope showed up to class in a blue T-shirt with a stretched-out collar, her fingers bare of the silver rings she usually wore. She slung her pea coat and purse over the back of her chair and looked at me expectantly.

"I'm wearing flat brown shoes with black pants," she said, smiling. "And this shirt doesn't go at all!"

I fidgeted with my pen. Did she think dressing queer just meant dressing badly? I was pretty sure she'd based her outfit, at least partially, on me.

Her nails were long and manicured, and she carried a purse with a dozen silver clasps. I would still read her as straight. "I thought you said brown and black don't clash."

"Brown shoes and black pants still do!" She eyed my V-neck sweater and boot-cut jeans, the same clothes I always wore. "You're not doing the assignment," she said, digging into her purse.

"It was optional for me."

She sighed as she dropped her pen and notebook on the desk.

"But I'm wearing tights under my jeans." I pulled up my pant leg to prove that I'd moved beyond the horror of "underdressed." I liked the feeling of compression, as if the tights held me together in addition to keeping me warm.

"What?!" Hope shook her head. "It's barely autumn! You can't wear tights *now* or you'll have nothing left to add in January."

Freezing now or freezing later didn't seem like a great choice. I wished I could make an informational phone call to McGill Nightline. What comes first, the long underwear or the tank top? The thin socks or the thick ones? The toque or the ear muffs? I wanted those easy answers, but someone might recognize my voice, maybe even Hope herself. To minimize mockery for my dumb Americanness, I told myself I had to figure out my winter wardrobe management system on my own.

Maybe my problem wasn't about clothes at all. Maybe I was physiologically different than the Canadian students and hadn't grown the necessary subcutaneous layer of fat that would protect me. Or maybe my miserable achiness was related to EDS, my connective tissue disintegrating in the cold. But I pushed that thought out of my mind. I didn't like my freakish genetic thing affecting my actual life.

In any case, my every West Coast defense, even with tights under my jeans, proved insufficient. I had to buy more clothes. Scarves and thicker gloves, a toque with a pom-pom on top. I added tank tops and long underwear under multiple sweaters worn at the same time, and to prove Hope wrong, I also bought warmer tights to go under my jeans in January.

Before Montreal, I'd been infuriated by tiny pockets in women's clothing—or worse, decorative ones—but with so many new layers, I struggled with a new pocket problem. Too many. Those layers created a minefield of black holes and panic. I'd get back to my apartment but not find my keys in my coat pocket, so I started undressing in the street, exposing my hands to the icy air as I patted myself down. I cursed my poor planning, worried that I'd have to retrace my steps to search for keys in snowbanks, but I always found the keys eventually, hidden in pocket layer two or three.

In December, I sat smoking on the steps of the Stewart Biology Building before my Medical Anthropology lecture. My smoking hand was glove-less, slowly turning numb, but the nicotine cinched my brain together in a way that helped me think. Through snowflakes so thick they obscured people in the distance like fog, my friend Daniel emerged. I hadn't seen him since the last game of Catch Phrase at his apartment, a charades-like game with a beeping console. He'd grown a short goatee since then. "See?" he said. "This is why I don't get smoking. Aren't you cold?"

I was always cold during Montreal winter. And didn't *he* see? If I could locate both my cigarettes and my lighter in their respective pockets, that cigarette before class symbolized me having my shit together. I'd found success at navigating both the cold and the pocket black holes, which meant that I was beginning to function in the big, freezing city. Some-thing of a miracle, just like the snow that fell and always stuck. "I'm training for the circus," I said.

He laughed in his single staccato bark. "Breathing fire," he said. "Good one."

I took another drag of hot fire while snow plastered my glasses flake by flake. They felt medicinal, those rare cigarettes I smoked, and it made me like Daniel even more that he hadn't walked up to me in the snow to tell me that smoking caused cancer. I wanted to shake people who did that. I wanted to scream at them, "You know what else causes cancer? Nothing! Six-year-olds get cancer and die just from existing in this toxic soup of a world, so do not try to tell *me* that *not* smoking will save me or anyone." If I'd made it this far without dying on a cartoon-themed hos-pital ward, useless poison seeping into my chest tube drip by drip, I was lucky enough. Besides, as the Medical Anthropology prof had lectured last week, correlation was not causation. I was happy to use this shining new piece of knowledge to counter any statistic thrown my way.

The winter deepened.

When I sat in my basement window seat now, the electric wall heater cranked up to maximum, I watched boots covered in salt stains skirting patches of ice. I'd heard horror stories about girls going out with wet hair and being able to break pieces off once they'd turned into hair icicles. I never tested this theory, possibly an urban myth, because I rarely show-ered before leaving my apartment.

Why bother, if my skin was always five layers deep?

Now on my walk to school, I passed frozen maple tree silhouettes and icicles on the twisting wrought iron staircases. The gravel and salt sprinkled over the sidewalk ice worked its way up the back of my jeans in half-moon arcs. Moisture from my breath froze between my scarf and my face so that during the last half of my walk, my chin and cheeks nestled not against warm wool but a sheet of ice. I had moments of doubting my decision to go to school in a place capable of freezing nose hairs and eyelashes on a bright sunny day. I'd definitely wanted to go *away* for school. Montreal had seemed exciting. But I'd gotten my passport stamped with that shiny four-year student visa and moved to Quebec without knowing what I was in for.

I turned right on the cobblestoned street, now cleared of restaurant tables to make room for pitted snowbanks. I envied the furniture that got to stay inside all winter long. The wind tunneling down the Saint Lawrence River gusted with enough force to detach my muscles from their bones and tuck ice between the crevices.

The speeding sidewalk plows were like mini Zambonis that smoothed the sheets of ice under the snow into a city-wide hockey rink. I fell a lot, slipping on the ice even with the metal ice cleats I'd bought for my boots. Not only did I have to navigate the ice itself, but I also had to be ready to tumble into dirty snow banks at any moment to avoid the manic drivers whose face-covering balaclavas made them all look as if they were fleeing a bank robbery.

As I got closer to campus, deeper into the stream of commuting students, I overheard conversations behind me. Small talk had started to revolve around snow removal. "Think of how much better it would be if the city installed heaters in the streets to melt it," I heard someone say.

Or we could all stay home until spring?

By the time I got to school, my whole body ached and my ankles stabbed. Pavement and asphalt and cobblestones had no give to them, and my bones felt every shock.

I took a seat in Phonetics I. The lucky students who'd made it to school without freezing in place or being run over by sidewalk plows streamed in, flush-cheeked. I watched them remove sweater after scarf after toque until no desk or back-of-the-chair space remained. Anything dropped got dipped in the winter floor sauce of dirty melted snow, salt, and gravel. I let my warming bones sink into the overheated building.

After class, Hope pulled out a pair of hand-knit mittens from her many-buckled purse and handed them to me as we got up to leave. "I made these for you," she said. "They're warmer than gloves."

I grinned, speechless, as I rubbed the sky blue wool, tightly looped and stiff from not yet having been worn.

She shrugged like her gift was no big deal. "They're obviously home-made."

I hugged her before slipping them on. "That's what makes them so great!" I said. "I love them." Inside that insulated wool bubble, my fingers would share their heat instead of shivering in separate compartments. Mittens weren't childish after all.

"You can be an honorary Canadian," she said as she pushed open the heavy door of the Arts Building. We hit the cold air and descended the wide stone staircase. Maybe I could belong in this cold city after all.

WILTING FLOWER GIRL

At four, my first appearance as a flower girl was photographed so it could be laughed at later.

On the hours-long drive to my uncle's wedding in the Yakima Valley, my little brother Zach crashed and whooshed his Matchbox cars next to me in the backseat. The noise pulled a screeching barbed wire around the back of my ears and neck, an invasion my body reacted to as if I were about to be run over by a full-size rumbling truck. Fight or flight or freeze.

I drew a line with my finger in the upholstery to delineate our respective sides over which no hands or toy cars should cross. "Stop making sound effects!"

He jumped, turning his wide blue eyes toward me, his blond hair glowing in the sunlight. I had big sister authority, so he followed my orders for a few seconds. I looked out the window at the hills with long, deep crevices that I thought looked like bum cracks. They were covered with scrubby brown bushes that, from a distance, looked more like freckles than foliage. My stomach quivered, carsick from staring out the backseat window.

Then he started up again. "Rrrrrrrrrr pffffhhhh."

"Stop!" I repeated, kicking my leg in frustration. I couldn't draw a line in the air space.

In the passenger's seat, Mom kept looking straight ahead at the highway. "Just don't think about it, Alyssa."

I'd already tried not thinking about it, and it didn't work. How was I supposed to sit quietly in the backseat when I was about to get run over by noise? We crossed the Columbia River at the Dalles, then over Satus Pass, and by the time we descended into the Yakima Valley, the evergreens had been fully replaced by dusty hop fields, evenly spaced rows as high as telephone poles that flickered as we passed.

I wished for a little sister instead.

The day of the wedding arrived. I stood in front of the bridesmaids in a white frilly dress with my basket of flower petals, many of which remained because I'd been frugal in my sprinkling as I walked down the aisle of lawn in my grandparents' backyard. I couldn't see my uncle and soon-to-be aunt in their fancy clothes from where I stood. I couldn't see anything but the people seated in the front row, unrecognizable faces save my grandparents. Grandpa Abe with his long legs and Grandma Tillie with her long glass-beaded necklace. No one looked in my direction.

The priest murmured.

The drive had been interminable, but it couldn't have been as long as the wedding itself. Behind me, koi shimmered in the artificial pond; behind the audience, a weeping willow bent its unraveling branches toward the ground. Beyond the yard for acres in all directions, hop fields stood tall and laden with dark green foliage, filling the air with fumes my cousins said smelled like skunk.

I wished I could redo my walk down the aisle and sprinkle more petals. What was I supposed to do with them now?

The priest still murmured.

I was ready for the wedding to be over. My knees had locked, my legs ached, and I wanted to sit down. My fancy shoes hurt my feet, even though I loved the grown-up clack they made when I walked on cement. My head felt fuzzy, like I was drowning, sinking into the koi pond with the shimmering fishes. I'd scattered at least some of those rose petals, so it felt like my role as flower girl had been fulfilled.

I couldn't see beyond the front row, and no one looked in my direction. Maybe it didn't matter what I did up there in front of the bridesmaids. My heart swirled as I considered my options. I'd been instructed to stand there. Maybe if I didn't actually touch the ground, it wouldn't count as sitting? I took a cue from the weeping willow, its floppy trunk bending to brush its long branches on the lawn, and relaxed into a squat with the skirt of my frilly white dress ballooning around me. The blood rushed back to my head, and I spent the rest of the ceremony running my fingers through the pile of leftover petals I'd dumped on the lawn.

And that's how my parents acquired a photo of my four-year-old self squatting with a hoard of flower petals in front of the wedding party.

They started early, the weird feelings I got from standing in one place.

Part II

FRAMED

I liked the way Mags strutted across the classroom. She had short blonde hair, layered and shaggy, and wore a navy blue sweater zipped over a bright yellow T-shirt that read, "I am the supreme bean." I eyed her sky blue corduroy pants as she took a seat in front of me in our one shared class, Literary Montreal. They were well worn and very appealing, those cords.

"Hey," she said to Anja, who sat next to me.

Mags smiled at me as she removed her smoker's gloves, the kind with a mitten flap that folds back to reveal fingerless gloves underneath. Tough and practical and warm. I eyed the smoker's gloves too, yet another winter accessory I'd never before considered necessary but that, all of a sudden, I desired with surprising force.

I held my breath as Mags tucked a strand of hair behind her ear. Was that a wink?

In class, I had a hard time focusing as the professor talked about *Main Brides* by Gail Scott, set on "The Main" of rue Saint-Laurent, the historical geographic division between anglophone and francophone Montreal. Mags had slung a vinyl messenger bag over the back of her seat, and the apple green paint near its zipper distracted me. I wanted to ask where it came from. I wanted to pick at it. I knew that Mags drew comics, and I wondered if she painted too.

"Do you think the bar in the book is Bifteck?" Mags asked us after class. "I play pool there a lot."

Of course she did. Of course she lived a life that wove right into a book we analyzed for class. "Probably," I said, even though I had no idea. I was bad at pool. "We should all do some research sometime."

Mags took her paint-splattered messenger bag to her next class, strutting her long legs as if in slow motion, and Anja raised an eyebrow at me.

"I have a bit of a crush on her," I said.

Anja hesitated, putting the last of her papers into her bag. She chose her words carefully. "I think Mags would be into something . . . casual right now."

I didn't say anything, my stomach sinking as if right before a fall on sidewalk ice. Casual? Maybe Anja thought Mags was too cool for me, with her smoker's gloves and pool-playing and well-worn cords.

"She just broke up with her girlfriend," she said. "And they were together for a while."

I nodded. It sounded like good news to me.

I sat in the tiny bedroom I'd painted creamsicle orange and reread lecture notes on alkene and alkyne reactions. My head hurt. I hadn't taken chemistry in high school, because I missed the only year it was taught, so I struggled in McGill's chemistry courses designed to weed out first-year students rather than make sure they understood the significance of Avogadro's number. I was a fourth-year cultural studies major, but I wanted to go to naturopathic medical school, and I needed the prerequisites. That year, I flipped back and forth between dry introductory science lectures in huge auditoriums and Lacanian vs. Saussurian critical theory. I really just wanted school to be over and my real life to start.

When the screen door from the apartment below me slammed, I pushed myself up from my desk to see who had walked into the small courtyard beneath my second-floor window. A guy in baggy jeans dropped a twenty-four-case of Molson on the cigarette-scarred picnic table, then cupped his hands around his mouth and took a deep breath so his voice echoed all the way up the brick walls.

"Who's ready for beer pong?"

I slammed down my window. Who knew how many bellowing management students would join him now? I grabbed for my bulky noise-canceling headphones. "I just felt so sorry for you," my mom had said when she'd sent them as a gift. Just before I slipped them over my ears, my roommate turned on the TV that sat right outside my bedroom door. She was always home, always watching TV. I was still annoyed with her from yesterday.

"You looooove taking pills," she'd said to me after I rummaged under the bathroom sink for the vitamin E for my skin, magnesium for energy, and vitamin C for collagen.

They weren't pills, they were supplements. She made it sound like I was an addict when I'd actually conducted extensive internet research on the herbs and vitamins that might clear up my skin, my exhaustion, and my continual achiness. They hadn't helped yet, but that only meant I needed to try more combinations. When I went to the campus health center, they'd just wanted to put me on antidepressants, so I never went back.

The noise-canceling headphones buzzed in my ears, but they didn't block out the pops of opening beer cans in the courtyard below or the hum of the TV against my wall. I took quick gulps of air. City soundwaves wafted like a gas leak, and I suffocated in them. My creamsicle-orange walls, a color I had chosen and painted myself, glowed oppressive rather than warm. I couldn't concentrate. My notes blurred from being read too many times, and I fantasized about silence. Coming home to a quiet, breezy room full of books where I could sit and recover from the dense energy of the city, where I would actually have the headspace to teach myself the language of whatever I needed to learn. Instead, bellowing management students tortured me with beer pong and I couldn't calm down my overreactive system.

Was I about to be weeded out of Organic Chemistry?

The three of us—Mags, Anja, and I—walked across campus in a heavy autumn rain. When it rained in Montreal, the angry raindrops fell with purpose in sheets, unlike the wandering drizzle of the Pacific Northwest. I could barely make out the downtown buildings that scraped the edges of campus. Red maple leaves plastered the asphalt underneath our feet.

We walked fast, talking about our group presentation on Lise Tremblay's *Mile End* when, out of nowhere, I twisted my ankle and fell, dropping the umbrella that did nothing to keep me dry. My ankle bones cracked and I landed on my forearm.

"Oh!" Mags said as I went down. She held out her hand to help me back up, her eyes wide. "Are you okay?"

I got up quickly and wiped the asphalt grit off of my palms. I inspected my clothes. A rip in the elbow of my awkward-fitting velvet jacket but no rips in my own skin. How cool would it have been to end up in the hospital because I'd tripped over my own feet and a puddle?

Anja handed me my bent umbrella and looked at Mags. "I've never heard you make that sound before."

Mags shrugged and readjusted her shoulder bag.

I folded up the broken umbrella. "Let's keep walking," I said, shivering. "I'm fine."

Anja parted ways a few blocks later, at avenue du Parc, leaving me and Mags on the corner in the pouring rain. My wet jeans clung to my skin, and we stood only steps away from Bar des Pins, a sticky sports bar firmly within the radius of anglophone student territory around McGill.

"What are you doing now?" I asked. "Do you want to get a drink before the walk home?"

She smiled big. "Sure."

And then we were sitting at a small table against the wall in an almost empty bar, two whiskeys and an order of frites between us. My twisted ankle throbbed right along with my quick pulse, Mags right in front of me and all to myself.

"So, you draw comics?" I knew she was making one for another class.

"Yeah!" She reached into her bag and handed me a photocopied sheet of paper. *Geek Girl.* Sparse lines drawn with a Micron pen. She pointed at the face of the main character. "That's me," she said. "I'm easy to draw with my big square head."

"Ha." I wanted to tell her I liked her lines, but I thought it might come out wrong. I took a sip of whiskey.

In the comic, her character sits in a café "flirting" with a girl across the room by staring at her, hoping that the intensity of her gaze will bore into the girl's soul and get her a date. It doesn't work. The sign on the wall of the café says a different thing in every panel, first ADD IT UP, then YOUR FAULT. I didn't quite know what Mags was getting at, but I liked the absurdity of it, the inside joke noticeable only to those who looked closely. I wanted to be in on the joke.

"This is so cool," I said.

"I'm making one about the Montreal comics scene too," she said. "You can see it when I'm done."

My blood buzzed from the whiskey, and my wet jeans set my legs ablaze with itchiness. I folded a paper napkin into an accordion, then remembered to be embarrassed by my cold purple fingers, so I shoved my hands between my thighs to warm them up and glanced at my nails. Had I trimmed them recently? I didn't want Mags to associate me with jagged fingernails.

"Do you draw?" she asked.

I shook my head. "I can't draw." I reached for the cigarettes in my bag. I smoked rarely, but I still carried them around for moments like this one when I craved more heat and something to calm my nerves.

"Anybody can draw," she said, leaning forward to light my cigarette with her Zippo lighter. "I could show you."

I thought she was wrong about drawing, but I'd let her show me whatever she wanted. As I took a drag and savored the burn on my lungs, I kept getting distracted by the screen on the wall behind us. People on ice skates brushed push brooms up and down a hockey rink.

I gestured toward the screen. "Is this show some kind of joke?"

Mags tilted her head at me. "Are you serious?"

"They're sweeping a hockey rink like they're on speed."

"It's curling!"

I couldn't tell if she was messing with me. "It's a real sport?"

"I forgot you're not Canadian," she said. "Where are you from again?"

"Portland," I said. "Oregon, not Maine." I always said Portland because if I said Vancouver, everyone thought I meant the city in British Columbia, not the suburb in Washington State.

"Isn't that like the coolest city in the States?"

I nodded.

"Well. You need to watch *Men with Brooms*," she said. "I think you should come to my apartment for a movie night sometime. I mean, if you want."

My stomach flipped. I did want.

"Think of it like cultural studies homework." She winked at me. "It's a new Canadian classic."

We gathered up our wet coats to leave. "How much further is your walk home?" she asked.

I hesitated, embarrassed. "I just moved to Saint-Dominique and des Pins," I said, embarrassed that it was the closest I'd ever lived to campus.

I didn't want to be seen as one of those students who never left the anglophone bubble. "It's awful. You?"

"Along Saint-Joseph. Why is it so awful?"

"I'm surrounded by managements students, and my roommate is always home watching TV."

Mags reached over to grab the last frite. "What does a person even watch on TV these days?"

"Reality shows," I said. "*A Baby Story* and *A Wedding Story*. The TV is right up against my bedroom wall, so I hear every word."

"Yeah, that's bad," Mags said, her face blank. "Breeder TV."

I choked on my last sip of whiskey when I laughed.

She smiled back. "You'd probably like my place. It's pretty quiet."

In my creamsicle-orange bedroom, I put on clothes and took them off again. Even in my fourth year, I still had trouble dressing in autumn, always over- or underdressed. Fingerless gloves or nothing? Sneakers or boots? I put a safety pin in the ripped elbow of my velvet jacket, the one that fit funny in the shoulders, but I couldn't decide if it looked punk rock or sad. What was the right thing to wear for a "movie date" at Mags's house that may or may not be a real date? She said she'd order takeout. It was probably a real date. I ended up wearing the same thing I always wore, sneakers and the safety-pinned velvet jacket.

On the twenty-minute walk to Mags's place, I zig-zagged streets and tried to remember to breathe. I walked along the cobblestones of avenue Duluth in the Quartier Portugaise, past Chez José Café and its bright orange octopus painted on brick. I would have bought empanadas and almond croissants for later, but the window was dark, the wooden chairs stacked on tables. As I walked further north, the two-story buildings turned into three-story walk-ups with bright spiral staircases, ochres and teal. I was glad I didn't have to shovel one of those metal staircases every day of a Montreal winter.

I walked along Saint-Denis, then down avenue Rachel past La Banquise, the best place for poutine in the city. Fresh cheese curds, crispy fries, and dozens of gravy options, including "poutine spaghetti," a dare I would never take. Quebecois gourmet. My previous apartment had been nearby, and I missed eating poutine in Parc la Fontaine while I watched the ducks. Hope had told me the park was designed by the same guy who designed Central Park in New York City. The pond froze into a skating rink in the winter.

Just before the park, I turned up Mags's street and, several blocks north, arrived at the three-story red brick building with no exterior staircase. The second I rang the bell, Mags stepped onto the third-floor wrought iron balcony as if she'd seen me coming. "Come up! The lock's broken."

I climbed a narrow stairwell with bicycle wheel-scuffed walls, and she opened the door before I even reached the landing. "My roommate's gone for the night," she said. "I'll give you the grand tour."

Before I even dropped my messenger bag on the light parquet floors, breathless from nerves, I could tell that Mags's apartment was Montreal-perfect. The living room had one burgundy wall and three tan ones, just like the third-floor apartment across the street we could see right into. An old enamel bathtub sat on hexagonal black-and-white tiles in the bathroom. The galley kitchen overlooked a narrow alley filled with ductwork, and bulk grains in mason jars lined the counter. On the white board in the kitchen, either Mags or her roommate had written "weed guy" and a 514 phone number.

Her bedroom made me gasp. Bright and alive, the dark purple duvet cover on her bed popped against the apple green walls, the same apple green as the splotch on her messenger bag.

"You painted your room!"

She looked at me. "How did you know?"

"Your bag."

"I can't believe you noticed that," she smiled. "Yeah, it was a disaster. I stepped backward into the paint can."

"It sounds like something I'd do." My eyes landed on her bookshelves. Two cherry-stained shelves lined one wall, with the book spines lined up flush with the front of the shelves. "Wow. You alphabetize your books?"

"I used to work at a bookstore," she shrugged. "So I'm well trained. My dad made the shelves."

I wanted to linger, to read everything she'd ever read and alphabetized. She pulled down the wooden flap of her secretary desk and grabbed a small silver cigarette case. "And your desk!" I said. I wanted to know where a person even got a desk like that.

"Oh yeah! I dusted it off from my parents' drive shed. It's from an old nunnery."

I tried to imagine what it would be like to go to school so close to home, with a dad who built you bookshelves. To go shopping for pine furniture from old nunneries in your parents' drive shed. To bring all the favorite books from your childhood bedroom and line them up in alphabetical order, flush with the front of the shelves as if everything in your life could be pulled together into one bright, vibrant room. I envied her Montreal groundedness. I walked over to her window and looked out onto the fire escape.

"I usually sit out there to smoke up," she said, opening the silver case to reveal two joints, a roach, and a packet of rolling papers. "Do you want any?"

I did and I didn't. Pot usually made me paranoid and speechless, but maybe this time would be different. Canadians "smoked up," which I kept hoping would be a different experience than "smoking out," which is what one did at home. "Sure. A little."

We climbed out the window, careful of the hot and clanking metal radiator.

"That's pretty too," I said rubbing my finger over the engraved flowers on her cigarette case.

"Thanks," she said. "It was my grandmother's." She lit the joint and handed it to me, clicking the metal case shut. Her Zippo lighter matched her grandmother's cigarette case, and the sunset reflected in her bedroom window, glowing.

We sat for a moment without speaking as the pot lifted me up, not out.

"I see comics when I look at window frames," Mags said, as if she were deep in the middle of a conversation we were already having. "Like, from inside my bedroom, the rooftops and Mount Royal are two horizontal panels on the same page."

I squinted. "I've never thought of it like that before."

"It's like the entire city is a comic book grid."

I glanced back inside at the rows of her books still visible through the open window. "Like everything we do is a story and we're the main characters," I said.

"Yes!"

"Can you give me a graphic novels reading list?"

She lit up like the sunset. "Comics, you mean? Absolutely."

Uh-oh, my paranoia kicked in. "'Graphic novels' isn't the right thing to say?"

She took another drag. "Calling them 'graphic novels' is just a marketing attempt to make comics more socially acceptable, when people should really respect comics as an art form in and of itself." Just then, a ring on the doorbell that made Mags jump up. "That's the takeout."

We moved to the rooftop to eat tom yum soup and egg rolls, drinking through a six pack of Coup de Grisous and watching the sunset. I picked at my beer label, then stopped myself because Hope had told me that picking at labels is a sign of sexual frustration.

From the rooftop we could see all the way to the city's horizon, the darkening sky where the Old Port met the Saint Lawrence River. Skyscrapers towered along the southern perimeter of the McGill campus, and to our right sat the white illuminated cross on top of Mount Royal, the most iconic Montreal landmark. I filled my lungs with chilly air. Maybe we really were the main characters in an epic story. "I can't believe you can see the cross from here," I said. It felt like Mags's world was filled with furniture and views too good to be part of my real life.

"Did you know it glows purple whenever the pope dies?"

"Like by magic?"

She laughed. "I think they just change the light bulbs."

Maybe it was the pot or maybe it was the view, but the coriander buckwheat beer with the picked-at label was the most delicious beer I'd ever tasted. Two bottles in and my stomach barely hurt at all.

"You're shivering," Mags said, scooching closer to me. "Do you want an extra sweater?"

I shook my head. I felt her body heat. "I never really know what to wear in this city." I pulled my slightly too-small velvet jacket over my chest. "I'm either too hot or freezing cold."

Mags reached over and rubbed the goosebumps on my forearm, and I startled at the warmth of her fingertips. She wasn't wearing her tough and practical smoker's gloves, but they were still warm. I kept talking like it was no big deal that her fingertips were touching my skin.

"And this jacket," I said, pulling my knees to my chest. "I can never decide if it's cool or if I look ridiculous."

"I like your clothes." She took another swig of beer. "On campus you walk like, 'these are my clothes and fuck off.' You just own them."

I was glad it was too dark for Mags to see me blush. We stared straight ahead at the horizon for a beat too long.

"I can't wait for summer," Mags said, finally. "My roommate says you can watch the fireworks competitions from up here every Friday."

I nodded in the dark. She touched my hand, then grabbed them both. "Your hands are freezing!" she said, rubbing them between her palms.

When I looked up, her eyes held my gaze. "I need gloves like yours," I said. I wanted to kiss her. Now was the time.

She stopped rubbing but still cupped her hands around mine. "Warmer?"

I nodded. What was I waiting for? There would never be a more perfect rooftop moment for a first kiss. Her face leaned a little closer to mine, and I tried to keep breathing. Stay cool, Alyssa. I could hear my own heartbeat and the slight crunch of gravel.

When Mags spoke again, she whispered. "Should we watch the movie then?"

I could tell by her voice that she wasn't really thinking about the movie, but I pulled back a little, skittish that I'd missed my window. Would I really have to sit through a whole movie about curling when I really wanted to grab her hair in both hands and pull her toward me? I held my breath and reached for the thigh of her well-worn cords. When I leaned in, her lips parted as if she were one step ahead of me yet again, deep in the middle of a conversation we were already having.

I closed my eyes against the twinkling dark. The city silenced itself, and the traffic stilled.

She tasted like ginger and lemongrass and the best beer I'd ever had. Bright orange sheets hid underneath the purple duvet cover in her bedroom, another vivid layer of warm color for us to curl into. And when the cool breeze from her comic book frame of a window washed over us, it didn't even raise goosebumps on my skin.

We could watch *Men with Brooms* another night.

If Mags's bedroom window framed an iconic view of Montreal and told the story of her grounded life, mine framed overflowing ashtrays and transient assholes.

I didn't want that story.

Before the end of the semester, I was packing moving boxes again. I'd only lasted a few months in my creamsicle-orange bedroom, and my move coincided with final exams and paper deadlines.

My new apartment would be in Pointe-Saint-Charles, a neighborhood across the Lachine Canal from Saint-Henri, the setting of Gabrielle Roy's *Tin Flute* about an impoverished francophone family during WWII. My new neighborhood was almost as far as you could get from McGill management students while still actually living in Montreal Centre-Ville, and I hoped it would be quieter. Daniel lived down there already, as did other friends, so I envisioned a whole new life for myself. Quiet, relaxing city weekends along the canal. Space to study, since I had managed not to get weeded out of Organic Chemistry.

One large garbage bag of junk in each hand, I descended the steep stairs from my second-floor apartment. My hands were too full to lean on the railing for balance, and my head was too full with an overstuffed to-do list to focus on my every single step. I stumbled, then slid face-first down half the flight of stairs, garbage bags tumbling alongside me.

Thump, thump, thump like a bag of disconnected bowling bowls. I skidded down head and shoulder first. My nose bent, and my skin split open above my eyebrow, on the bridge of my nose, and above my upper lip.

I needed stitches. On my face this time, not my shins.

I debated calling Mags, who I knew was working on a paper about Mordecai Richler's *The Apprenticeship of Duddy Kravitz*, about a young aspiring Jewish entrepreneur on rue Saint-Urbain. Did I actually need her help, or could I make it to the hospital on my own? I called her. She hailed us a taxi to Montreal General, and I leaned on her in the waiting room. After an hours-long wait, a short, abrupt doctor with circles under his eyes didn't give me enough lidocaine to numb my nose before sewing it up.

"I can still feel it," I said.

He kept sewing.

I didn't know then that local anesthetic doesn't work as well in people with EDS. My cells leak. They're not good at containment, keeping lido-caine—and whatever else they're supposed to contain, like electrolytes—in place. I needed more local anesthetic and to wait longer for it to take effect. All I knew then was that I could feel every stitch of the black thread he pulled through my thin, stretchy skin. I jerked in pain and my eyes watered. The stitches sounded like shoelaces threading through grommets. My arms and legs lifted with each stitch, like they were at-tached to invisible strings. A tortured puppet. But aside from stitches all over my face and my shoulder and side bruised purple, I was fine.

Tough, I told myself.

Mags's warm hand squeezed mine while the silent doctor finished sewing up my face.

Bruised and stitched, moving day didn't shift—smack in the middle of final exams—but my friends rallied, Mags included, to move my stuff for me. I watched mittened hands stack boxes of books in the back of a rented U-Haul van while I stood on the icy December sidewalk. My breath swirled in the cold with the lightness of gratitude. Every box stacked made my injuries throb a little less.

The following year, Mags would move into that new apartment with me. This would not be the first time that I leaned on her to save me from the dangers of moving.

LITTLE MISS PERFECT

In the second-grade play, I came forward from the choir and closer to the hot stage lights, pretending to be in my own little world as I crouched in front of a pile of wooden blocks.

Another kid approached. "What are you doing?"

"I'm making a friend," I said

The parents laughed.

At first, I'd been embarrassed by the part. Would people think I didn't have any friends at school? But I liked following a clear script of what to say and do next, and I liked getting the laughs. It made me feel older, sophisticated, like I was in on the joke.

The scene ended with me making a "real" friend in the form of an actual classmate who I didn't really like offstage, then I sang a song called "Make a Friend Today." I finished my solo and returned to my place in the front row of the choir, where the rest of the concert dragged. My legs sunk and my head floated, and I ached to sit down. Instead, I fixed my gaze on my poor little half-constructed block friend who I'd abandoned all alone under the spotlight.

I understood the joke, but still. I would have liked to finish fitting the pieces.

The apple vending machine in the school lobby was one large bin of Granny Smith apples behind a glass front, and I tried to buy one every day before school started. I'd heard my teacher say, "An apple a day keeps the doctor away," and I'd been rushed to the emergency room more than once in the previous year for stitches. Why hadn't anyone told me the apple-eating rule for self-protection against doctors sooner? Maybe I could have avoided all of those emergency rooms.

Indirectly, my report card also reflected my loyalty to apples. Often the time it took to buy my apple made me late for class, breathless.

"That's the second bell, Alyssa."

But no matter how fast I moved my feet in those LA Gear high-tops after the school bus dropped me off, I couldn't keep up. Even before I took off my backpack in the morning, I juggled too many rules: Eat an apple a day; walk down the long hallway instead of run; be at my desk by the second bell. My budding anxiety grew deeper roots when I saw the number of days tardy tallied on my report card. I inspected the neon pleats of twisted leather on my shoes.

What did "tardy" mean?

I didn't want to ask my parents for a definition, thereby drawing attention to how I'd done something wrong at school, so I made my best guess. "Tardy" was clearly shorthand for retarded, a cutting-edge insult from the playground that meant "you're an easy target and nobody likes you."

Second-grade devastation.

Mrs. Hamilton thought I'd been acting tardy for seven of the days I'd spent idolizing her. I redoubled my efforts to make myself perfect and, thus, more lovable.

Anything new I tried in secret, and that included fashion. The year before, Steph, a girl who sat two pods over in my first-grade class, had worn bright pink slouchy socks over gray leggings. I liked the way you could see her knee bones while she lined up a row of wide-eyed trolls along her desk during rainy day recess. I wanted to copy her look, only I had baggy red cotton pants instead of leggings.

I could make that work?

I didn't try my new style until I was on the school bus, riding eastward, scooched up against a right-facing window to watch the horses grazing soggy grass. I tucked the hems of my red pants into pink ankle socks, and even though my pant legs bunched funny, ballooning out like MC Hammer's, I squeezed them in and went with it.

As the bus pulled into Ellsworth Elementary School, an L-shaped brick building with blue doors to every classroom, I told myself that good outfits didn't always feel natural at first. Confidence was key.

I'd forgotten it was class picture day. Yes! I had timed my new fashion with the annual photo shoot, and I always stood in the front row.

Despite my tardiness, I liked second grade better than first, when my old teacher, Mr. Zapp, had raced across the room to rip the eraser out of my pencil whenever he saw me using it to correct my practice letters.

"I need to see your mistakes," he said.

Whenever I was under such tight observation, my experiences never felt like my own. Mrs. Hamilton, on the other hand, mostly ignored me, aside from the occasional glance over the top of her spectacles. She had salon-set white hair and aligned her classroom desks in straight, evenly spaced rows. I had dominion over my own school supplies and didn't have to show my mistakes to anyone.

I loved cursive lessons more than anything, more than *recess*, where the monkey bars hurt my hands and I often asked the playground monitor if I could go to the health room so I could lie down with a stomachache. But I could fall right into those swooping cursive letters. I watched closely at Mrs. Hamilton as she scratched loops across the chalkboard. Writing too firmly made my hand cramp and my fingertips bend funny, so while the other second graders filled in their worksheets with blunt pencils and firm lines, I pressed my finely sharpened graphite lightly, squeezing faint letters onto the worksheet. Then I walked to the pencil sharpener on the other side of the room, repointing the one I'd just used and some others too for good measure.

No one reacted to my continual grinding of pencils, but I hated anyone who disturbed my peace with noise. Sara sat in the desk behind me, and I couldn't stand how she mouthed the words from her book during silent reading. She was always sniffling, tucking used Kleenex up her sweater sleeves for later.

I turned around to face her in one fast twist. "Read *silently*," I said.

She glared and rolled her eyes before tucking her straight, light brown hair behind her ear and resuming her loud silent reading. The faces from her New Kids on the Block T-shirt kept eyeing me, threatening to blast their speakers. Sara and I wouldn't become friends for a few more years.

After Mrs. Hamilton pinned our worksheets to the cork bulletin board across the room, I could see the dark lines of everyone's practice letters but my own. From where I sat, my letters were invisible, my assignment a blank page. I rolled my hand over the pencils lined up inside my open front desk like a float of logs and gathered the whole precious bunch in my fist like a bouquet to sniff their woody, pointy tips. Not like flowers, but comforting.

I wanted to go perfectly unnoticed, but invisibility felt weird too.

PUPPETEERS

They called it a victory lap, the extra year I wanted to take at McGill, but I felt more stressed than victorious. I worried that my soon-to-be expired student visa would get me deported from Canada before I reached the finish line.

I waited for Daniel in a corner diner on Wellington Street in Pointe-Saint-Charles, the one called Le Café. Montreal business signs had to be in French. If English appeared on a sign, the French font had to be three times larger and in a brighter color; *Office québécois de la langue française*, known to anglophones as "the language police," monitored these regulations. The law-abiding bilingual signs read a bit like double vision.

So I sat next to the window in Le Café, with its single-vision sign understandable in both languages, and added extra creamer to my weak, bitter coffee. I gulped it fast because I liked my coffee one degree below scalding. Cafés in my old neighborhood had espresso to which I didn't have to add any cream at all. But I liked my new neighborhood, which had fewer students and more working class francophones. Across the street from our apartment, whenever the garbage crew overturned cans or missed bags, a homebound neighbor threw his voice out the open window, his words chasing the truck's squeaky brakes down the street.

Ostie! (body of Christ). *Câlisse!* (chalice). *Tabernac!* (tabernacle). Roman Catholic cultural influences ran strong in francophone Quebec. Such missives didn't get under my skin nearly as much as those from bellowing anglophone management students.

Out the café window, I could just make out the Via Rail tracks that crossed over Wellington Street two blocks down. The tracks ran through the West Island suburbs; further westward, they followed the Saint Lawrence River all the way upstream to Lake Ontario, past Kingston, then Toronto. Going east, the tracks headed for downtown, toward

McGill. Further eastward, they followed the Saint Lawrence River all the way past Quebec City, then New Brunswick, where it finally empties into the Atlantic Ocean north of Nova Scotia.

Daniel arrived by bike, his right pant leg tucked into his sock. He'd lived in Pointe-Saint-Charles the whole time I'd known him, since my very first semester, so he'd introduced me to Le Café. He floated off the bike like he weighed nothing and secured it to the stop sign—*Arrête*—with a U-lock, wiping his wire-rimmed glasses on his T-shirt before coming inside. He slung his helmet over the back of his wooden chair.

"Hey, Lyssy," he said.

Only three people called me Lyssy. Mags, my little brother Zach, and Daniel. This endeared him to me. "Hi, Danny."

The waitress plunked down and filled a mug for him without asking, and I slid him a copy of my new zine, freshly photocopied legal-sized pages folded in half like a book and stapled. The zine contained my partially informed rant about the evils of harsh pharmaceuticals and their enantiomer-causing side effects. I had a thing about starting side projects when, or possibly because, I already had too much going on. He started to read the zine right away, and I made like it was no big deal to watch him read what I'd written from across the table. I stared at the cover illustration of a tiny person trapped in a pill bottle until my eyes glazed over. Mags had done the illustrating since I didn't draw. She drew people spilling out of giant capsules and drowning in a ball pit of pills. She'd made her own zine alongside mine as well, a comic noir story about a verbally abused toaster that finally gets revenge on its owner through an incident with a fork.

Under his dark, neatly trimmed beard, Daniel's face remained expressionless. I tapped the handle of my fork on the table. The waitress came over. *"Plus de café, ma belle?"*

I stopped fidgeting while she poured me more diner coffee. *"Merci."*

Dishes clanked in the open kitchen, and smoke wafted from the next table. "Maybe you could finish reading that later?"

Daniel put down my zine and took a sip of coffee. "I considered going to naturopathic medical school for a while too," he said. "But then I changed my mind because what's the point of being a doctor if you can't prescribe actual medicine?"

I thought he was missing the point, since I still saw actual medicine as basically useless. But I wondered if the laws were different in Canada, prohibiting naturopaths from prescribing medication like they could in Oregon and Washington. I made a mental note to look it up.

"Anyway," I said. "I need a few more prerequisites, but my student visa expires in six months." Daniel was American too, originally. "What did you do when yours expired?"

"Getting a work visa was pretty easy once I had a job offer," he said. He'd majored in linguistics and was working for a speech recognition software company.

I'd minored in linguistics but didn't have the skills or the inclination to seek out a job at a software company.

He tilted his head as if trying to see the problem clearly. "It's doable to extend your student visa for a year. You just have to get a letter and explain your case."

That sounded awful, having to explain myself well enough to be allowed to stay in the country where my life was happening. I didn't really need to finish my prerequisites at McGill. Technically, I'd finished my degree requirements. What if the immigration people didn't like how I explained my case? I'd have to go back home. I'd have to break up with Mags over an immigration technicality. She had one more year to go, and I wanted to stay with her.

"I guess it makes sense that I need extra time, since I took off that whole semester my first year," I said, working on my story.

"Yeah," he said, nodding once, like punctuation. "That was legit. But the process might take a while. You should start now."

Anja rented a red Ford Focus to drive us the six hours from Montreal to the rolling hills of the Haliburton Highlands cottage country. She'd promised us a weekend at her childhood home in the woods with her Finnish-hippie parents, where we'd spend two days stoking the wood-fired sauna and frolicking amongst autumn leaves. In the city, I felt continually on the verge of getting sick, but I hoped to regenerate in the crisp air and crackling silence.

Mags slung our duffel bag into the back, and Anja looked at me expectantly. "Where's yours?"

"Oh!" I said. "That's all the stuff."

Anja paused, her hand resting above her head on the lifted hatch. She tilted her head and raised one eyebrow. "You guys packed the same duffel bag?"

"Yeah . . ." Did Anja have a problem with efficient packing? I'd rolled up our hoodies and jeans, and separated our socks and underwear into the end pockets for easy retrieval. We didn't really need two bags' worth of stuff for one weekend.

"Okay, then," she said, shaking her head.

Was it weird to share a duffel bag?

We drove up Saint-Laurent, past the dive bars and Schwartz's Deli, then further north past the three-story walk-ups with bright spiral staircases and groups of Hasids in black rekelech and braids, past Parc Lahaie and Dieu du Ciel, the pub where Mags and I always went for beer and cheese plates.

By the time we hit the highway, the sky already hinted at dusk. The low sun backlit the signs for Tim Hortons and tech companies along the West Island as we all sang along to Buck 65's "Wicked and Weird," a unanimous road trip choice.

"What do your parents do again?" I asked.

Anja hesitated, checking the rearview mirror before speaking like she'd had this conversation a million times and didn't really want to have it again. "Do you guys remember Crinkles? The puppet?"

I shook my head and imagined an old-fashioned puppet with strings dangling from a wooden X. I thought puppets were kind of creepy, but Mags gasped. "Oh my God, your parents made *Crinkles*? The little dog with the wrinkly face?"

Anja gave a single nod. "Yup."

Mags grasped the sides of the front seat, giving me a little shake. "I used to have one on my bed!"

I turned to look at Anja. "Your parents make puppets?"

"They were big in Canada in the eighties." She swapped out Buck 65 for Will Oldham in the CD player.

I tried to imagine Mags as a child, thrilled by a crinkly puppet she could jerk around on strings, but I couldn't picture easygoing Mags as a controlling puppet master. It seemed like an awkward thing to have on a bed, the strings tangling up in the pillows. "Can we see where they make them?" I asked.

"Sure," Anja said, like it was no big deal that she grew up in a puppet factory in the woods. "I mean, they sold the rights to Crinkles, but they make other puppets now."

Mags put her fist in the air. "This trip is going to be the *best*."

After a breakfast of goat cheese on Ryvita and home-canned Ontario peaches, the three of us sat on Anja's parents' porch overlooking a field of tall ochre grass and a foot trail leading downhill to the sauna. Beyond, the maples had turned red and orange, and sparse evergreen daggers jabbed the bright blue sky.

"I love Adirondack chairs," I said while sipping a second cup of steaming coffee. I leaned back against wooden slats and rubbed my fingertips on the armrests' cracked woodgrain.

Anja turned to me. "You mean Muskoka chairs?" Muskoka sat due west of Haliburton, another region of Ontario Lake country.

"Muskoka chairs! Is that another dialect thing?"

Mags nodded. "And in Quebec, they're called Laurentian chairs."

I loved that chairs had different names depending on where you sat in them. My body sunk heavy in the chair, like the calm silence was edible and I'd been starving. The only sound was Anja's dad chopping wood near the garage. He stood almost as tall as the roofline, his worn flannel shirt tight around his upper arms. Anja pointed in his direction. "You guys want to go see the puppet studio while I start the fire?"

Mags nodded. "Sure."

I wondered where her enthusiasm from the day before had gone, but she still strutted like she knew where she was going. She wore ripped jeans and a down vest with brown corduroy shoulders, an Ontario country girl in her natural habitat sauntering toward the wood pile. As we approached, Anja's dad split a maple round, the wood so dry that the pieces echoed hollow when they hit the ground. He embedded his axe in the stump and turned toward us.

"Not much to see," he said, "but go on ahead. We're starting back up again in a week or so for the holidays."

Inside the garage, plastic bins overflowed with fabric, the worktables clear. Two industrial sewing machines sat covered in thick plastic, and the only finished product in the room was a stuffed animal sitting on a shelf by the doorway. Where were the wooden Xs dangling puppets from strings? And where were the old-fashioned sets with dusty curtains for the puppet shows? Mags grabbed the stuffed animal from the shelf and stuck her forearm up its bum. Her fingers opened its mouth. "Hello," she made the puppet say, "I'm Crinkles."

"Oh! *That* kind of puppet." Not the kind on strings. This was just a normal-looking stuffed animal without anything creepy to say.

I inspected the studio more closely. Concrete floors with a space heater in the corner. Windows that hadn't been cleaned in possibly forever. Dust floated through the open room, a workspace on holiday. I loved the idea of a backyard studio. I would want a cozier one though, with bookshelves, an electric tea kettle, and a recliner in the corner. What craft could I learn that would let me live this life? A life where I could take extended breaks and start up again for the holidays. Could I be a potter? Woodworker? Weaver?

"How amazing to just make things with your hands," I said.

Mags nodded but didn't add anything. I looked at her stoic profile, then stomped on a dry leaf on the studio floor, crackling it into tiny pieces. I was pretty sure that being a puppeteer, or any other kind of artisan in the woods, wasn't the sort of career that came with a work visa from Immigration Canada. I startled at Anja's dad's voice behind me.

"We'll be coming to Montreal for the holiday bazaar in December, if you girls are looking for a couple weekends of work in our booth."

"I'd love that," I said, imagining a day people-watching and soaking up artisanal secrets.

Mags and I headed down to the sauna to meet up with Anja, rustling the tall ochre grass. I had no idea what she was thinking, and I wanted to. I felt her presence when we shared dinners, when we made zines side by side, when we talked about books. But then there were times like this when I couldn't seem to get ahold of her. We brushed against waist-high milkweed pods that had dried and cracked open to reveal white fluff, and when I plucked out a tuft, the silky fibers rolled smooth and slippery between my fingertips.

Smoke now billowed out of the sauna's chimney, and we joined Anja on the hammocks in the adjacent screened-in porch to wait for it to reach full heat. We stripped off our clothes when it was time to go in, and the scars on my shins caught the light.

"What happened to your shins?" Anja asked.

I looked down as if the scarring was new to me. I'd stopped wearing anything that exposed my shins years ago, so I was no longer used to answering that question. "Oh, those," I said. "I had a lot of stitches when I was a kid."

"Those are from when you were a *kid*?"

I nodded at the familiar reaction. "They've faded a lot."

Back at home in our apartment in Pointe-Saint-Charles, I liked to get rid of stuff. I scanned our bookshelves while Mags put away her T-shirts. Did we really need two copies of *But Is It Art?* No. Out went our duplicate copies of *Cunt, Main Brides, The Tin Flute, Mile End*. My head cleared up just a little bit with every donation box I filled, knowing that one less box meant one less thing to move and slightly less risk of falling on my face while I moved it. Book collections merged, we were in it for the long haul. If Mags minded these purges, she never said so.

I floated, playful, while I watched Mags fold laundry, fastidious but only halfway.

"This is my impression of Mags folding a T-shirt," I said, as I took her "I am the supreme bean" T-shirt out of the hamper and pursed my lips.

She smiled, curious.

I made slow, careful folds with my pinkies extended, then turned toward the T-shirt shelf in the closet. In mock anger, I stuck out both lips, furrowed my brow, and bunched the T-shirt into a rough ball before shoving it in with the other ones.

She doubled over laughing, collapsed on the bed.

I gave the T-shirt shelf an extra battering with my fists for good measure. Then I walked over to her. "Are you angry with your T-shirts, Mags?" I asked, mock-concerned.

When she caught her breath, she pulled me toward her and kissed me. "You like me," she said. "Admit it."

"I admit it."

In December, I caught the bus on Wellington Street that took me to the holiday craft fair at Place Bonaventure, *Le salon des métiers d'art*. So much road spray coated the bus windows that the city passed by through a curtain of dirt. Pitted snow piles lined the train tracks, and the freeze of the Lachine Canal looked permanent.

When I relieved Anja of her shift, she looked tired. She grabbed her messenger bag from the curtained closet behind the wall of puppets and took out a pair of suede mittens. They had bright stitching along their seams and wool felt linings that extended the mitten eight inches up her forearm. When she slipped one on, it reached halfway to her elbow.

"Those mittens are amazing," I said.

She clapped the soft suede together. "I refuse to be cold this year."

I liked her confidence, her simple refusal of winter. More than four years in Montreal and I still hadn't succeeded in refusing the cold. My smoker's gloves with the mitten flap kept my hands warm enough in autumn, but the true cold of winter had no problem seeping its way in.

No mittens required in a crowded craft fair though. Anja's dad swung in to show me how to work the credit card machine and where he stashed the extra-large boxes in the curtained closet. He put on a show for the holiday shoppers who strolled by, holding long, involved conversations with the biggest puppets—the elephant with the swinging trunk, the giraffe with the long neck—opening their enthusiastic mouths as wide as possible.

I tried to mimic him after he left, since he'd hired me to sell puppets, but my thumb dislocated when I opened and closed the elephant's heavy mouth, like it had charged me with its tusks and rammed the joint out of place. Not a friendly puppet. I choose the rat instead, one of the smallest. But while its mouth was friendlier, I couldn't think of much to say to him in front of a passing audience. The entire city strolled in front of me, and every time I heard "*c'est cute*," my energy wilted a little more. I felt like a puppet myself, hollow and waiting. My hips and back ached after only a few minutes of standing in one place, so I flopped down in the chair, half-hidden by the rotating display. Even people who made puppets in the woods for a living had to face large crowds and small talk?

I kept talking to the rat, but quietly, as if we were having a private conversation over tea. "Do you want this to be your life?" I asked him. "Do you like putting on shows for strangers?"

The rat shook his head. "I want to be an artist who hides."

After four hours, Mags relieved me of my shift. I was too exhausted to stick around to watch her version of a puppet show. Like usual after a day of stress and standing, I had developed a fever and a stomachache. The fevers and chills would usually last a day or two but then pass without me ever having actually developed the flu. I loaded up on health foods and supplements recommended by the internet, but I would need much more than the usual introvert social recovery window.

On the last day of the craft fair, Anja's dad slipped us rolls of cash. He also handed me the small white rat puppet with pink hands and sharp whiskers. "For the both of you," he said, winking.

Mags named the puppet Ratso, and he sat on our dresser. I liked him best like that, still and silent, when neither of us had to think about what to say to attract attention from holiday shoppers.

It took a few months and one sweaty interview with an immigration officer downtown, but I succeeded in extending my student visa for one year. While I finished up my science prerequisites, I read books on wood working and daydreamed about the smell of sawdust, the satisfaction of having something to show for an afternoon's work. Not an academic paper that I would forget about a week later, not a two-hour chemistry experiment soon to be rinsed out of an Erlenmeyer flask, but a finished bookshelf, a stool, a cabinet. While I rinsed out beakers in the lab, I craved the grit of sandpaper. I wanted a tool belt, not a lab coat.

I hadn't totally abandoned the idea of naturopathic medical school, but I wanted to take a year to decide which school and maybe get the artisan bug out of my system. Maybe I could also do some pre-studying with the *Anatomy Coloring Book* so I wouldn't feel behind from the beginning like I had in those first-year weeder courses at McGill. But the problem of my immigration status remained. If I didn't have a job offer and wasn't going to school, I had no legal justification for staying in Canada.

Unless...

I leaned on the other side of the kitchen counter as I watched Mags chop onions and carrots for chili. I snitched a carrot round. "Maybe we should just get married."

Mags paused her chopping and looked at me. She didn't say anything. I wondered if she'd heard me, or maybe she thought I was joking. It's not like either of us had spent our childhoods dreaming of white wedding dresses. She cracked herself a beer and rummaged in the fridge for the jar of olives. She was making me a martini to soften the blow of telling me she didn't love me enough to help me get the piece of paper that would keep me in the country. But when she handed me the Bombay martini with three olives on a toothpick, she held her beer in the air.

"Let's do it." She clinked her bottle to my glass.

I took her face in my hands to kiss her as the first sip of gin hit my empty stomach.

While Mags finished chopping, I sank into the corner armchair that wobbled on a stack of books in place of its missing fourth leg. Eventually, I could get citizenship through marriage, and I'd never have to make a case for my presence in Canada again.

THE SUGAR SITUATION

My dad drove me and Zach to Great-Grandma Ila's house on a hot August morning. I gazed out the car window as we wound through streets of single-story houses with mossy roofs, front lawns browned from heat. At a stoplight, Dad turned to where I sat in the front seat. "You kids know Grandma Ila used to smoke but doesn't anymore," he said. "Right?"

I nodded. How was I supposed to know? I'd never seen her smoke.

He scrunched up his face in mock disgust. "Eeew," he said. "Smoking is disgusting, turns your teeth and fingers brown."

I'd never noticed the color of Grandma Ila's teeth or fingers, and made a mental note to check.

"We made her quit." He turned left into the cul-de-sac, then up the narrow driveway to her pea-green house. "She'll probably live forever now. Ha."

A split-rail fence bordered her front yard; in the back, a gigantic blue spruce held a secret fort between its trunk and low-swooping branches. The screen door squeaked, and, once inside the front door, my eyes adjusted to the dim room. She kept her blinds closed against direct sunlight, and a large standing fan wobbled back and forth. Zach and I kissed her soft wrinkled cheek and climbed onto the swivel barstools at the kitchen counter. "Maxine just left," she said to Dad as she lit the sandalwood incense she kept next to the cookie jar.

Maxine was her next-door neighbor, younger than Grandma Ila but still an old lady. She wore bright red lipstick and shoes that clacked on the linoleum, and, unlike Grandma, she still smoked, a cigarette always dangling from her mouth. She was always just leaving, puffing in and out of Grandma Ila's house at random.

After Dad left, while Grandma slapped cards onto her gold-flecked Formica countertop in her continuous game of solitaire, Zach and I stepped into the open living room to play with her special chair. The rest of Grandma Ila's furniture was from the 1940s, with carved wooden feet and burnout velvet upholstery, but her special chair had bloated beige cushions and a mechanical frame that hummed up and down at the push of a button.

We loved that thing. I sat on the hearth next to the book-sized obsidian rock while Zach took his turn on the most thrilling slow-motion ride in the world. On the wall above me, a ceramic mood barometer was set in between "bossy" and "touchy." While the barometer's arrow never shifted, I still monitored it closely just in case its little black arrow ever pointed at "hysterical" or "malicious."

"Whoa, whoa. Grandma, look, I'm falling!" Zach's legs dangled off the tilted chair, his toes almost, but not quite, touching the sculpted tufts of wall-to-wall brown shag carpet. Grandma Ila glanced up for half a second before returning to her card game.

No matter the heat, lunch was always homemade chicken noodle soup from the freezer, reheated on the stovetop but with a single ice cube in the middle of our bowls to cool it down. She clacked woven straw placemats on the counter in front of our barstools. "Do you want crackers?"

"Yes!"

She gave us the plastic-wrapped tower of Saltines so we could crumble as many as we wanted on top. The soup was good, but my stomach always hurt after eating, sharp spasms so consistent I didn't always mention them anymore. Like usual, I curled into a ball on the couch to wait for them to pass.

"Be good," she said later, before disappearing into her bedroom with its creaky four-poster bed and quilted hot pink coverlet.

My stomach spasms had weakened, so the second she clicked her bedroom door shut, the gold specks in the countertop started dancing. Zach and I tiptoed into the kitchen to assess the sugar situation. She usually had not only freeze pops that turned our mouths blue but also a well-stocked cookie jar and multiple cartons of vanilla ice cream in the freezer. The treatiest things at home were toaster waffles or peanut butter mixed with chocolate chips, so Grandma Ila's dim house shone bright with sugary possibilities.

We didn't get ice cream every day, though. It was something to aspire to. We peeked inside the owl-shaped ceramic cookie jar, which sat underneath the hanging macramé planter that Grandma Ila had knotted herself, complete with wooden beads. I lifted the lid carefully so as not to make the glassy ding she might be able to hear from her bedroom. Inside, the usual. Crumbly pecan cookies that were better than no cookies at all. We didn't take any, simply wanted to determine what we had a reasonable chance of receiving later if we begged.

We resumed riding her special chair. But when she returned from her bedroom, I caught a glaring glimpse of the carton of Breyer's vanilla ice cream in her hand. She snuck it back into the freezer quickly, trying to make so we wouldn't see.

But I saw.

"Did you see that?" I whispered to Zach. He stilled the mechanical chair and shook his head, wide-eyed.

"Grandma was eating ice cream in her bedroom without us."

Zach's sticky fingers gripped the cold, hard buttons on the mechanical chair like the best slow-motion ride in the world had lost its thrill. "Why?"

Grandma Ila reclaimed her spot behind the counter. I approached slowly and crawled onto a swivel stool, watching her hand as it slapped down each card. The skin on her fingers looked more yellowish than brown, and the wrinkled skin on her forearm drooped toward the counter.

"Did you want something?" She looked up over her thick glasses.

"Can we have some ice cream too?"

"Hmpf," she said, looking back down at her orderly solitaire piles. "Maybe later."

It was as if she didn't think she owed us any explanation at all. We went outside and crawled into the hidden fort at the base of the blue spruce, crunching its long, slender pine cones under our feet as we talked about the unfairness of it all. But the next time Zach and I had the kitchen to ourselves, while Grandma Ila stood in her backyard talking to Maxine over the fence, I decided we should help ourselves to the ice cream.

It was only fair. Compensation for betrayal. I dragged over a swivel stool that boosted us high enough to reach into the back of the freezer.

And when I opened the door, the gust of cold air held me in place while I processed what I saw. "She has *three* ice creams in here?"

I went over everything we'd done since arriving at her house that morning. We rode the mechanical chair, we sprinkled Saltines on top of our chicken noodle soup, and we hid in the secret fort at the base of the blue spruce. The usual. What had we done to make her so angry that she wouldn't share her sugary bounty? The mood clock's arrow still pointed between "bossy" and "touchy." No changes there.

"Did you break Grandma's special chair?" I asked Zach, proposing the worst thing I could think of.

He shook his head and gulped.

Freezer burn crystals hovered above my head. Maybe it was all okay. Maybe we were just two kids getting ice cream on a hot summer's day. Nothing wrong with that. In any case, no turning back now.

"Go get us spoons," I ordered.

Zach climbed down to fetch two spoons from the silverware drawer while I kept watch out the kitchen window. The fence obscured Maxine except for her head of short dark curls. She and Grandma Ila still cackled, the smoke rising in puffs between them.

Spoon in hand, I dug my fingers underneath the lid of the nearest container. Snowy ice cream that we would plow into our mouths before Grandma Ila crunched back through the brown grass toward the house. The container made a gaping sound when I peeled it open and released its seal of air.

I recognized the smell first—like Maxine, only sharper—before I saw what was inside. It wasn't vanilla ice cream. "Oh my God," I said, nearly losing my grip on the spoon as I recoiled.

We looked at each other in horror and leaned so far back that we almost toppled the swivel stool. That round Breyer's container was a massive frozen ash tray, filled with cigarette butts and vinegar-soaked paper towels that did little to hide their stench.

My stomach lurched.

"I don't want ice cream anymore," Zach said, his voice quivering.

I couldn't bring myself to look inside the other two containers, even the brick-like one that unfolded like a cereal box. "Me neither."

We crawled out of the freezer, and I dragged the stool back to its place under the bar side of the gold-flecked Formica countertop while Zach returned the spoons to the drawer. "Hurry, before she comes back inside."

We slunk back to the TV in the dim living room. I claimed the special chair but didn't push the buttons as we sunk into daytime game shows. Soon the sound of playing cards resumed clacking on the Formica countertop behind us.

I thought about how Dad said he'd made Grandma Ila quit smoking, but he hadn't. My stomach still wobbled from the lingering smell of infinite cigarette butts, but I admired the quiet way in which Grandma Ila did whatever she wanted. Maybe you couldn't make someone quit doing anything they still wanted to do.

BIKER CHICK WEDDING

My extended student visa expired the same year same-sex marriage became legal across Canada, so the summer after Mags and I graduated from McGill, we had the queer version of a shotgun wedding. Only instead of a baby, I got another mountain of paperwork from Immigration Canada. If I were straight, I never would have gotten hitched so young. But validating a queer relationship the same year it became legal for us to do so? It felt more like rebellion than a preemptive settling down.

We lived in the country north of Brockville with Mags's parents—Howie and Margaret—academics who worked in Ottawa. Their late 1800s Gothic Revival sandstone farmhouse sat on close to three hundred acres. They'd bought and furnished the house in the 1970s, when rundown farmhouses and antique pine furniture in rural Ontario could be had for cheap. It had ornate white gingerbread fretwork and two wood stoves, but the first thing I fell in love with was its silence. After years in Montreal, I craved the silence like air and took deep gulps. The only sounds at night were the aches of the cast iron wood stoves as they warmed or cooled, and the dream-thumping tails of their golden retrievers. Decades of claws had gouged the wide-plank cedar floors.

"Just focus on the dogs if you don't know what to say," Mags suggested the first time I met her parents.

I never really knew what to say, so I focused on the dogs a lot. I also focused on the wood stoves, bringing in armloads of wood from the front porch, my grabby wool sweater covered with both tufts of yellow fur and dried bits of bark. The house smelled not only of wood smoke but also, always, of Mags's dad slow-roasting something in the oven.

It felt like home.

After the wedding I'd be able to apply for a temporary work visa and then permanent residency. The unknown variable was how many months the work visa would take to process, and I couldn't work a regular job until then. I'd take whatever under-the-table work came my way.

Mags took a job at a provincial campground on the Saint Lawrence River, and Howie asked me to write an index for his management textbook. I thought it would be busy work, but I wasn't really in a position to say no to a job offer. Indexing turned out to be more than creating a list of words. I had to conceptualize the whole book and how people were likely to use it, and I liked the challenge. It relaxed me, to spin my head around within the finite limits of a set number of pages. Then I helped Margaret research an article she had to write on urban policy. I found and summarized the previous research, pulled the best quotes, and compiled it all into a binder for her to peruse. "That was the easiest article I've ever written," she said.

Working in my pajamas on my own schedule, in a beautiful and quiet sandstone farmhouse, suited me. Maybe I'd keep freelancing forever.

Even though my mom thought I'd been brainwashed by all the "pinkos" on campus when I first came out, when I told her about the wedding, she wanted to host a reception for us in Portland that fall.

"Maybe," I said. "But I have to wait for my work visa, otherwise I might not be able to come back into Canada. Can we figure it out later?"

When I told my dad about the wedding over the phone, he asked, "Is that the sort of thing you'd want me to be at?"

"You don't have to," I said. He'd gone relatively silent for years after I came out, and I didn't want him there making things weird.

I just wanted to sign whatever paperwork and be done with it, but the City of Kingston required a ceremony so we found a Unitarian minister willing to marry us, without rings, in her backyard on Lake Ontario. We only needed two witnesses. I searched online for generic vows, like I expected there to be some sort of official template for a nonreligious queer wedding.

At the farmhouse, Mags and I sat with her parents on the brick patio eating a lunch of bread and cheese and boiled eggs and tapenade a few paces away from the small apple orchard across the lawn. Across the ditch to the left was the large vegetable garden and, beyond that, old crop fields gone wild into a brambly forest.

"Neither of us likes to be the center of attention," Mags said to her parents to explain our minimal wedding plans.

Margaret fed cubes of extra sharp cheddar cheese to the golden retrievers. "I know you don't want a reception," she said, "but we should at least go to dinner afterward."

Mags and I made eye contact. "Sure."

When I wasn't indexing or minimizing our wedding planning, I did DIY sorts of things. I helped Margaret in the vegetable garden, mounding the potatoes, pruning the tomatoes, and covering the carrot seeds with burlap. One of the golden retrievers made a game of eating the asparagus tips poking out of the ground before we could stop him.

Mags taught me how to knit, and I made hand warmers and ribbed toques and my first sweater out of black mohair that made me look like a gorilla. Then I made a box for my yarn out of leftover tongue-and-groove floor planks from the scrap pile in the barn. We went to summer studio tours, peeking in local artisans' shops and studios, and I couldn't decide which craft I liked best. I loved the bumpy woven shawls, the wonky handblown glass, the speckled glazes on tea mugs. Could I create a studio that somehow incorporated all of them?

The morning of our wedding, Mags and I went yardsaling along two-lane country roads. I wanted some time alone together before our brief ceremony, and I needed to clear my head. I had awful cramps and so much allergy-induced congestion I could barely breathe. My eyes itched an angry red and my nose bled. I hated the oppressive heat, and I felt more like curling into a ball in a cold cupboard than getting married that afternoon. A hot water bottle jiggled on my lap, soothing the cramps but adding unwanted heat to the rest of me.

Mags passed a group of bikers because she knew I hated the grating engines and suffocating exhaust that ruined peaceful, head-clearing drives. We meandered through the network of marshes and lakes and canals, passing limestone outcrops, soy fields, and chip trucks, and I put my head in between my legs to keep from vomiting.

I sat up. "I wish those chip trucks were espresso stands."

Mags didn't say anything. She'd heard it before, how much I missed lattes on every corner, even along two-lane country roads.

"That looks like a good one," I said, pointing to a few folding tables and some soggy "free" boxes. "Let's stop there."

The air smelled like sap and freshly mowed lawn. I sneezed. Among the array of chipped mugs and ripped lawn chairs, I made for the black leather motorcycle jacket on a meager clothing rack. Metal grommets and a wide collar. I liked the idea of finding something special on my wedding day, but I wasn't sure the jacket suited me. I tried it on. It weighed me down and only zipped up if I held my breath. "What do you think?"

Mags stepped back. "You look tough."

It seemed like an identity-changing kind of day. Maybe once I was a married woman, I'd be able to pull off badass biker chick? But it was way too hot and humid to stand around in a leather jacket considering the perfect fit. I unzipped the heavy jacket and paid $25 without bothering to haggle.

Back in the car, my congestion fully renewed from the grass-filled air, it took me a few minutes to realize that my new-to-me motorcycle jacket reeked of stale cigarettes. My sense of smell returned, combined with the winding roads, to trigger intense nausea. I pushed the jacket to the floor and held my head in between my legs to settle my stomach. Not until I heard a sound like raindrops did I realize my nose had started to bleed again, splashing heavy drips onto the black leather jacket that I'd never wear.

"I miss the ocean," I said. "We have to move to British Columbia."

"Okay, Lyssy."

Our definition of fancy was anything new instead of secondhand, so for the wedding we'd splurged and each bought one new thing from American Apparel—Mags, a brown short-sleeved polo shirt dress and me, a white long-sleeved keyhole T-shirt. When we got back to the house, we changed into our wedding casual. Mags added a leather flower choker, and I put on a sea-foam green corduroy skirt, polka dot tights, and blue Doc Martens.

I thought we looked pretty good.

Before the ceremony, Margaret gave us four handblown wine glasses—small, wonky, and triangular—that we'd seen at a studio tour earlier that summer. I loved them, ready as I was for everything in my life to be handcrafted. We succeeded in keeping the ceremony small, with only the Unitarian minister, and Margaret and Howie as witnesses.

I only remember one line from our internet-retrieved vows: "May our lives be more full for having lived them together." Yes, I thought, I could say that out loud without dying of embarrassment. I could say that out loud and mean it.

We kissed. "Do it again," my new father-in-law said. "That was too fast."

We reenacted a kiss that lasted long enough to be photographed, and we clinked our handblown wine glasses on the shores of Lake Ontario.

My new mother-in-law put her arm around my shoulder, "I never thought I'd have another daughter," she smiled.

The lake sparkled over her shoulders, and a gust of wind rustled my hair. Even though I never expected to get married at all, my chest expanded at belonging to this new family.

To mark our first interprovincial move, Mags loaded the majority of our belongings—books and diplomas and furniture—into the attic of her parents' drive shed. I supervised while she labored.

"You fall every single move," she said. We'd been through three moves together so far. "So I'm carrying stuff up the ladder."

With me uninjured and our boxes stacked where they had a good chance of being shredded by mice before we came looking for them again, we drove off toward British Columbia in our over-stuffed station wagon. I'd packed my new tongue-and-groove yarn box and the wonky wine glasses, but I left the smoky biker jacket behind.

TRUST ME

My parents were getting divorced that year.

At least I thought so.

They fought. From my bedroom, I heard yelling and thumping, and I'd watch my dad's car screech down the street. One day, my mom, Zach, and I returned from the mall to a ransacked house, the shelf that had held my dad's boxy silver stereo with shiny knobs stood empty, and leftover cardboard boxes gaped open in the living room like he might be returning for them, and for us.

I hovered around my mom, waiting for an explanation. Was she crying? My stomach sank. I wanted to ask what was wrong, but I didn't. Maybe I knew. This was divorce, right? The worst possible thing? The childhood apocalypse? After my mom went into her room and shut the door, my five-year-old brother Zach and I wandered around the house in silence to see what had gone missing. None of our toys.

At my large, institutional daycare, however, I got confused. Maybe I'd made it all up and my parents weren't getting divorced at all? They often arrived together to pick us up, smiling and laughing like we were a happy, unified family. I didn't understand why they both came in to get us when we'd only be driving home with one of them. Confusing. Confusing the same way dad would laugh and joke with the adults at the daycare but then stop being happy the second we were alone in the car. It seemed like I always did something to make him mad the second we got away from other people.

I mentioned to one of the daycare workers, Patty, that my dad lived in his own apartment.

"Your parents aren't divorced," she said.

"Yes, they are!" I said. "Even ask Marianne."

I wobbled, unsure of what I knew, not having any proof besides my own experience. What if she asked Marianne—one of the other women who worked at the daycare—and Marianne didn't back me up?

I liked a school picture of myself for the first time that year. I wore a black turtleneck and my hair frazzled in a loose ponytail. I had a real smile on, and I thought I looked like a writer or an artist. My disheveled look meant I was too preoccupied with creative thoughts to pay attention to superficial things like combs.

I buckled into the front seat of my dad's car, where he had a fresh yellow sticky note stuck to the dashboard that read, "COUNT to 10!" I handed him the large envelope with the cellophane window and waited for him to exclaim over how cute I was, but when he saw my duplicated grins, he grimaced and covered his face. I jumped when he spoke.

"Your teeth are yellow!" He reached for my shoulders. "Come here and smile."

I gave a wide false grin.

"Ugh. There's so much gunk on your teeth I can scrape it off with my fingernail." He pushed me away in disgust. "When's the last time you brushed them, huh?"

I slumped and looked out the car window at the stoic profiles of other people in their cars. Did they all brush their teeth every single day? I didn't like the sound of the bristles echoing in my head or how toothpaste dribbled globs onto my pajama shirt. So why should I bother to do it more than occasionally?

My dad had covered his face when he'd seen my first-grade school pictures too, in particular the class photo, me in the front row with baggy red pants tucked into pink ankle socks.

"Socks go under your pants," he'd said, as if I were an idiot instead of an avant-garde fashion warrior.

But why did I still embarrass him, even when I wore a black turtleneck and looked like a classic genius? Before Dad picked us up, I'd shown Marianne my school picture, cellophane crinkling as I pulled the envelope out of my backpack.

"So cute," she'd said, inspecting it closely. "You look happy."

Marianne was the greatest.

Marianne was a different kind of adult. She had short hair and wore tight jeans and dangly earrings, and she went to the local community college. Just that word "college" sounded impossibly sophisticated. I loved her. I wanted her attention, all of it, all the time.

In fact, I longed for attention from almost every older woman or girl I came across. When a couple of teenagers went door to door in my neighborhood, I tried to impress them by lying stomach-down on the grass and pulling myself along like a snake. I hoped this would earn me loving gazes. "What a silly, creative child!" I imagined them thinking. And then they would laugh and give me piggyback rides for the rest of the afternoon. Instead, they looked at each other with raised eyebrows; after my mom returned with her billfold, they walked away without looking back, leaving me just a weird kid with grass stains all over her shirt.

I loved Marianne because she talked to me like I mattered and also because she knew my middle name. She ran a deluxe version of the name game in the daycare, where she sat a small group of us in a circle and we went around saying our full names.

"Alyssa *Jean* Graybeal," she repeated.

Something about her calling me Alyssa Jean made me feel like she really knew me. When she said my middle name in a kind voice, she scratched the surface to all my secrets and loved me anyway.

I also liked it when she noticed my shoes coming untied, which happened often because the knots I tied myself were too loose. It hurt my hands to pull the laces tight, and I didn't want to crush my feet. In any case, I tripped over my own ankles more often than untied shoelaces.

"Alyssa," Marianne said later, "this is the fifth time today I've had to tie your shoes."

I grinned as she kneeled at my feet.

"Do you know how to tie double knots?" she asked.

Of course I did, but I preferred to stick with the single version.

In daycare the year before, I'd squeezed myself in between the bookshelves to read about Ramona Quimby. Ramona lived nearby, in Portland, and I looked out for her whenever we drove across the green trussed bridge. Whenever the endless rain got too sad, I thought of her across the river, staring out her living room window at the same endless rain, and my mood lifted. I related to her look of untied shoes and messy straight hair, but I wasn't sure my own curly frizz had the same lovable effect.

Even while reading, I kept close tabs on Marianne. On the way outside for play time, Marianne stopped me before I reached the cement steps leading from the wide-open basement playroom to the backyard.

"What are you reading?" she asked.

I showed her the cover. *Ramona Quimby, Age 8.*

"Oh, I love Ramona!"

I glowed. That meant she loved me too, since I was the same age. Actually, I was only seven, but my dad always told me I was too smart for my own good, so I thought my smartness probably made me more like an eight-year-old than a seven-year-old. So I carried my chapter book outside with pride, even though I wished Marianne didn't have to stay inside to vacuum. I would have preferred to follow her around the yard and try to prompt another admission about how much she loved Ramona Quimby.

A swing set sat at one end of the long, narrow yard, and patches of moss grew along the fence. The towering fir trees didn't let in much light, and I could never find a dry place to sit on the damp ground, so I had to find something else to do besides read.

I didn't have the energy to play tag with the other kids at the far end of the yard. Plus, running hurt my ankles. So I walked over to the swings. I gripped the chains as tightly as possible because I loved the white impressions they left on my palms. I got off, admiring my temporary blister-like bumps, and watched Patty, who was in charge of watching us while we played outside. Maybe if my hands were disfigured enough, she'd ask me about them.

No. Patty was having a moment inside her own head.

She leaned against one of the swing set's wooden posts, slanted at a seventy-five-degree angle. She looked so cool leaning against that post like nothing mattered. I tried to copy her, only instead of leaning back I leaned face-forward against my post, turning my head to the side to rest my ear on the wood. I let my arms flop forward, hanging lifeless as a sock monkey.

I didn't feel as cool as Patty looked, but it didn't matter because I didn't stay in my limp-limbed position for long. I gasped and pushed myself to standing.

Noises sprung from inside that post.

I looked behind me to see if anyone else had noticed, but no one paid any attention to the magic happening inside the swing set. I leaned in again to confirm that, yes, aches and groans echoed inside the post like little elves had climbed in through the wood's knife-like sliver holes and formed a miniature factory of voices and squeaks and clangs, one that probably looked more or less like the Keebler elves making cookies in that TV commercial.

"Patty, you have to come listen to this! There are elves in the swing set."

She raised one eyebrow.

She didn't believe me? I knew how it sounded. I mean, I was almost eight years old. I knew elves weren't real, just like I'd pointed out my parents' handwriting on the gift tags supposedly written by Santa. I wasn't stupid. But still. I really could hear a factory of elves inside that post. Should I believe what I knew—that elves didn't exist—or should I believe what I could hear with my own ears?

"For reals! I mean, that's what it sounds like."

Patty didn't move from her cool seventy-five-degree lean. "Come on, Alyssa."

I wished the other kids would stop swinging for a minute so I could concentrate on figuring out how to convince Patty of the truth, but I couldn't think straight with their rhythmic kicking. I leaned into the post one more time in an elaborate display of listening. I opened my eyes wide and nodded in time with the elves' clinks and clanks.

My voice started to quiver. "No, really. Listen!"

"You're trying to trick me," she said.

She thought I was a liar. I widened my stance, hands on hips. "Elves!"

"I'm not going to do it."

"Fine."

I stomped away to hide in the little cabin-like structure in the middle of the yard that no one ever played in. I was done with Patty. I inspected the rotten wood of the cabin walls and breathed the damp evergreen air, then started tying and untying the knots of my shoelaces. Through the cabin window that never had glass and never would, I watched as Patty

/9j/

sidled over to the post where I'd been leaning ear-first. She looked over her shoulder to make sure no one was watching before touching her own ear against it.

Her mouth made an open "O" just like in the cartoons, and she jerked back from the post.

She'd heard the elves.

When her eyes scanned the mossy yard for me, I ducked down underneath the glassless window so she couldn't see me, and I hid there until the end of play time. I only emerged to file back inside with everyone else, down the cement steps to the basement.

She smiled at me. "You were right about the elves," she said, her voice lighthearted, as if we were still friends.

But it was too late for us to share a moment. She hadn't trusted me when it mattered. I rolled my eyes. "I *know*," I said, as I walked past her into the wide-open basement playroom.

On New Year's Eve, Marianne sat in the throne-like wicker basket chair in the corner of our living room talking on the brick of a portable phone from the kitchen. She babysat for us sometimes too.

"What are you guys doing later?" she asked the phone.

I sat near her and tried to figure out what her friends were saying on the other end of the line. Something funny. When she hung up, she looked at me and Zach milling around her like excited puppies.

"What's so funny?" I asked.

She pushed down the phone's antenna with her palm. "You guys aren't going to want to stay up till midnight, are you?"

"Yes, we are!"

I knew Marianne was only teasing. She smiled a little, clearly thrilled to get to spend an extra-long evening with us. When she'd arrived, both of my parents had descended from the master bedroom as if they'd been getting ready together, even though my dad had arrived fully dressed at the front door only a few minutes before Marianne.

"His clothes aren't up there anymore," I informed Marianne after they left on their date night. I needed her on my side, especially when I suspected that my parents would be talking about me over dinner.

Marianne nodded, but she also asked me hard questions. "Does your dad live in Portland?"

I frowned and fiddled with my hands. The drive to my dad's apartment did take longer than the bus ride to school.

"Do you have to go over a bridge to get there?"

Two different bridges crossed the Columbia River to divide Portland from Vancouver, a suburb even though it was in a different state. I didn't want Marianne to think I was so babyish that I'd never crossed the river. I had, lots of times. We usually drove over the green trussed bridge, and I always looked for Mount Hood in the distance even though you couldn't see it if it was raining, and it was usually raining. No matter the weather, I always bobbed my head in time to the rhythm of the beams passing over the car, pretending I had to duck to avoid them. But did I have to duck under those green trusses every time I went to Dad's new apartment? I couldn't remember.

"Yes?" I said.

Marianne nodded. I worried that if I didn't give the right answers, her belief might be retracted. But even if the details were hazy, my dad definitely lived in an apartment instead of our house.

At first, I couldn't sleep at my dad's apartment, and I didn't want to go.

"It's too loud," I said. "I want to stay in my own room."

My mom looked up from where she sat reading her newspaper at the kitchen counter. "I spoiled you, always letting you have your own room," she sighed, returning to the giant pages. "You'll get used to it."

So I had to go anyway, even if I couldn't sleep.

"The neighbor's TV is too loud," I said to Dad from the sleeping bag on the floor of his new apartment's second bedroom. The sound knotted up the space between my shoulder blades.

Dad bundled up my bedding and made me a nest of blankets in the middle of the scratchy living room carpet, as far as possible from all the thin walls.

"Better?"

I nodded once but felt uneasy to now be floating in the middle of the carpet the color of sand. What if he accidentally stepped on me in the middle of the night? I wanted my own bedroom, with its pink walls and pink bedspread and matching curtains my mom had sewn for me. Only my head peeked out from the top of the sleeping bag. The noise still bothered me from there.

Eventually, I stopped complaining about the rhythm of my childhood. I had a packed overnight bag in the corner of my bedroom at all times and got ferried to Dad's on Tuesdays and Thursdays and every other weekend, even after he really did move all the way to Portland and we commuted over that green trussed bridge. But I left most of my things, clothes and books and notebooks, at Mom's house. I needed to know where my pens were when I needed them.

I couldn't bring myself to move half of my stuff for the sake of an even fifty-fifty split.

Several months after my dad moved out, I floated in the bathtub waiting for my mom to come in and wash my hair. Too grown up for bath toys, I just wanted to float and feel the hot water on my ears. My fingertips wrinkled, which I loved the same way I loved the white marks on my hands from gripping swings' metal chains. I kept my hands under water as much as possible to maximize the effect.

Mom came in to sit on the edge of the tub and rub shampoo into my hair. She finally spoke, her voice serious. "You know your dad and I are divorced, right?"

I held my gaze on my wrinkled toes near the faucet and nodded. Maybe I had done something bad, because why was Mom talking about this now?

"Good," she said.

I gripped the bottom of the tub with my wrinkled fingertips, feeling more buoyant in that bathtub now that I had confirmation that I hadn't been lying to Marianne about the divorce after all. Mom rinsed out the shampoo by leaning me back under the faucet, and I closed my eyes tight to prevent the bubbles from rushing in.

Then I went to bed without brushing my teeth.

HALFWAY HOT SPRINGS

I had a hot springs fantasy: pristine pools filled with rare healing minerals, available only to those willing to blaze a trail through dense backwoods to get to them. They'd be like a spa, only instead of a heady mix of essential oils and petrochemical beauty products, I'd inhale deeply of fresh pine and damp leaves. Instead of wearing fluffy acrylic slippers, I'd walk barefoot over glistening rocks. And instead of being ushered into a private room by a polished employee, I'd soak in the majestic privacy of the entire forest. The water would be held lovingly by rocks deposited in perfect hot tub formation by receding glaciers. Or maybe a group of bearded gentlemen in tie-dyed T-shirts had crafted a rock-lined oasis to facilitate my enjoyment of the Kootenay Rockies?

It would be perfect.

Mags and I landed in a small cabin built by an old hippie who didn't believe in building codes. The water was heated by propane tanks we changed ourselves. Gnarly lacquered branches twisted up either side of the ladder-like stairs. We'd originally intended to go all the way to the ocean, but I'd gotten into woodworking during the summer we got married. Whittling away my time on Mags's parents' farm, I'd fed my craving for working with my hands, and I liked the smell of fresh sawdust and the layers of scrap wood leaning against the wall in the barn. Maybe I'd become a fine woodworker? The idea had prompted me to look up community college programs in British Columbia, where I'd discovered a free, semester-long skilled trades program in Nelson, one that included courses on carpentry and woodworking, as well as wiring, soldering, and plumbing. The prospect of learning such practical and nonacademic skills interested me. But it turned out I couldn't enroll in the program to get free practice with a blow torch because, even though

Mags and I were legally married, I still floated in immigration limbo, not yet a permanent resident of Canada. We moved to Nelson, British Columbia anyway, and Mags took the yearlong program instead. Our lives and desires had become intertwined.

While Mags went to class, I stayed in the cabin to stoke the old wood stove, its only source of heat. No matter what we did, we couldn't get it to bank its coals overnight, but the heat rose and aggregated above our bed nestled under the A-frame roof. We'd fall asleep sweating and wake up to our frozen breath until one of us could be coaxed out of bed.

"It's your turn to start it."

"No, yours."

It was the perfect—and quiet—antidote to five years in a big city. We were living the life. Because I couldn't work legally, Mags's parents continued to funnel under-the-table research assistant work my way. I also completed a correspondence course on back-of-the-book indexing, learning the organizational minutiae of letter-by-letter vs. word-by-word alphabetization, indented vs. run-in subheadings, and cross-referencing. I was very good at it. From our folding black card table in the cabin, I fantasized about what it would be like to stay in Nelson forever. I imagined myself as a freelance indexer or a librarian and, in the evenings, writing in a little shed (built by Mags) that overlooked a wild vegetable garden.

I became obsessed with the creativity workbook *The Artist's Way*, which I'd checked out from the Nelson Public Library, and I started doing its assigned "morning pages," three pages of stream-of-consciousness writing that, someday, I imagined I'd be able to mine for insights about my psyche. In the afternoons, I tried to write stories, or I sketched clothing and pattern ideas, and daydreamed about how I might make a living selling hand-knit sweaters. Maybe I'd never need a "real job" if I was able to make my own meaning through writing and sweater design. Maybe I could live the freelance artist life forever. I didn't want to be a naturopathic doctor anymore. My aching limbs needed to curl up cat-like in a chair after only a few hours of freelance work. How would I handle medical school when I worried my body wouldn't even be able to handle a full-time job? But I hoped after a restful year, my body would bounce back and more energy would come.

I calmed myself with the repetitive motion of looping string around needles, but I hated it when a half-used skein turned into a knotted mess. I made the knots worse as I went, pulling at the loose ends as if I could unravel them by force. Fortunately, Mags liked being asked to untangle them, accepting a dense pile of string like a puzzle she'd been waiting for.

"Ta-da! You just have to start from the center."

She made it seem so easy.

To make our situation even more idyllic, while our landlord had gone off volunteering in Africa, we'd temporarily inherited a loving German shepherd named Shyla and an affectionate long-haired cat named Mittens who peed in the shower. Because Shyla needed daily walks, we explored many hiking trails, both official and unofficial, so after only a few months we fancied ourselves locals, at least in terms of geographic knowledge.

The one thing I disliked about the cabin was its missing bathtub, my primary pain management strategy, which I missed intensely. I complained about it so much that Mags bought me a gift certificate for three fancy soaks at the spa in town. Hot water was on my mind as the ultimate luxury. "Let's take a day trip to a hot spring," I suggested.

Our official sources of information were a thirty-year-old guidebook from the public library, whose pages were faded and spine cracked by generations of secret-seekers, and a twenty-something girl with blonde dreadlocks and crocheted headbands who worked at the Dominion Café and served our lattes along with confident, yet vague, directions that seemed so clear we didn't even feel the need to write them down. Finding the hot springs would be simple. What we wanted would simply come to us through the laws of attraction, the workings of which were only just being revealed to us.

"Just follow the flow of traffic," our landlord had said when directing us to the nearest grocery store. Likewise, he'd said the crystals in the mountains could direct us like homing beacons, if only we were attuned to them. So we told ourselves to trust the crystals.

On the appointed October day, it rained. We'll call it a drizzle, but it looked like it had no intention of burning off. No matter. I grew up in the Pacific Northwest. I thought I had immunity to the rain. I loved its sound, its smell, how it took the harsh, exposing glare out of the sky, and how it encouraged the meltable sugar cube people to stay inside their homes, leaving the streets quiet. But I also loved it for keeping me inside. I didn't relish soaked denim as much as I did being curled up in a chair with a book and a pot of tea and a cat in my lap. On rainy days, gazing out the window washed me clean of any guilt that I should be leaving the house and interacting with humankind.

The rain facilitated my introverted dreamland.

So in my decidedly pro-rain stance, I had let it slip from my mind that hiking in heavy rain is unpleasant, no matter how poetic it sounds. I packed a bag with bath towels and changes of clothes, as well as water and snacks. We cruelly abandoned Shyla that day, our canine trailblazer, in a miraculous act of foresight on our part. Four-plus hours in the car might have been too much for her, despite the reward of a walk, and we also worried she might want to join us in the steaming pool, which would've spoiled the romantic effect.

We set off steeped in the spirit of adventure. My intuition, which had been honed by two months of drinking the water, told me the rain would clear and we'd be guaranteed a soak under the soft, feathery fronds of old growth red cedars. Mags drove west on Highway 6, taking a hard right at Playmor Junction to follow the highway north. Had we continued south, we would have passed through the town of Castlegar, notable to me because when we'd driven through on a previous exploratory road trip, I'd done a double take at the tiny sign on a bridge under which a small river rippled. The sign read Columbia River.

Was that the same Columbia River of my childhood, the one that divided my parents' houses in Vancouver, Washington and Portland, Oregon? It felt like a little piece of home to have discovered the familiar river looking small and inconsequential way up here. According to the map, it earned its name Columbia River right there at the bridge, at the junction of the Kootenay River and Upper Arrow Lake. Six hours further north, the same waters ran in what looked like an unbroken string winding its way through Kinbasket Lake. Up here, the river gave no hint of the power that would eventually grow to feed fourteen hydroelectric dams before it met the Pacific Ocean, four miles wide, on the northern shore of Astoria, Oregon.

But this time we headed north through the Slocan Valley to Nakusp while I watched the rain increase in direct proportion to how far we'd travelled from the cabin. The forest closed in around the highway.

"It's so crazy how you could just disappear into these woods and be lost forever," Mags said.

I shrugged. "It's so beautiful though. The mist."

I wanted Mags to love British Columbia so much she'd insist that we stay. Eventually, I hoped to drag us all the way west to the Pacific Ocean, not back to humid Ontario.

"That could never happen in Ontario," she said. "Someone would find you."

"Right, but who just walks into the woods and gets lost?" I had a sense of ownership over any rainy, evergreen landscape. Getting lost was for tourists. The fewer people, the better. We were safe. The drops on the window shield had hypnotized me, so only when Mags pulled off onto an unmarked logging road did I snap to and realize we'd soon have to get out of the car. The logging road carved into the side of a mountain obscured by fog, and the potholes slowed us down.

"Do you think this is the right road?" I asked.

Mags didn't answer, her knuckles white on the steering wheel.

"We're looking for surveyor's tape next to a big fallen tree," I said. "And she said it would be halfway between kilometer marker eight and nine."

Distance was the official nomenclature of the area. Hamlets were known as Three Mile and Six Mile according to their distance from town. Even though by 2005, Canada had been switched over to the metric system for decades, they hadn't renamed Three Mile to Four-Point-Eight Kilometers, which didn't have the same ring to it. But right then we were in a distance-based, in-between no-man's land.

"Between kilometer marker eight and nine," Mags repeated. "Doesn't every logging road have a big fallen tree marked with surveyor's tape?" Seeing no trail marker, Mags finally stopped the car. It took a while for it to sink in that we were no longer moving. Nothing to do but head downhill because we knew the hot springs pooled next to a river.

"Do you want a granola bar first?" I asked.

Mags declined. She looked pale and not at all hungry. But when I reached into the back seat to retrieve our towels and changes of clothes, I didn't see the backpack on the floor behind the driver's seat. Then I didn't see it on the floor behind the passenger's seat. And then I didn't see it on the entire empty expanse of the backseat itself. Why would Mags load the bag into the cargo space of the station wagon? What a pain. I crawled back, sure it would be there.

But it wasn't. "Mags," I said. "Where'd you put the backpack?"

She turned to look at me. "I thought you packed it."

"I did! But you were supposed to put it in the car."

Her eyes grew wide and she almost laughed. "But I thought *you* put it in the car."

I rubbed my face with both hands. We'd get soaked walking down to the hot springs no matter what. "We can't drive home in wet clothes. We'll get hypothermia!"

I closed my eyes and tried to will us back in time to when we were leaving the cabin and made sure to put our dry clothes, towels, snacks, and water in the car. When that didn't work, I forced us into my plan B. "Okay, here's what we're going to do. We'll walk down in our underwear, T-shirts, and shoes, and leave our jeans, hoodies, and socks in the car. Then we'll have something warm to change into when we get back." I paused to make room for her enthusiastic agreement. When it didn't come, I continued. "We'll be cold on the way down but fine on the way back because we'll be all warmed up from the hot spring!" I started unzipping my hoodie. "Ready?"

Mags remained silent and stripped along with me, probably wishing she was still whittling next to the wood stove. When we stepped out of the car, my first surprise was how quickly white underwear turns transparent in the rain. My second surprise was how quickly the tops of my thighs turned purple from the cold shock of exposure.

"We have to go fast," I said.

We slipped down the steep hillside. The rain had turned the entire slope into mud, and tree branches acted like gutter downspouts to funnel even more water onto our heads. Amazing that the moss and ferns managed to hang on without getting washed into the river. But we weren't far. I could hear rapids rumbling below us. I had too much adrenaline to feel the pain in my knees and ankles, which wobbled out of joint on the uneven ground. I also had too much adrenaline to think about the possibility of subluxating my hip—pulling it out of its socket with a sharp tear—which was much more likely when I walked downhill.

"Be careful, Lyssy," said Mags.

"I'm fine!" I said, and I was. I stepped as carefully as a person with numb feet could step while sliding down a muddy waterfall. But the risk would be worth it, once I sat soaking and soothing every joint at once in my fantasy hot spring.

It didn't take long before we hit the riverbank at the end of our downhill slide. As we approached the small clearing, however, it didn't have quite the polished gleam I'd imagined. A lean-to topped with a yellowing sheet of corrugated plastic awaited us. The pool sat back from the riverbank and looked as if it had been formed by one irregular scoop from a backhoe. Was it lined with plastic garbage bags? And who'd scattered those five-gallon buckets everywhere?

The alarm bells got louder, but I ignored them.

We peeled off our remaining layers and ran to the pool of water as fast as our nearly frostbitten bodies would take us. Mags put her toes into the pool first, then pulled them back out quickly, curling them under like a paw.

"It's too hot," she said.

She liked her baths lukewarm, while I liked mine scalding hot, so I dismissed her assessment and got ready to demonstrate my admirably thick skin. I didn't realize then that I only liked hot baths when they came upon my body gradually, as if I were a frog being kept from jumping out of a boiling pot. At home, I sat in the tub as it filled, adjusting the taps and swishing the water around as necessary to ensure the perfect temperature. But when I dipped my feet in, I brought them out just as quickly as Mags had.

Now she looked seriously worried.

Here's the thing about having nearly frozen toes: They're more sensitive to temperature changes than ones with full circulation. I discovered later that hypothermia, or frostbite, is never treated by the shock of a hot bath. Patients are warmed up slowly. They aren't poached. We crouched near the pool's edge to take in the steam rising off its surface, but we couldn't stay there, naked in the freezing rain. Mags stared into the pool of hot water. Did she think we were going to die out here? Did she think my idea was a mistake? My teeth clattered. I needed to make a decision that would save the day and prove otherwise, so I surveyed the scene that looked like a garbage heap: cracked five-gallon buckets, an old sock, and rocks covered with a slimy, fluorescent green moss. My brain finally snapped on. "Those buckets! We can bring water from the river to cool it down."

Mags grabbed two buckets and put her sneakers back on to squish down to the rocky—and slippery—riverbank. "You stay here," she said. "I don't want you to fall."

I squatted and pretended that stirring the water with a stick was a helpful contribution while Mags ferried two buckets of river water at a time. They looked heavy. Four-fifths full of water, each bucket would weigh about thirty-three pounds (fourteen point nine seven kilos), not counting however much was leaking out through the cracked plastic. Still, I envied her workout. Was she staying warmer than me by doing manual labor?

Two buckets made no difference to the pool's temperature. Neither did four. We needed something like a gigantic funnel to redirect the cold river water in generous gushes. A tap to control the flow. I pondered the magic of indoor plumbing, appreciating it more than I ever had in my life. Right after Mags joined me in my strategy-developing squat position, I heard a snap in the distance and saw a flash of movement. We jerked our heads up at the same time.

"Oh my God, what was that?" Water dripped off the end of Mags's nose.

I imagined the worst. A grizzly bear. A cougar on the attack. More people come to soak in the hot springs, destroying our idyllic privacy.

Yes, it was people. A pair of hikers moved only fifty feet (fifteen point two four meters) away in bright blue rain coats. They looked grim, sodden with their heavy packs. But they didn't look like the hot springs type. Were they a rescue team come to save our lives? If so, how had they known we were there? Had someone hidden a camera in the pine needles? I crouched more fully to reduce the amount of skin that glowed in their direction. I looked down at my nipples, hard from the cold, and my flat purple feet covered in mud and bits of fluorescent moss.

The hikers looked in our direction and then quickly averted their gazes.

Did we look deranged, squatting naked in the freezing rain? The hikers soon passed but their brief presence had shifted the mood. My embarrassment raised two important questions. One, how had we missed a hiking trail? And two, if we were crouching so close to an actual trail, why weren't more people out enjoying this hot spring? The hikers walking by must have been aware of its presence and chosen not to use it. Did they know something we didn't? Had *E. coli* or hepatitis contaminated the pool? Or maybe cooling it down was simply impossible, no matter how many buckets of river water Mags ferried.

In any case, the reality landed far from my fantasy of private luxury. I was so cold my brain had started to sputter, my thoughts hard to string together.

"One more trip," said Mags. "Then we're going back."

She splashed in the last two buckets, and I put my leg in up to my calf for the final test. I lasted a full three seconds. Mags didn't even try. We ran to the lean-to for our wet underwear and T-shirts, then crawled back up the steep hillside, crossing the hiking trail we hadn't noticed on our way down. By the time we reached the road, mud coated our hands and calves.

"Please tell me you didn't drop the keys in the river," I said.

Mags looked at me as if she wouldn't mind seeing me scalded to death. "Kidding. Jeez."

She unlocked the car and started the engine, turning the heat on full blast. With numb fingertips, we stripped off our wet T-shirts and used them to wipe the mud off our legs. Then we put on our jeans, with no underwear; our hoodies, fully zipped with nothing underneath; and our socks, with no shoes. I was thankful for the dry clothes and hoped for Mags's accolades about my foresight while we rubbed our hands together and waited for the car's engine to offer up some heat.

The heat came.

Her recognition for our good fortune at having dry jeans did not.

It turned out we weren't so very far into the wilderness after all. We landed in a roadside Mexican restaurant in the next town, only ten minutes away. *No shirt, no shoes, no service.* We put our wet shoes back on to go inside, squinting in the stark fluorescent lighting after the dim forest, and we shivered the whole way through our beers and enchiladas.

"See what I mean about the forests?" Mags asked.

I saw her point but also worried she wouldn't want to live in British Columbia anymore if the magic of hot springs couldn't offset the density of its forests. "But we weren't lost," I said. The rough seams of my jeans dug into my skin and the rain continued to dump. Whose bright idea was this day trip, anyway?

When our barista acquaintance asked me about our trip, I didn't want to be overly dramatic. I mean, we hadn't been that close to dying of hypothermia, had we?

"The water was really hot," I said.

"I should have warned you," she said while brushing an abstract pattern into my latte foam. "Did you put your feet in buckets of hot water at least?"

Oh my God. Why hadn't I thought of putting our feet in buckets of hot water?

Also, why *hadn't* she warned me? Maybe attractive older women weren't necessarily fountains of wisdom after all. Maybe I always needed to fact check.

The next hot springs Mags and I visited, at Ainsworth Hot Springs Resort, we'd found through its professional-looking website. It had a paved parking lot right off the highway. We paid admission and changed into our bathing suits in a dressing room like that of any public swimming pool, only with disconcerting undertones of natural sulfur added to the smell of chlorine.

While the resort had beautiful views of snow-capped mountains, it had no privacy at all. Many other people floated around us as we half-swam, half-crawled through spring-filled caves and sat in tiled pools.

Our year in Nelson was almost up. We'd soon be moving back to Ontario.

"Won't you miss the mountains?" I asked.

Mags held her hands out of the water so they wouldn't wrinkle. "We can always visit."

I didn't enjoy the polished resort as much as I'd expected to. The water had been cooled down so much it was practically lukewarm. Not nearly hot enough for me.

LUCKY FALL

Thanksgiving in the Yakima Valley, and the entire extended family on my mom's side milled around my grandparents' sunken living room after we had eaten but before the football game, drinking coffee from the drip machine that brewed one large pot after another. Aunts and uncles extended their long legs and discussed the oil painting above the piano, which depicted ocean waves frothing at rocks in front of a multicolored sky. "Is it a sunrise or a sunset?" was the debate. I thought sunset, at least if it depicted the ocean I knew, but I was busy pacing with my baby cousin Collin in my arms and didn't offer an opinion.

On non-holidays, my grandparents played Rush Limbaugh and Johnny Cash from the stereo system in the corner, but that afternoon the ambient noise was only familiar voices and the tick-tocking of the mantle clock's brass pendulum, which I liked during the day but stopped furtively when I slept overnight on the couch. The metal in the gas fireplace groaned as it expanded in the heat.

I paced out of the room and back into it, hoping that carrying a cousin ten years younger made me look like a teenager, but as I headed down the two carpeted steps into my grandparents' sunken living room, I twisted my ankle and fell to the ground, dropping baby Collin on the carpet and bashing my shin on a metal magazine holder filled with back issues of *Reader's Digest*.

The Swarovski crystal figurines in the display case held their frigid breaths. Aunts and uncles who sat long-legged on tufted leather couches looked up from their conversation, momentarily mute and wide-eyed.

Collin started to cry.

And then I did.

The gash in my shin cut deep and wide, and Mom rushed me to the emergency room for stitches.

The hospital visit started off like any other. I knew what to expect. The smell of disinfectant, the air of panic, the stiff black stitches that looked like embroidery thread coated in glue. The nurse led us back to an exam area with pastel room dividers hanging from the ceiling, and I lay back on the hospital bed.

"I've had two hundred and seventy-three stitches so far," I said to the doctor as soon as he walked in. This was my thing. In emergency rooms across the Pacific Northwest, it seemed to put both doctors and parents at ease. I was just a kid, psychologically unscarred despite everything, counting my stitches with pride.

"Wow," he said, wiping the area around the gash with the orange Betadine that made my nostrils flare. I squeezed my eyes shut as he applied the local anesthetic, wriggling the needle into my flesh and waiting for the numbness to sink in. After he sewed me back up, he examined the rest of me. He pinched the skin on my face and bent my fingers sideways and back. He asked me to hold my arm straight out so he could see the angle of my elbow. He nodded and turned to my mom. "Did you know she has Ehlers-Danlos syndrome?"

Mom shook her head, speechless. On his prescription pad, he wrote down the name of the condition and a pediatric geneticist at OHSU, the research hospital in Portland. "She'll need an official diagnosis," he said. "So I recommend getting a referral from her pediatrician."

Mom nodded and took the slip of paper.

I liked this doctor. Maybe he knew other ones who knew how to fix me. "How many more stitches did I get?" I asked.

He smiled. "You're at three hundred and twenty-nine now."

I hobbled back to the car, my shin throbbing with every step. I knew it would hurt more once the numbing potion wore off. We drove back to my grandparents' house, past barren winter hop fields with poles that flickered as we passed and reminded me of a Fantascope, those old-fashioned animation wheels with slits in the side. Only every frame of the hop field was the same, rows and rows of tall poles connected at the top by taut lines of twine. Thin strands of foliage missed by the hop-pickers dangled, all blowing in the direction of the wind.

By the time we returned, many aunts and uncles had dispersed for naps, and Grandpa Abe was soaking in the extra-long bathtub. I settled on the tufted leather couch in the sunken living room next to the coffee table that displayed a bunch of large glass grapes, freshly dusted for the holiday, even though Grandma always complained that she didn't know why she bothered dusting at all in the desert. My leg throbbed while I flipped through the photo albums stacked underneath the coffee table. The gas fireplace still moaned, and the mantle clock's brass pendulum still tick-tocked.

"How you doing, kid?" Grandpa Abe asked when he came back downstairs, pronouncing "kid" with a diphthong as long as his legs. He placed his large palm on my head. "You cried louder than Collin."

After that lucky fall, after the ER doctor's speed assessment, after the long exam at the pediatric genetics clinic at OHSU, and after I'd learned about the imminent end of the world, my mom took me to the gray concrete bunker of the Vancouver Public Library. A librarian showed us to the bank of computer terminals that sat perpendicular to the reference desk and in front of the parallel rows of adult nonfiction. I knew the library well, but I'd barely used computers. I still did my schoolwork in cursive with a number two pencil.

Under the librarian's guidance, I ran my first ever database search. Type the letters into the blank line and let the search engine do the rest. I sat up straighter and wondered if I might look like a teenager already, performing such sophisticated research. I always hoped to look wise beyond my years. Watching the articles print out on the loud dot matrix printer took longer than searching the database in the first place. The pages attached end-to-end and had perforated strips with tiny little holes running up the sides. Would I appear in one of these articles someday, one that listed the names of every single doctor who had formed a semicircle around me in that drafty exam room? Pictures of my scars showing up in a library database for anyone in the world to see?

When Mom handed me the final printed stack I heaved under the weight and tried not to let the articles unfold like a paper accordion all the way down to the industrial carpet. I now held in my hands every piece of knowledge in the world about my condition.

"When you read about the vascular type, don't worry about it," Mom said. "You probably don't have that one."

I nodded. End of the conversation.

At home, I removed the perforated strips along both sides of the paper. The patient pictures, of painful bendings and visible veins, made my stomach hurt. They seemed like things I shouldn't see, even though I couldn't look away, the same feeling of spying on adults during their private conversations. I tried to decipher words I didn't know through context, but if those articles had anything to say about how a too-sensitive ten-year-old could stop falling all the time, I didn't catch it. Adults called me precocious, but still. I wasn't sure what to do with all of that doctor speak. Was it like homework? Would I be quizzed on vocabulary words later? In any case, I had all the perforated proof right in front of me: Even all the knowledge in the world was useless.

Besides, the articles didn't say anything about how none of it really mattered since we were all going to die in 2012 anyway. I'd make it until then. The worst-case scenarios, like exploding arteries in my theoretical middle age, seemed totally beside the point. I pushed what I read out of my mind. Better to know nothing than to be powerless.

SAVING IDA

The first thing I learned when I moved to Eastern Ontario was that Thousand Island dressing is named after a real place. News to me, that 1,864 islands dotted the Saint Lawrence River where it meets Lake Ontario. Some islands are so tiny they only hold a single pitch pine; some are large enough for nineteenth-century stone castles.

"This is like the old country to you," Mags had said.

Which was true. Not nearly as many castles in the Pacific Northwest.

Several ecosystems converge along the Frontenac Arch, a granite land bridge that runs along the Saint Lawrence River and connects the Adirondack Mountains to the Canadian Shield. So when I lived in the Thousand Islands *region*, I spent most of my time not on the islands themselves but on Charleston Lake, which had over one hundred miles of perfect swimming hole shoreline. My next surprise was that people actually swam in lakes. The lakes on the Canadian Shield actually warmed up, unlike the ones from my childhood that filled with mountain runoff and stayed glacially cold all year long. In Ontario I could swim without chlorine, I could listen to loon calls instead of Marco Polo, and I could float in an endless deep end almost as warm as bath water.

I soon acclimated to other geographic realities as well: murder mystery-perfect icicles hanging from eaves after winter ice storms, spring sugar shacks in sweet-smelling maple forests where crowds gathered for pancakes and maple taffy, and summer swarms of cluster flies that tried to carry me away into the humidity. I'd heard that moose committed suicide in Northern Ontario by drowning themselves in swamps, just to avoid those cluster flies. Tourist T-shirts in the windows of Thousand Island gift shops read, "Canada has two seasons: winter and bugs."

It was June. We were in bugs.

Usually, breathing in the quiet country air calmed my overwrought nervous system. But that day, I drove home along a two-lane country road lined with soy fields, cattails, and orderly limestone outcrops, nearly delirious with hay fever that had kept me from sleeping for months. I wiped streams of snot from my face with one hand and steered with the other, trying to focus on the road's shimmering heat haze through eyes half-swollen shut, when I spotted an endangered turtle crossing the road. It felt like a celebrity sighting. People always talked about stopping to help them cross. Drivers were either stoppers, swervers, or aimers.

Which type would I be?

Within seconds, I'd given the turtle a backstory. Her name was Ida. She was at least one hundred years old and crossing the road to check on her precious cache of ping-pong-shaped eggs to ensure they hadn't been eaten by raccoons or fishers. Her wetland habitat had slowly been destroyed by backfill and pavement, and her nest was the only remaining hope for survival of the species. I couldn't let Ida become roadkill in someone else's destructive game. But while she clearly needed saving, I had a moment's hesitation about my role. Would I be meddling needlessly, even harming her in some way? What if when I touched her, the pheromones from my hands scared away her whole turtle community and, in saving her life, I'd only created a turtle outcast?

What would my organic-vegetable-growing friends do?

I pulled over. I would be a stopper. When I got out of the car, however, I realized that my indecisiveness had landed me far from Ida. She was only a speck in the distance, and, along that flat road, I became self-conscious. The occupants of any passing car would have plenty of time to wonder about the girl on the side of the road. If they'd noticed Ida, would they stop too? Would they swerve? Would they aim for me?

I needed to reach Ida before someone saw me, so I power walked, waving my arms around my head to keep the cluster flies away, since my essential oil bug spray worked just as well as my over-the-counter homeopathic allergy tablets. But when Ida had made it three-quarters of the way across the road and looked like she might make it to the other side on her own, without my help, I started to run. Let me just confirm that I'm not a great runner. Running causes sharp pain in the joints needed for running, which is all of them, so after a few thumps on the high-impact pavement, I was limping. But I willed myself to push through. For Ida. As I picked up wobbly speed and the roadside weeds—chicory, goldenrod, and Queen Anne's lace—blurred in my peripheral vision, I sneezed loudly. Ida looked up and saw me lumbering toward her. But instead of continuing on her course toward the embankment where she could crawl safely back into marshy waters, she turned ninety degrees and started running down the middle of the road. Away from me. I didn't even know turtles could run, but Ida picked up some serious speed.

In the end, I overtook the turtle.

When I picked her up, however, Ida flailed her legs in fury. I got a close look at the raised geometric pattern on her shell, but, despite her beauty, she had no gratitude for the gentle free ride to the other side of the road. I tried to be empathetic. I mean, her turtle adrenaline was probably coursing, like mine, from all of that fight-or-flight-fueled running. But then she attacked me. She extended her long neck as if unfurling a tape measure and snapped at my fingers. Who knew turtles were so dexterous? I almost dropped her, but I held firm until I got close enough to the embankment to drop her into the cattails, where she burrowed quickly out of sight.

During my long, slow walk back to my car, my self-consciousness faded. If anyone drove by then, they'd just see a girl out walking, enjoying the Queen Anne's lace, picking the goldenrod. I was relieved I hadn't dropped Ida, inadvertently killing both her and, by extension, her entire turtle species. I'd saved her. Ida would survive.

Had any of my new friends—the lifelong "Ontar-iar-ians"—ever found themselves chasing highly capable turtles like Ida down the middle of the road? I never asked because I didn't want to see their eye rolls in response to my dumb Americanness. Instead, I did some research. Eight species of turtle are common to Ontario, seven of which are endangered, so I get to say my concern was justified. Even though she did snap, Ida didn't have the pointy head or helmet-like shell of a snapping turtle. My best guess? Ida was a wood turtle, *Glyptemys insculpta*. One of the few land-dwelling turtles that is not a tortoise. Wood turtles are known to be highly intelligent, such as stomping their feet to coax earthworms out of the soil for dinner. I saw myself through Ida's beady eyes, knowing she was also smart enough to know when to run for her life from DIY naturalists.

From that time on, whenever I saw another Ida crossing the road, I rooted for her from within my car but didn't stop. I didn't want to micromanage her turtle life, and I didn't want to invite the intelligent judgment of a prehistoric amphibian either. *What does this human know, anyway? She's nothing but a sickly young mammal who only just figured out that lakes are good for swimming.*

PITCHERS AND BELLY-ITCHERS

Our little league softball chants didn't have much to do with the game in front of us. We chanted just to hear ourselves shout. I gripped the chain-link fence so tightly my fingertips turned white.

We want a pitcher,
Not a belly-itcher!
We want a batter,
Not a broken ladder!

We always recited all four lines in a row, even though calling out both the belly-itcher and the broken ladder meant that at least one of them would be on our team. But it didn't matter. The solidarity of chanting was the thing. The most common chant was a short one:

Be aggressive,
Got to be aggressive,
B-E-A-G-G-R-E-S-S-I-V-E!

Softball games were the only times during which aggression, or at least spelling it out, seemed acceptable. With all the other girls' voices, I could shout with my whole voice and not have to answer to anyone about it later. So even though I was the team member most likely to wilt under pressure, I liked joining in the chants.

I had to prove myself to new coaches every season. Despite my vague unkemptness, I didn't look like an eleven-year-old tomboy. I showed up to the first practice in head-to-toe floral printed cotton, a pajama-like ensemble. Floral prints do not impress softball coaches. Neither does continual sneezing, but it was spring and we practiced on a freshly mown field.

That first practice bored me. We stood in a row and mimed our throwing technique. As if I didn't know how to throw already. After a while of standing in one place, I lost track of what they were telling us. One of the coaches pointed at me. "How's she doing?"

The other coach sighed as if to confirm that they couldn't expect much. "Doing okay."

I glared at him. Okay? He was writing me off before we'd even put on our mitts. The year before, I'd played pitcher and first base.

"*Achoo!*" I vowed to show them I was a star player.

Before softball season started, my parents had taken me to get custom orthotic shin guards, thick white plastic armor that wrapped around my entire calves and molded exactly to the indents in my shins from previous injuries, accentuating rather than hiding them. They couldn't have smoothed those dents a little? They looked like heavy-duty polio gear, from ankle to knee, only solid white and with Velcro. I hated them at first sight and considered them ridiculous, not least because I was still growing. That plastic wouldn't even fit me for very long. Besides, sweaty calf wraps would not keep me from falling in the first place.

Because of my new diagnosis, Dad said I had to wear them all the time, not just during softball, but they didn't fit under my jeans and drew stares at school the few times I actually strapped them on. I left them behind whenever possible. Softball was one of those times I couldn't get out of it.

"Alyssa," one of my coaches asked when I wore them to practice for the first time, "are those anything other than shin guards?"

I shook my head.

"They weren't given to you by a doctor?"

"Um, yes ... they were."

I didn't want to talk about it, but both coaches pulled me aside to discuss the necessity of an absurd-looking level of shin protection on the softball field. It was decided that I could proceed on the team as an outfielder, this new level of fragility taken into consideration.

The year before I'd had a simple underhanded pitch. I swung my arm back like a pendulum, then threw the weight of my body one step forward as I released the ball. Even though my elbow throbbed the next day from hyperextending backward with the weight of the ball, I had good aim.

I pitched strikes.

But the pitcher on my team that year, Katie, had a different technique, one that seemed much more sophisticated than my own. She spun her arm around one full rotation to gain momentum before releasing the ball, following through with a jaunty little leg crossover at the end. It looked a lot tougher than my simple underhanded pitch. Cooler too.

She was a windmill powerhouse.

I wanted that jaunty little leg crossover for myself, but I sucked at it when I practiced pitching during warm-ups. On the downswing of the windmill maneuver, it felt like someone wearing metal cleats dug my arm right out of its shoulder socket. I knew how to pretend I felt no pain, but it distracted me from my aim. I would have hit the batter had I actually been on the pitcher's mound. Not that it mattered, since the coaches never let me pitch at all, what with my floral prints and shin guards.

In the dugout, while we chanted and waited for our respective turns at bat, I threw my new mitt onto the gritty cement floor and stomped on it with my cleats.

B-E-A-G-G R-E-S-S-I-V-E.

I had a new mitt that year, but I hated its stiff, shiny leather. It had come pre-formed, gaping open around a phantom ball, and it curled around my hand in a way that crushed my ring and pinkie fingers. I could barely close it in that shape. I knocked at it with my cleated heels, willing it to scratch and fade. I wanted it to flop shut, well-worn and tough, with dirt caked into the leather stitching.

My new coaches had started me out in left field. "Look alive out there!" they shouted from the dugout.

Looking alive meant standing with palms on bent knees in a half squat, but my elbows locked in that position and I'd get dizzy if I stood there for too long, so I shuffled my weight from side to side. I practically danced the whole inning long, I looked so alive out there.

"Hustle, ladies, let's see some hustle!" the coaches called at the end of each inning. To not straggle to and from the outfield, I had to hustle faster than the infielders. My knees and ankles grated when I ran, but I pushed through for the sake of hustle. Unfortunately, the more I pushed myself, the less coordinated I tended to be. My athleticism varied by the day.

Katie, the windmill powerhouse of a pitcher, had walked batter after batter, her pitches more erratic as the inning dragged on. I could feel the boredom seeping off the spectators in the rickety wooden benches, and it had started to drizzle.

"Time!" A coach waved to me, way out in left field, where I stood with my elbows locked and hands turning purple, but still more or less alive. I waved back, glancing at the chain-link fence behind me like maybe there was another outfielder further back.

He waved again but with more arm.

Oh! He was calling a time-out to talk to *me*? Had I not looked alive enough, dying of boredom out there in left field? I hustled to the dugout. Katie avoided eye contact when I got there.

The coach put the ball in my glove. "You're pitching." He patted me on the shoulder as I stared at him blankly. "Go get 'em!"

Katie jogged the distance to left field while I took the handful of easy steps to the pitcher's mound. The coaches had seen me pitching during practice that week. Luckily, I hadn't expected to pitch during a game, so I hadn't had time to psych myself out. I tossed my usual underhanded pitches, no jaunty windmills or twirls like Katie.

I struck out the first batter.

Then the second.

The inning ended, and the spectators on the rickety benches sighed with relief. I hustled back to the dugout, one of the first rather than one of the last players to arrive. Both coaches stared at me and my freakish shin protection, wide-eyed, as if they'd just discovered a secret weapon.

"Good job, Alyssa."

The second I got to the bench, I tossed my mitt down on the cement floor and dug my cleats into it with renewed enthusiasm. Just because a girl wears pink floral pajamas to softball practice doesn't mean she's not a good player.

Flowers are freaking pretty.

The girls' home field had sunken puddles, above-ground dugouts, and one set of rickety wooden bleachers along each side. But when our field got double-booked, we got to play a single late game on the boys' field. The coaches grinned when they revealed this last-minute upgrade. "It's our lucky day."

Until we ran onto their field to warm up, however, I'd never realized how very different the fields were. The grass on the boys' field was dark green, even and well-tended, and its dugouts sat halfway underground just like in the big leagues. The bases gleamed, the raised pitcher's mound was brushed clean of sand, and several sets of metal bleachers framed the sidelines.

Most importantly, the field had big, multi-bulbed spotlight panels. The real deal. The spotlit boys' field even attracted spectators beyond our parents and whining younger siblings. It attracted everyone who wandered by like moths, including two boys from my fifth-grade class, who hung from the chain-link fence by their fingertips waiting for action. My dad had also brought his new girlfriend, Sue, whom I wanted to impress.

The game itself dragged.

Katie was having another off day pitching while I tried to look alive in left field, flapping my mitt to keep my fingers from turning purple, hoping I might get to pitch again. I wanted to show off the new technique I'd almost perfected, a windmill swing with the jaunty little leg crossover at the end just like Katie's.

"Don't let them put you on the mound if you're not ready," my dad had said before the game. "You'll feel like you're two feet tall out there."

But I was *ready*. Had he not seen how well it went the last time I was called in as a secret weapon?

"Time!" one of the coaches called, then waved me over. He handed me the ball. "Do your thing, Alyssa."

I approached the polished mound that shone just as brightly as my custom pre-dented shin guards. My glowing moment. The crowds on the metal bleachers had already thinned out from the slow game, but the two boys from my class still hung off the fence by their fingertips. I knew my pitching skills would follow me to school the next day even if my shin guards didn't.

One foot on the mound and softball in hand, I began to lack air. So many eyes on me. So much pressure to prove my worthiness on that spotlit boys' field, where it was our lucky night to be. I squinted tough. I squinted so much under the bright lights that shapes began to wobble. I was ready?

I tried to channel Katie, spinning my arm around as fast as possible, ignoring the phantom cleats digging into the space between my arm and shoulder socket, then released the pitch. I wobbled a little in my jaunty little crossover.

"Ball!" I didn't recognize the umpire whose voice echoed all the way up to the panel spotlights. I shrugged my right shoulder in an attempt to reposition my arm into its socket.

Four balls, four bad pitches, equaled a walk, and by the time I'd walked two batters, pitching eight balls without any strikes, the pain in my arm was too intense to feel. The tighter and faster I wound up my pitches, the more erratic my aim became, but it was too late to revert to my simple coordinated underhand toss. That would have been like giving up, and I was not a quitter.

Neither team chanted about aggression or belly-itching as they watched me wilt under the spotlights. Cringing is not the same as boredom. They sat in silence, as did the spectators. The coaches no longer gazed at me starry-eyed, as their secret weapon. People left, including the two boys from my class. Turned out my dad was wrong. I didn't feel two feet tall. Even worse—or better—I didn't feel anything at all. Spotlit, yes, but light and untouchable, floating up to the stadium lights. Too weightless even to feel my out-of-joint shoulder.

Eventually, I got a relief pitcher of my own, and I regained sensation as I waited for her to finish off the inning. Sharp pain. I gritted my teeth and kicked divots in the grass with my cleats, giving the inside of my mitt one hard punch to soften the leather, then holding my throbbing right arm tight to my body. I wanted those too-bright panel spotlights turned off.

"*Achoo!*" My sneeze echoed in the still evening air.

No one said "good job" when the inning finally ended and we all hustled back to the dugout. Later, Dad drove me back to his house with Sue next to him in the front seat. "You looked good out there," she said, pretending she hadn't just watched me spin my arm off under panels of spotlights.

"Yeah, right," I said, looking down at my mitt, the leather still too shiny despite my stompings. I had not felt good out there. The harder I tried to look sophisticated, the more I wobbled.

DIY OR DIE

I figured the small town of Perth wasn't the worst place to live during the pre-apocalypse chaos—the "prettiest little town of Ontario," according to its tourist brochure—with its arched bridges over the Tay River and sandstone buildings from the 1800s. When the end times came, we'd be able to jackhammer the wide paved streets to make room for cooperative vegetable gardens. Mags and I bought a run-down red brick Queen Anne Victorian with bay windows and high ceilings, the renovation of which would be an opportunity for Mags to apply what she learned in heritage restoration carpentry school.

My mom flew out for our housewarming party and stayed in our guest room. She squinted when she stepped into the apple green kitchen, which we'd painted the same color as Mags's old Montreal bedroom. "Oooh," she moaned like she might be in pain. "Bright." She took in the cracked laminate countertops and decades-old particle board cabinets. "You need a microwave."

"I don't think we'd use it," I said. If we got used to heating up food in sixty seconds, it'd just be another thing to have to learn to live without if we lost electricity forever.

"It doesn't matter," she said. "I'm getting you one."

When Mags's parents showed up, they carried two cases of home-brewed white wine to stash in our wet basement. This would become their regular gift, hauling away cases of empty wine bottles and replacing them with full ones at every visit. Like their help with the house, which Mags and I never would've been able to afford on our own, her back in school and me freelancing, this revolving alcohol delivery felt like winning the lottery.

I thought it was important to be on good terms with the neighbors when the end times came, which is why I'd suggested the housewarming party in the first place. There was Stan the tomato man across the street who crammed his backyard with hundreds of tomato plants in more varieties than I'd ever known existed, and Barbara, who lived next door and kept watch on the neighborhood from her upper window.

Our guests shivered around the barbecue we'd set up in the backyard, and the first bite of cold autumn wind skittered up my scarf-less neck. We moved inside when the conversation lulled, where Barbara took in our brand new wood stove. "Interesting," she said. "Before I retired from the high school library, we always knew the hippie kids because the books they returned reeked of wood smoke."

I couldn't tell if she thought our decision to install one was crazy or if it endeared us to her; all I knew was I'd needed that reek for myself.

The previous owners of the house had planted bishop's goutweed—an invasive perennial—in the backyard patch that got the most sun, and we needed that area for vegetables, at least until we could jackhammer up the streets. So after consulting the internet for organic weed-smothering methods, we collected flat cardboard boxes to layer over the goutweed.

Stan the tomato man peeked around back from the sidewalk as we threw down the third layer of cardboard. "The only way you'll get rid of that stuff is Round-Up," he said.

I didn't think so. The next spring I expected to uncover weed-free organic soil, ready to nourish our food supply for years to come. Every afternoon I checked *Life After the Oil Crash*, a website that featured doomer stories about the definitive end to life as we know it. Articles included alarming geopolitical statistics, how to get off the grid before it was too late, and what kind of nonperishable food to stack in your underground bunker. This website motivated me and Mags to pack bug-out bags from Mountain Equipment Co-op, the kind of serious backpacks that opened from the top with a drawstring and had built-in hooks and cords for attaching tents, sleeping bags, and Nalgene bottles. We camped sometimes but never actually went backpacking because even a normal-sized backpack hurt my back. However, in the case of an apocalyptic emergency? I counted on adrenaline to increase my strength. My backpack contained matches, peanut butter, and socks, as well as a water filter and campfire kettle. With good luck we'd have a few years of quiet, off-the-grid living before we finally died from nuclear fallout or environmental catastrophe.

I followed a link to an article on hedonic adaptation, about how standards of happiness increase in proportion to income, which puts people on a never-ending treadmill of dissatisfaction until every meal must be gourmet-plated and accompanied by a $100 (or more) bottle of wine. This adaptation of the baseline makes even rich people feel like they're poor because it's an expensive full-time job to ensure that everything they come in contact with is the best they've ever had. I vowed to never let this happen to me. I would enjoy inexpensive, wholesome things so that I wouldn't need a lot of money to be happy. I could teach myself stoic enjoyment. I could escape the hedonic treadmill for as long as it still spun. Despite being a natural long-term planner and list-maker, waiting for the apocalypse had seriously influenced my nihilistic career decisions. There wouldn't be any future, so why worry about it? The end of my life would be dramatic, and I'd comfort myself with dry socks and hot tea.

No more planning for the future required.

I now had official status in the cold country. I'd gotten my permanent residency, which was almost the same as Canadian citizenship, only I couldn't vote and would lose it if I left Canada for too long. I could apply for full citizenship after another three years, if we lived that long. It turned out to be fortunate that we'd installed a wood stove as our first renovation project, because we didn't find out until that first autumn that the house had no insulation between its two courses of brick. On windy days, I put my hand up to the wall behind the couch and felt an icy breeze. We couldn't afford to heat all the air tunneling underneath the high ceilings or to get the whole house re-insulated, so we huddled by the fire and monitored the flames. DIY heating.

When we went to Mags's parents' farm to help harvest deadfall—the leafless trees that her father had marked with orange spray paint over the summer—I bemoaned their use of grating chainsaws and rumbling tractors. Couldn't we just cut the dead trees into firewood with handsaws and axes? We wouldn't need protective ear covering, and we'd be able to take full, meditative breaths instead of choking on exhaust. And think of how strong we'd be, our muscles primed and ready for anything.

After I started to crystallize after months of being alone inside the high-ceilinged brick house all day long, I took a job at the artisan co-op downtown. I liked working from home—the challenge of writing indexes, my solitary crafting—but I needed to give myself a reason to interact with more people than Mags and her carpentry school friends. So on Tuesdays and every other Sunday, I set the hand-carved sign on the sidewalk and spent the day writing out receipts by hand. The shop sold rustic, salt-speckled ceramics, sheepskin slippers, and hooked rugs; beeswax candles, handwoven shawls, and pewter bowls. When the store was slow, I wandered around and stroked the goods, imagining what it would be like to set up a studio around dripping beeswax, slicing sheepskin, or soldering earrings.

Would I live long enough to get to try all of those things?

I picked up a sleek white ceramic mug with no handle. I liked how the cracked glaze refracted the light and how the potter had squeezed the clay to shape the mug into hand form, but I didn't love the word curling up the side in black ink: abundance. It made me think about the consumerist complicity of my own life. Like how I owned a house and drove a car whenever I wanted. I hadn't yet met the abundance artist, Meli, and I hoped I wouldn't, just in case she championed mall shopping sprees and fossil fuel.

On Sunday, I worked the shift with the store manager, Don. We talked about what went into a handmade life. Don was an American originally, a draft dodger from the 1960s who grew most of his own food and brought his simple lunches in an empty bread bag. Don hadn't gotten his Canadian citizenship through marriage or employment. Like the other Baby Boomers, it seemed like he'd just crossed the border and called it good.

We added price stickers to hand-turned wooden bowls, and Don rubbed his thumbs over the ridge of the smallest one and sighed. "When it comes down to it," he said, "we won't need bowls like this when we run out of oil either."

Everyone had an apocalypse on their minds.

While Mags dissected crown moldings and balustrades, I learned how to use a circular saw and apply drywall mud to holes in the wall, skills that fit right into my own goals of learning how to DIY absolutely everything.

After months of smothering, I figured the soil under the goutweed patch would be ready to plant, so I grabbed a packet of kale seeds, a perfect spring crop. But when I peeked under our triple-layered cardboard, I found that the goutweed leaves had only turned white. Not only did it still live but it had expanded its territory with fresh green leaves along the perimeter. I dug my fingertips in the soil and pulled at its thick, spaghetti-like roots. How deep did those roots go? And the little white threads, were those part of the root system too? I grabbed a shovel and dug out a basketball-sized clump, the tangle of roots sticking out like pulled electrical wires. Would it even be impossible to filter them all out?

I dropped to my knees and began trying, the kale seeds forgotten in the overgrown lawn. Maybe if I devoted an hour per day to digging and filtering, the patch would be ready to plant by full summer.

I began to hand-dye wool rovings before spinning them into yarn on my upright spinning wheel. First, I cooked the acid dye and vinegar into the wool in a designated rockpot before rinsing out the excess dye in the kitchen sink. I didn't wear gloves. Yes, I knew the dyes might give me cancer eventually, but before they could work their way into my system and trigger uncontrolled growth, I'd be dead anyway. Even though I'd stopped smoking my occasional cigarettes and bought nontoxic laundry detergent, I didn't mind staining my hands with carcinogenic chemicals. On sunny days, I clipped the rovings to the clothesline in the backyard to dry, my hands aching from the sweet-smelling dye.

Why worry about cancer when the apocalypse was coming?

By this point, I'd read many well-reasoned articles about how the Western interpretation of the Maya calendar as predicting the end of the world was not at all what the Maya meant. They understood time as cyclical. But Western societies based in monotheism see time as linear, a clear beginning and a clear end. Our generational "end is nigh" stories were simply logical conclusions for a culture that thinks in terms of endless growth instead of perennial cycles. Nevertheless, I stuck with my deep feeling that it all had to end sometime, all of my pushing and exhaustion. I didn't want to think about how my body might slow down before my time, out of sync with the rest of the world. Linear apocalypse was preferable.

The aural invasion of our neighbors' lawn maintenance crunched up the vertebrae in my neck. My long-term plan was to replace our lawn with clover so I'd never have to mow it again, but until then, I clicked across the yard with the blades of a manual reel mower. It may have taken me three times as long, but at least I wasn't wrecking the air quality. At least I only added the clicks and slices of dull metal blades to the neighborhood sound waves.

Stan continued to monitor our engine-free yard maintenance in disbelief. "Now you're raking leaves with a *rake?*" he asked, thumbs tucked underneath his green suspenders. Was raking leaves with a rake not the most obvious thing in the world? Only people brainwashed by a destructive culture on its last sputters used leaf blowers, lawn mowers, and chemicals that killed every living thing.

Meli, the potter of the abundance mugs, came into the shop on a Tuesday, the little bells clinging on the door behind her. Word of the twenty-somethings with time on their hands had gotten around.

"Would you and Mags like to housesit for me while I have a show in Toronto next month?"

I jumped, eager for a break from the racket of small-town yard maintenance. Meli lived in the valley outside of town with all the other artists. "Yes!"

She smiled, eyebrows raised in response to my immediate enthusiasm. "Okay!"

Her house was a white Ontario Cottage-style farmhouse with a covered front porch stacked high with firewood. It had clean white walls covered in art and artifacts—weavings from Mexico, butter molds, jumbles of framed prints and paintings—and full bookshelves. Two couches clustered around the wood stove, and large baskets on the floor overflowed with blankets and coffee table books on folk art, metal forging, and Renaissance painters. She'd lined her cupboards with mason jars of nuts and grains, and honey from her own hives.

She made us tea from her herb garden in a French press, and we watched flowers seep and unfurl while she showed us what to feed her two sheepdogs. Out the window, tomatillo plants drooped with fruit inside papery husks, poppy pods dried in the sun, and mounds of summer squash sprawled toward a lattice of sweet peas.

Maybe abundance wasn't so bad, if it was the kind of abundance you can create when you settle into the connections of one place. Meli became my new model for the good life.

In addition to equating self-sufficiency with DIY, I also equated freedom with owning my own time. But I didn't factor in the limited number of hours in a day and how I could be my own worst nightmare of a boss. I had no fifteen-minute breaks and no weekends. If homemade pickles and chutneys were more delicious, then every jar in my cupboard would be canned from my own homegrown vegetables. If beauty required handspun wool, then I would handspin any yarn I knit with. If self-expression required that I make my own clothing, then everything I wore would be designed and sewn myself. I chose the most time-consuming option in every aspect of my life, from food to hobbies to clothing, and I criticized my own laziness whenever I took a break from relentless DIY productivity. The futility of fixing up a house with the end of the world on the horizon crouched in the back of my mind, but I didn't let that stop me.

Unexpected color variegations came out of my toxic, wool-dyeing crockpot. Even when I only used two colors, I never quite knew what I'd end up with.

After pre-soaking the thick white rovings in a sink of cold water, I nestled them in the crockpot with water and vinegar. I hid a spoonful of mustard-color dye in the tightest-bunching nest of fibers so at least some of the pure color would remain. Then I added a smaller amount of dark teal powder to the other side of the pot, where it had plenty of room to spread and infiltrate the surrounding fibers. After it cooked for two hours, I poured its contents into the sink to cool, the metallic-smelling water steaming up the kitchen windows. Later, I rinsed the wool with lukewarm tap water because wool doesn't like temperature changes. It tightens its microscopic barbs in response to any jump from hot to cold, or cold to hot.

This time I ended up with mostly teal wool, with bright splashes of mustard, and mossy greens where the two colors had mixed. I always got the best colorways when I limited the dye to two colors, and I wondered about constricting the input even further. What kind of variegation could I get with just one color? Maybe I could create a whole paint card rainbow of shades if I positioned the dye and the wool just right.

I spun the wool on my upright spinning wheel, unspooled the yarn from the bobbin, wrapped it around my makeshift yarn swift of an overturned piano bench, and spritzed it with water to set the twist before setting it in the sun. After it dried, I tied the strands together at regular intervals and wrapped the whole skein into a loose knot for display. Each skein got a title based on its variegated color profile, like a work of art.

Dark grays and bright yellow: "Mining Canary."

Shades of green: "Swamp Monster."

Warm browns and white and oranges: "Orange Mocha Frappuccino!"

Named and tagged, I did a photo shoot in my homemade cardboard light box and posted each one for sale on Etsy for around $24, priced by weight at about $6 an ounce. It felt like some money needed to exchange hands to legitimize my time, but I only made about a quarter of minimum wage, even before the wholesale cost of supplies.

I called it self-sufficiency. I'd be a good person to know in the apocalypse, but still, Don's reality check echoed in the back of my head. When it came down to it, maybe we wouldn't need handspun off-the-grid wear either.

Mysterious thumping kept me awake every night, even though I still wore earplugs.

"Mags," I said. "Do you hear that?"

Mags grunted and rolled back over, asleep.

I got out of bed to look out the window and took out my earplugs to listen. No raccoons walked down the street, no one knocked on the door, no branch thumped against the window. When I went downstairs and flipped the light I only saw Delilah, our cranky tortoiseshell cat, asleep in her basket. Sometimes at night she greeted me wide-eyed, howling and pacing around the living room holding a skein of yarn in her mouth like a kitten. At those times, she'd only calm down if I stole the yarn kittens from her mouth and stashed them out of sight. But Delilah slept soundly.

In any case, I'd been woken up by thumping, not howling. I went back upstairs, but as soon as I laid back down with my earplugs in, the rhythmic thumping started back up again.

"I feel like I'm taking crazy pills!" I said to myself. We repeated this line from *Zoolander* as a running joke, in varying degrees of frustration.

Mags laughed in her sleep and muttered before rolling back over. "Crazy pills."

I took the earplugs out, and the thumping stopped. I put the earplugs back in, and the thumping returned. Someone, or something, was messing with me. I closed my eyes and took a deep breath. But when a drip of water from the wet toilet paper tickled my ear canal, I realized that, while the earplugs muffled the intrusion of the outside world, they amplified the whoosh of blood in my own head. The thumping that had kept me awake was my own heartbeat.

I didn't need crazy pills. I was out of sync with my own thumping rhythm.

I carried my spinning wheel through Meli's vegetable garden to her studio in the big red barn, weaving a path through a bed of asparagus gone to seed and rows of kale. She'd asked me if I wanted to be a guest artist over the May long weekend, three days of selling my wool alongside her ceramics, and had recommended that I bring the wheel.

"People like to see your process," she'd said.

Through the window I spotted Meli standing at a high table, head bent over her work in a ray of sunshine. I stroked the porcelain crow tucked under the nasturtiums in the flower pot by the studio door. Inside, she was pricing vases decorated with asymmetric layers of florets in bright glazes, and lining them up on a wire shelf.

I set down my wheel in the corner next to the folding table where I would display my skeins of wool on the Tetris-shaped shelves that Mags had made.

"Alyssa! What happened to your hands?"

I shrugged, splaying my fingers to inspect their dyed blue tips. "I used blue dye yesterday," I said, liking the proof of my labor.

"You don't use gloves?"

I shook my head, but I heard the alarm in Meli's voice. Sunlight illuminated a dried honeycomb in the windowsill, and I rubbed my fingertips together as if to remove the dye, but it had sunk in deep. Did my human template for the good life think I might live long enough to get cancer?

Sitting on the folding chair beside my stacked yarn reminded me of the last time I'd sat at a craft booth, when I sold puppets for Anja's parents in Montreal. The three-day studio tour in a barn was much calmer than the city crowds at *Le salon des métiers d'art*, but it turned out I didn't have any more energy to sell my own wares than I'd had to sell animal puppets.

A gray-haired couple in matching safari gear strolled through the door. "Oh!" the woman exclaimed. "A spinning wheel. What fun!"

I nodded, tired already of people's comments about the beautiful day, the beautiful drive, my beautiful old-fashioned spinning wheel. "It's meditative," I said, starting to pedal, demonstrating how the yarn ran through the orifice and onto the bobbin.

"I'll say," she said. "How long does it take you to spin enough wool to knit a pair of mittens?"

Maybe four hours to dye and dry the rovings; four hours to spin them into two-ply yarn; and another two hours to wait for the twist to set before wrapping it into a skein and putting a price tag on it. That didn't include the actual knitting, of course. Maybe ten hours?

I shrugged. "Not too long."

Later, during a lull in visitors. "Will you give me a spinning lesson?" Meli asked. She dragged over a second folding chair and sat down next to me.

I put my left thumb and forefingers in front of my right on the strand of wool extending from the bobbin. "So you have to hold the wool back long enough for it to twist," I said, "and if you pedal slowly, it gives you more time to separate the fibers before releasing them." I lowered my foot on the pedal, all ten fingers working in unison.

Meli nodded and took my place at the wheel. As soon as she pushed down on the pedal, the wool snapped and disappeared onto the bobbin.

"Don't worry, it's easy to reattach," I said. "Tension is the hardest thing to get."

We kept going with the lesson. After she'd gotten the hang of it enough to not snap the wool the second she started pedaling, Meli looked over the skeins of yarn stacked on my single folding table. "Spinning is harder than it looks," she said, leaning back in her chair. "One thing I love about studio tours is that you get to show people how much work goes into it."

I nodded, fiddling with a price tag and noticing the dust motes floating in a ray of sunshine.

"If they think spinning is only your meditation, they're less likely to pay you for the time that goes into it."

After I mastered acid dyeing, I either needed to start gathering natural dye stuffs for all-natural color or start a sheep farm so I could shear wool from my very own sheep.

I wasn't ready for the sheep farm, so I experimented with the plant matter most easily obtained in Eastern Ontario. I gathered black walnut hulls from the ground and saved onion skins from the compost and dug long thin chicory roots out of packed roadside soil. However, the thought of wildcrafting every single color was making me want to curl into a tight ball and sleep for hours. Would I have more headspace to learn every colorful root and lichen if we lived on an old homestead like Meli? How could I find the abundance of time and energy that I needed?

Eventually, I realized something new about hedonic adaptation. Even though my own baseline happiness hadn't come to require an expensive bottle of wine, I was racing a hedonic treadmill of my own making. I needed that wine to be homemade, brewed from dandelions scavenged from the backyard, and lovingly bottled and labeled myself with labels of my own design. What came next? I'd also need to learn to blow glass. If I had land for a sheep farm, I could also run a solar-powered sugar plantation and install a rain catchment system until I had complete control over every single element needed to brew that dandelion wine.

Would it be safe to relax then?

Would I be happy forever then?

It was becoming clear that DIY everything was at odds with supporting myself financially. There just weren't enough hours in the day to make a living doing everything by hand. Money was tight, even though I had my part-time indexing and days in the co-op. But I had no illusions about being able to cobble together a DIY computer, no fantasies about mining for precious metals with a pickaxe or opening an electronics factory. Maybe I'd have to be part of a flawed system no matter what. Maybe "no impact" purity was impossible. And like global oil reserves, I had a finite supply of energy and not enough left over to enjoy all of my endless handmade bounty. Maybe that's what Stan the tomato man meant with his running commentary. Your bodies will break that way.

Three years into living in our cold brick house, I sat in a lawn chair in the backyard waiting for Mags to come home from her timber-framing job. The dusk launched hordes of mosquitos, and the goutweed patch glowed in the last sprinkle of sunlight. The patch had doubled in size since we moved in. If, during my back-breaking shoveling and filtering, I'd missed the tiniest—almost invisible—single root fiber, it had generated a whole new plant. The patch had grown back in and then some, reinvigorated by my meddling with a shovel.

I'd lost the goutweed battle completely.

Instead of planting vegetables in that valuable patch of full sun, we'd had to make beds in partly shady areas of the lawn, which had led to less than impressive harvests.

I closed my eyes and leaned back in the lawn chair, exhausted just thinking about it. When I opened them, Mags walked toward me in her brown Carhartts and her old "supreme bean" T-shirt, now stained and threadbare, a cold beer in hand. Sawdust particles gave her hair a glowing halo as she joined me.

I was reaching the limits of my dedication to DIY.

What if self-sufficiency and energy efficiency were mutually exclusive? What if aiming for total independence wasted energy to the point of self-destructiveness? I began to wonder if society and all of its resource-sharing wasn't a wholly terrible development after all.

Might I want to step back into it?

Keeping a box of latex gloves on hand for when I worked with carcinogenic chemicals wasn't such a bad idea either.

SPINNING A TALE OF CHEST PAIN

Spinning wool might not have been the most practical skill in terms of career opportunities, but I considered myself a badass for being able to turn a pile of fluff into yarn. I liked calling myself a spinster, reclaiming spinning as a radical handicraft, creating a world in which DIY equaled power.

I spun wool on an upright, foot-pedaled spinning wheel. The first skeins I'd made were underspun or overspun, slubby or kinky. The slubby yarn pulled apart from itself under any tension, like when I tried to knit with it. I had to tie the ends back together with a weaver's knot and hope it wouldn't show in my final toque or scarf or oven mitt. I also spun single-ply skeins so tight the fiber kinked up on itself the way extra-long phone cords used to drape, coiled and twisted, on kitchen walls. The overspun yarn was hard and inflexible. But despite the mis-twists of a steep learning curve, I kept at it. The meditative rhythm of spinning calmed my nerves, making both me and the fibers stronger and more resilient.

I rarely thought about the spin of fibers that held my own body together.

⸻

Collagen molecules are made up of three polypeptide chains in a triple helix. Three-ply for strength.

⸻

I sat in our cold brick house with our cranky tortoiseshell cat, Delilah, curled up by my side. I suspected that Delilah had the feline version of EDS. Her posture and movements were out of whack, and she felt floppier than other cats when I picked her up. I handled her gently. She spent most of her days in the basket by the wood stove, only moving for laps or spinning sessions. Her curled body impeded access to my pile of wool rovings, but I didn't move her. I liked her warmth.

My relationship with Delilah had recently improved. She'd taken to the basket by the wood stove soon after we'd brought her home from the animal shelter. At first, I'd sit next to her on the floor saying unconditionally loving things about the quality of her fur, but as soon as I touched her, she'd let out a tone-deaf howl. Why wasn't she soothed by my sweet nothings? After I figured out she was deaf and stopped sneaking up on her, she became more affectionate. If I wanted to pet her, I just had to move my hands in front of her face to catch her attention. She liked spinning because she could tell by the bounce of the couch cushion if something in the flow was about to shift.

I'd gotten better at spinning even twists that made yarn both soft and strong, neither slubby nor kinky. I prepped to spin a two-ply skein of wool and silk blend. Silk fibers, which are long, can be spun loosely and remain strong, but it's hard to knit with silk on its own because its fibers are slippery and have no elasticity. They're more likely to snap than bounce when pulled, and they don't take instructions well, kind of like how girls with shiny, straight hair complain that hot roller curls won't ever set. One way to make silk stronger is to ply it with wool, which is grabby and impressionable, filled with barbs that only want to hold onto other things as tightly as possible. That's why it felts with heat and water and agitation. It'll do whatever you tell it to do if you set its new form with water and let it dry that way. But wool fibers are shorter than silk and need more twist to hold them together.

So wool and silk blend well, building on each other's strengths.

⚌⚌〰〰

Collagen fibers aren't monolithic; collagen comes in over twenty different types that intertwine to structure not only joints and skin, but also cells, membranes, blood vessels, organs, bones.

⚌⚌〰〰

I integrated the wool and silk fibers using my carding paddles, which looked like fine metal hair brushes and sounded like Velcro. I lay tufts of each fiber on the bed of metal spikes that distributed the barby wool and the slippery silk when I brushed the paddles together. Carding got out the tangles. It stretched and aligned the fibers, and that alignment made them ready for spinning into fine yarn that could handle the tension of knitting and the wear of clothing.

In addition to twist, fiber alignment also creates tensile strength.

Delilah glared at me, irritated by the jerky movements of carding when she'd come for rhythmic pedaling. But just as I'd finished integrating the wool and silk, and lined up the fluffy tufts on the back of the couch within easy reach, I felt a stabbing in my chest. It stabbed right at the level of my heart and held steady. I held my breath and waited for it to pass. When it didn't, I tried breathing deeply, but expanding my lungs only increased the depth of the stab. Delilah pretended to sleep, eyes open just wide enough to monitor my unexpected behavior.

I told myself the chest pain was nothing. My body hurt continually. Why should this be any different? I told myself to ignore it in favor of more important things, like my morning plan. After I spun the first ply, I'd need to spin the second ply on a second bobbin, then spin them both together on a third. Two-ply yarn is much stronger than single-ply, but it takes three times as long to spin.

With my metal hook, I fished the lead string through my spinning wheel's tunnel-like orifice and started pedaling. I attached the tufts of loose fiber to the freshly twisted strands being pulled through by the spin of the wheel. The fiber twisted left or right depending on whether I spun the wheel clockwise or counterclockwise. And the fiber twisted loose or tight depending on whether I pedaled slow or fast, and whether I released a lot of fiber into the orifice with each spin or a little. I preferred clockwise Z twists and textured slubby yarn best used to knit a particular style of lumpy winter accessories. But that morning I aimed for precision, spinning fine, blended strands strong enough for anything.

Delilah shut her eyes, finally relaxing into the warm rhythm she'd come for.

━∿∿━

Triple-helical collagens bunch together to make fibrils, which are meant to be striated end-to-end like stairs.

━∿∿━

But when, in addition to the chest pains, my left arm started tingling, I stopped spinning. I leaned back on the couch, trying to reposition my arm to bring back sensation. My shallow breaths were making me light-headed. Was I hyperventilating? Should I call an ambulance? Should I call someone to interrupt Mags at work?

Delilah opened her eyes a sliver, willing me to keep going with the wheel.

In general, I avoided doctors. They couldn't fix a genetic disorder, and "be careful" was all they had to say. So I rarely sought medical attention and had no primary care doctor, even though I was finally a permanent resident of Canada and had the same theoretical access to health care as everyone else.

"We call patients like you orphans," my one-time nurse practitioner told me inside the RV that had been converted into a roaming mobile clinic. It sounded about right. Were young medical orphans even allowed to go to the emergency room for chest pain? My head kept spinning while my body froze.

I knew the chronic burning of nerve pain. I knew the acute pain of misarticulated joints and sudden falls. But this sort of chest pain was different. It came stabbing every couple years, threatening to slice me open. But now the stabbing was sharper than it had ever been.

I knew I was at risk for spontaneous arterial rupture, but I thought the risk was small. I'd already gone to the hospital once for chest pain when I was eighteen, and the doctor had said that all of my valves looked fine but to come back if it got worse. This was probably the same false alarm.

But still, I wavered. I walked slowly to the computer, left arm guarding my chest, because I wanted Google's opinion on whether I should go to the hospital with acute chest pain and a tingling arm. Maybe the internet could talk me into taking myself seriously. I needed reassurance that, if I went, I wouldn't be dismissed. That it wouldn't be a waste of time. My search confirmed that, yes, I had emergency-room-worthy symptoms. And when I let myself feel that this could actually be an emergency, I started to panic. Did I have enough time to walk to the hospital several blocks away, or would I die on the way there?

I called an ambulance, shaking.

Then, because Mags didn't work within easy access to a phone, I called a friend who lived near the workshop to run over and tell her to meet me at the hospital. I returned to the couch to wait for the EMTs to arrive, uneasy that I wouldn't be able to finish spinning my morning skein. That two-ply yarn, strong enough for anything, would have to wait.

⚊⚊

A genetic mutation may weaken triple-helical collagens in many different ways, such as through wonky alignment, attachment, length, thickness, or twist.

⚊⚊

When the EMTs arrived, my heart still raced. Delilah remained oblivious to the noise and intrusion of the siren and the pounding at the front door, and had returned to her basket by the fire. Before they put me on the stretcher, the EMTs taped wires to my chest and ankles to monitor my heart with their little machines.

They asked what I'd been doing when the chest pains had started. "Reading," I said. My radical spinsterhood was a liability now that everything I said would be judged as part of an official record on whether my pain mattered. Would doctors take me more or less seriously if they knew I was a badass married queer spinster? Probably less.

"Reading," the EMT repeated in a monotone voice.

What was my excuse for being a twenty-five-year-old woman "reading" at home on a weekday morning? Maybe reading was no better than being a spinster. My heart sunk at the misstep.

"She's tachycardic," he said to the other EMT, a woman who didn't speak.

Well, who wouldn't be panicking in the face of chest pain and a potential heart explosion?

"Do you need to call your parents?" he asked before loading me onto the stretcher.

"I don't live with my parents," I said, offended at the assumption. We rolled down the sidewalk and into the back of the ambulance, where the silent woman placed an oxygen mask over my face.

"What's the name of your condition again?" the EMT asked before repeating "Ehlers-Danlos syndrome," mispronounced, into the radio to whomever was on the other end of the line in the ER. I relaxed a little. At least they'd be able to catch me on the other end.

After he hung up, he hovered over the plastic dome that covered my face. "Do you have a tendency to exaggerate?" he asked, nodding for me with raised eyebrows. He looked away before I even answered.

My throat tightened. He thought I was just some hysterical girl, worked up over nothing. And we both knew I couldn't defend myself while strapped to a gurney under an oxygen-pumping face mask. I wished I had never called an ambulance in the first place. My heart rate amped back up as we pulled into the unloading bay.

⸻

A genetic mutation can also affect fibril formation, how the different types of triple-helical collagens bunch together.

⸻

At the hospital, I was wheeled in and out of little rooms for tests. Fortunately, the doctor took me seriously. My heart rate stabilized, and I started to breathe the same oxygen as everyone else. When he asked about family history, I told him about Marfan syndrome, the long legs, and risk of aortic dissection on my mom's side.

"But you don't have Marfan syndrome."

"No," I said, certain that I didn't.

"And what type of EDS do you have?" he asked.

"I don't know." I explained how my diagnosis hadn't included genetic testing, only clinical examination. And that my parents had told me the doctors didn't think I had the most serious type, the one most similar to Marfan syndrome in terms of its risk of arterial dissection.

"You were lucky to get diagnosed so young," he said. "But you still need to find out your type. Different types have different risks."

I nodded. But did it really matter? Floppy was floppy was floppy. No matter which type I had, the most important thing would be to push through and ignore it. By the time Mags arrived at the hospital, wide-eyed and out of breath, all the tests were coming back normal.

"I think your ribs might be out of alignment and poking or pinching a nerve," the doctor said. "But your heart looks fine. Be sure to come back if it gets worse."

And, like that, they released me.

Mags took me to a pub for poutine and beer, a warm, sticky juxtaposition to being hooked up to machines in a cold, beeping hospital. The beer tasted like I didn't deserve it. My stabbing chest pains had only been due to misaligned ribs, not a heart attack. Had I been exaggerating after all? How big was my risk of aortic dissection, really?

I had no idea.

When the chest pains returned, randomly, over the next decade, I never went back to the hospital. False alarm, I would tell myself. Just my ribs twisting and poking and pinching. Walk it off. Spin through it.

⹂⹂⹂

The type of collagen affected, and the location of a genetic mutation within that collagen's triple helix, determines EDS type.

⹂⹂⹂

The specifics mattered.

SOCKIE BABY

I got a kitten for my eleventh birthday.

Dad had picked up me and Zach at Mom's house to bring us to his house in Vancouver, the one he only lived in for a couple of years while renovating it. When we pulled into the driveway, he turned to me and grinned. "Check your bedroom."

As soon as I realized my birthday present didn't come wrapped, I hoped for a bunkbed. I imagined the thrilling slumber parties I could have, complete with blanket forts. My friend Sara and I would puff paint pillow cases while Sara described the plot of the latest Lurlene McDaniel novel, nostalgic romances about teenagers dying of cancer or teenagers' best friends dying of cancer. "I love them so much," she always said. "They're so sad!"

While she talked, I'd make us matching friendship bracelets out of embroidery thread in our self-contained bunkbed bubble.

"Alyssa was born to make bracelets," a friend in my class had said.

It was clear that I'd found my calling, so I made friendship bracelets continuously. A bracelet-in-progress always sat taped to my desk at school so I could resume my knotting when I finished assignments early.

Eleven would be a good year. More friendship bracelets and better slumber parties. But when I opened my bedroom door and saw my same old unmade daybed, one level of sleeping only, my shoulders slumped. I didn't see the tiny kitten until she brushed against my ankles trying to escape.

"Eeeeeee!" I forgot about the bunkbed, falling to my knees on the stubby new wall-to-wall loop pile carpet to scoop up the black-and-gray tabby with white paws. It took me less than a second to fall in love with my little escape artist and her socked paws that implied she wasn't fully dressed, not quite ready to make it on her own in the world—or the rest of the house—even if she did escape. I named her Socks but called her Sockie Baby when we were alone.

With her striped little face, Sockie Baby was all mine.

In the summer before I started sixth grade, we visited Sue's family house on the Puget Sound, where barnacle-clad rocks lined the shore.

On the carpeted stairs, I took the same sort of fall I usually had. A twisted ankle, a slide on my shin until I caught my weight on the banister. Only this time, despite the carpeted stairs, a large patch of skin had peeled off as I slid.

Dad and Sue drove me to the nearest hospital for stitches, and in the curtained exam area, my dad grimaced at the blood. At the sight of the syringe of lidocaine that would numb my shin before stitching, he moaned and turned toward the sink. My tiny reflection in the paper towel dispenser seemed to shrink.

"Do you need me to stay for the stitches?" he asked, teeth bared.

I sort of wanted him to stay, but I knew he would continue moaning and pacing if he did. "No," I said. "It's okay."

Sue held my hand when the doctor started stitching. "That was good of you to let him leave," she said, giving my hand a squeeze.

I shrugged like it was no big deal. I watched from a distance as the doctor pulled the thick black suture string, tied the first knot, and snipped off the ends. No matter my injury, it was good of me to put other people first.

After my dad and Sue got married, they moved into a new house in southwest Portland. A steep drive turned off the snaking main road, leading to a cluster of large houses tucked behind security fences and privacy hedges. The new house had a terraced front yard, a rose garden off the kitchen, and a heavy front door that creaked like one from a haunted house, shuddering whenever anyone walked in or out. Sue, now my stepmom, had decorated the house in a tight color scheme of forest green and aubergine. It was a much fancier house than the one in which Zach and I still lived with Mom.

Sue was pregnant, and I felt sure it would be a girl. I knew I would be an excellent big sister to her. I couldn't wait to carry an adorable baby around the house and read her picture books. When she was old enough, maybe I would teach her how to make friendship bracelets out of embroidery thread too.

I hovered as Sue unloaded the dishwasher in the long galley kitchen, trying to prompt another conversation about my new sister. "You know," I said, "there's a chance this baby might have EDS."

Sue startled. In each hand, she held crystal wine glasses with deep grooves that sliced the bowls vertically like sections of an orange. "I thought they said that was from your mom," she said, her brow furrowed. She eyed me warily while she put the glasses away, like I might be trying to trick her.

"They don't know that for sure," I said, certain of my memory. I crossed my ankles and leaned sideways toward the counter, bouncing off my left palm. A fidgety talker, especially in conversations like this. "The doctors still need to run more tests."

They'd diagnosed me with EDS, not the Marfan syndrome that ran on my mom's side of the family. But beyond that, the genetics weren't totally clear to me. Maybe EDS, then, was from my dad? Or it could be only mine. I wasn't sure. But it didn't make sense that my dad would tell Sue my weird genetic thing was definitely inherited from my mom if I didn't have Marfan syndrome. All I knew for sure was that EDS and Marfan syndrome were not the same.

Did Dad not want to claim any genetics with me because it made him look bad?

Sue sped up on her kitchen rounds, clicking the dishwasher shut and scrubbing at a copper pan with a sponge that didn't seem to be working. Our conversation had ended, and I wasn't sure what I'd said wrong. I didn't want my sister to be falling-down clumsy, with shins as embarrassing and scar-covered as mine. I'd just wanted to claim her, even if only by half. I hoped she'd have at least some of my traits, but they didn't have to be the weird ones.

I don't remember my mental gymnastics that came later. How did I get from knowing that we were waiting on more tests to the certainty that I'd already had them?

I went outside to see if I could find Sockie Baby.

Exactly one week after my twelfth birthday, my half-sister, Elizabeth, was born. My dad took a picture of me holding her in the hospital rocking chair, cocooned and sleeping in a blue-and-pink-striped white blanket. I wore a black, oversized men's T-shirt promoting a charitable run I didn't compete in, smiling with one of the few genuine smiles in pictures of me from that era. Gaps between my teeth, tendrils of frizzy hair framing my face, and fluorescent hospital lights deepening the circles around my eyes.

Next to the scars on my shins, I most hated the dark yellowish circles around my deep-set eyes. It looked like I'd been punched with expert symmetry and the bruises were still fading, localized jaundice, another manifestation of EDS. I'd seen enough commercials to know under-eye circles were meant to be fretted over and dabbed with special foundation.

"Do you wear makeup around your eyes?" a softball teammate had asked me while we sat on the bench in the dugout.

I frowned and shook my head, feigning interest in the twists of the chain-link fence behind us. I admired this teammate—one year older, outgoing and kind—with short brown hair that never frizzed like mine.

"It looks like you do."

Why would I wear makeup to create dark circles instead of cover them up? Did she really think I chose to discolor my face in this freakish way?

"You're so shy, it's cute," she said when I remained tongue-tied.

She thought I was cute?

Maybe shyness and eye circles weren't the worst afflictions in the world. But still. I worried that I'd never be pretty and lovable, since I already looked weird before I'd even made it to junior high. If I already looked like a suspicious character—a masked bandit or a raccoon—at twelve, how weird would my face be by the time I got my driver's license?

I thought baby Elizabeth was perfect, with her wisps of brown hair and fuzzy hints of eyebrows. The skin around her puffy eyes was the same reddish pink as the rest of her face. But it seemed like the timing was never quite right for my enthusiasm over the newborn in the wicker bassinet.

"She's only three days old," I overheard Sue say to my dad from the next room after I'd asked to hold her.

I understood her protectiveness, even though it hurt my feelings, because I'd channeled my own maternal energy toward Socks, who was not allowed in this new house in Portland's West Hills. Sue had told Dad she didn't want cat hair on the furniture. But I would not let Sockie Baby go homeless, so I constructed a series of cardboard houses, painted them red, and set them on the covered back porch filled with soft beds of my old clothes. If she had to sleep outside, I at least wanted her to feel loved. As soon as one cardboard box became so damp that its roof sagged, I made another one. Sometimes I added a cardboard mailbox with her name on it, duct-taped to the side.

"She looks like a little raccoon!" Sue joked whenever we spotted Socks climbing the crabapple tree overlooking the rose garden.

Socks did look a little like a striped bandit, especially after her undercoat became thicker from living outside. But calling her wild didn't make it so. Each time I got to my dad's house, on Tuesdays and Thursdays and every other weekend, the first thing I did was step out into the mist that clung to the edge of the porch and call for Sockie Baby, listening for her little chirp as she came running.

HURRICANE EARL

Despite the looming apocalypse, I'd decided to go back to school. I wanted to become a children's librarian so I could recommend the present-day equivalent of Ramona Quimby to eight-year-olds, and I already had the cardigans and glasses, so I moved to Halifax, Nova Scotia for a master's degree in library and information studies. However, situated within the Faculty of Management, the program at Dalhousie University only offered a single children's course every other year. I told myself it didn't really matter. After I had my degree, I could apply to whatever jobs I wanted.

Plus, Halifax was on the ocean.

The professors preached concepts like synergy, corporate social responsibility, and fake-it-till-you-make-it with straight faces. At school-sponsored networking events, I felt like a directionless fraud and gulped red wine to calm my nerves, which stained my teeth and gave me a jester-like purple stain at the corners of my mouth. I finally caved and got my very first cell phone, an almost-smart phone with a slide-out keyboard, and started faking enthusiasm for corporate synergy.

The shift from setting my own schedule to double-time work and school jolted my system. Leaving the house every day at specific times I had no say over? Maybe any type of rejoining the rest of the world would have felt jarring after three years of working from home in a small town, but once I started forcing myself out the door, I didn't quite know how to stop. I lived alone my first semester because Mags, who loved her job in Perth, had stayed on for a few extra months to finish a build. So my workaholicking didn't seem so crazy at first, with Mags not there to see it. "You could always stay here," I'd said back in Perth as I packed my surplus raw wool rovings into a large garbage bag. "It's only a couple of years."

She leaned against the doorframe and took a sip of beer. "I want to be with you."

So we sold our red brick fixer-upper in Perth and, once again, Mags and I stashed our excess stuff in her parents' drive shed. Before we left Ontario, I applied for Canadian citizenship, since I'd now lived in Canada long enough to make my belonging official and irreversible.

"A carpenter and a librarian!" a friend said. "You can catalogue the books, and she can build the bookshelves. How perfect."

My first semester at Dal, I took weekend drives to trace Nova Scotia's many ragged peninsulas. I witnessed the clashing flow of tidal bores, reverse waves traveling up a river as a result of the Bay of Fundy's dramatic tides.

The Atlantic has a different personality than the Pacific. Instead of rainy sou'westers that flood roads, Halifax has frigid nor'easters that bury them in snow and blow away cars. Apparently, living near the ocean didn't necessarily mean the weather would be temperate. Not an intuitive fact to my West Coast brain. And while the Pacific is on the leading-edge of the continent, keeping many of its secrets fathoms deep, the Atlantic slopes gently into the abyss and so coughs up more decay in its tides. It stinks more, with its deep piles of kelp, rockweed, and knotted wrack, more putrid life close to the surface. It also coughs up more human detritus from the populations along its coastlines, washed and worn by the churn of the ocean. On the Oregon Coast, I hunted sand dollars; in Nova Scotia, sea glass. Sea glass tumbles in the ocean for years or decades or centuries until its edges wear down and it takes on a frosty opaqueness. I collected all the colors and tossed them into a mason jar on the kitchen window where they fractured the light.

When I stumbled across the unmarked trails that meandered through the rocky coastal barrens outside Peggy's Cove, my heart beat faster at the unexpected discovery.

"I found an amazing trail just off the side of the road," I said to one of my bosses, who squinted as if she couldn't quite place the intelligence of a grad student thrilled by the discovery of one of the most photographed and tour-bus laden Canadian landmarks. But not having grown up in Canada, I'd had no knowledge of Peggy's Cove, with its iconic light-

house surrounded by gently sloping, cracked granite. I hadn't even seen
the lighthouse that day, but the trails approaching it were unlike any I'd
ever been on. Large granite boulders dotted the rolling hills; these gla-
cial erratics had been carried long distances and then abandoned on foreign soil. Moss and lichen and carnivorous pitcher plants blanketed the
sprinkling of topsoil; the spoon-leaf sundews, also carnivorous, looked
like sea anemones that had learned to breathe air instead of ocean water.
The Dr. Seuss-like foliage in dramatic shades of ochre and rust promised
an exciting new beginning. Oh, the places I would go.

Anything was more compelling if I thought I'd discovered it myself.

Early in my second semester, after a full day of classes and dying of thirst,
I returned to our apartment with views of the North End Library and
the Macdonald Bridge across the bay to Dartmouth.

Mags had arrived.

I gulped a pint of water at the kitchen sink while she made me a martini with three olives. Then we sat on the couch, my legs slung over her lap,
while she rubbed my painful feet between her hands, flattening my high
arches as if they contained no bones and loosening the knotted muscles.

"I figured out how to seem less anxious during presentations," I said. "I
just have to move and talk like I'm under water."

Mags nodded.

"But it doesn't really matter if I fuck up because I always have you to
talk to about it."

She nodded again.

Mags's presence stabilized me on my tightrope of overwork, and I
leaned into it. She'd even just helped me to identify gluten as the culprit
behind my continual stomach pain, and made me gluten-free comfort
food almost every night, moussaka and enchiladas and risotto.

"You used to have to lie down after every meal," she said whenever
I hinted that I might be still okay with the occasional piece of gluti-
nous bread. So I glowed in the best part of the day, a martini hitting my
bloodstream on an empty stomach and about to watch my adorable wife
cook food that didn't cause stabbing stomach pain. She hadn't found
her bearings in Nova Scotia yet, but I had an infinite number of ideas for
projects she could help me with. A skilled carpenter and cook?

I could plan her days until the end of time.

I started taking pictures of her in the kitchen, documenting what she cooked for dinner. From every angle, I recorded our little kitchen with the tiny two-person table under the windowsill where the sea glass I'd collected fractured the light. We ate out of artisanal stoneware pasta bowls we'd dragged from British Columbia to Ontario to Nova Scotia and used every night, pasta or not. That night, she made deconstructed sushi: piles of rice, seaweed, pan-seared tuna, and enough wasabi to burn my brain clean. "I express my love through cooking," she'd always said.

"You should write a cookbook, Mags. We can give them away as gifts and not even have to shop for Christmas gifts next year."

She nodded.

"You can use my pictures!"

After dinner my throat grated raw. Drinking many more than eight pints of water a day felt necessary, but the more water I poured into my mouth, the thirstier I seemed to get. And despite Mags's willingness to pose for my camera and nod at my ideas while rubbing my feet, we were becoming detached from each other in a way I couldn't quite pinpoint.

I holed myself up in the bedroom to finish my taxonomy paper, watching the spring snow out the window and fighting the urge to check up on Mags's weird shuffling around the living room. Later, I went out to find her asleep out on the couch with our nervous cat Vinnie on her hip. Vinnie had black-and-white markings like a Holstein cow and, when she saw me, jumped to the floor with a squeak and starting crying. She hated Halifax. Not only had we flown her on a plane, thinking it'd be less traumatic than two days in a car, but she'd also lost her small town yard to prowl around in. Unlike Mags, she'd gotten louder in her insistent unhappiness. She chirped and whirred and whined about everything I'd put her through.

I swooped down to scratch her head and let her rub against my knee. "I'm so sorry, my little Vin. I'll never put you on a plane again, okay?"

Vinnie started purring, but Mags flinched. She wasn't asleep after all. "Don't promise that if you don't mean it."

Vinnie and I both looked at her, startled by the sharp hostility in her voice. Mags was right. Despite my flippant promise to Vinnie about staying put, who knew where the next couple of years would take us?

On the weekends, Mags and I started exploring Nova Scotia's coastlines and collecting sea glass together. On our drives to far-flung beaches, we admired brightly painted saltbox houses adjacent to walls of stacked lobster cages, and we speculated about living in the tiny cottages we passed on country backroads. I daydreamed with more enthusiasm than she did, but she went along with whatever I wanted. It buoyed me up to have something fun to talk about, something that skirted the growing distance between us. Real estate cost less in Nova Scotia than it did in Ontario, where we'd recently sold our house, so we could buy a cottage if we wanted, especially if we found a fixer-upper we could justify as an investment. Maybe that could be Mags's job in Nova Scotia?

Nevertheless, I had moments of clarity about timing. As much as I loved the ocean, I knew it wasn't terribly likely we'd stay in Nova Scotia after my two-year program. Most of the jobs were elsewhere, and owning anything would be cumbersome when it came time to move.

Back at school, at work, I needed to prevent all the systems of the world from falling apart into chaos. First, I put Dalhousie University in order as a minute-taker for the University Secretariat, where I attended board and committee meetings and noted all the important stuff. I liked being behind the scenes and my new Fluevog shoes.

Second, I put the reference desk in order at Saint Mary's University, where I wrote Chicago Manual style guides, created interactive online tutorials about how to search databases, and answered research questions about P/E ratios from MBA students.

Third, I put the internet in order, "tracking user engagement with social discovery systems." As a research assistant, I tracked tags and ratings and reviews on a public library catalog's new social functionality that no one used.

In my fourth and fifth jobs, I found myself right back to the work I'd done before library school. I wrote a report for Dalhousie on student engagement. I worked as an assistant consultant doing legwork for a client report on software systems for digital archives. I'd spun away from my original intention in going back to school, too busy to reorient myself.

And while I met the required duties of all of these jobs, I was too strung out to fully engage in any of them.

Secretly, I worried about my ability to function in a regular job after library school. I could work five part-time jobs because my ingrained habit was to work at triple speed fueled by adrenaline. I never procrastinated because I hated working last-minute, and I always work as fast as possible so I wouldn't be stuck without the energy to complete it later. It was like a poverty mindset in terms of energy. Instead of spending all my money in fear of being broke later, I spent all my energy in fear of the exhaustion that would inevitably come. I didn't know how I would get through endless days of working nine to five at breakneck speed.

I often crashed during my late evening shifts at the reference desk, where I scrolled real estate listings, daydreaming about what it might be like to spend weekends within walking distance of piles of knotted wrack and scatterings of sea glass.

Mags never really picked up the cookbook idea, despite her nods, so I stopped taking pictures and stopped mentioning it. Was she mad at me for throwing so many ideas at her? For unloading too many details about my day over the martinis she made me with three olives? I rummaged through the closet looking for the extra pair of tick pliers to take on a hike at Duncan's Cove, a stunning landscape of coastal barrens and granite cliffs that sloped into the Atlantic, but I found a stash of empty vodka bottles instead. "Mags, what's going on?"

She shrugged. "Those are old."

I leaned against the wall for balance. Was I making a big deal out of nothing? If she said a stash of empty bottles wasn't a problem, then it wasn't. But why couldn't she just have her nightcaps in the kitchen like a normal person? In any case, she filled my evenings with foot massages and dinner, so I let denial do its dirty work.

Mind over matter.

Fake it till you make it.

I sat down at my desk, stared at the computer screen, and looked through more real estate listings. Something to ground me.

We drove along Highway 329 around the tip of the Aspotogan Peninsula the day the for-sale sign had gone up in front of a white 1950s shack with green trim that sat on large, speckled granite boulders.

I gasped when we drove by. "Oh my God. Back up!"

Adorable and run-down, the property came with five forested acres covered with poplars, pines, and deep peat moss, and a bright orange cast iron hand pump gushed well water into the kitchen. It had a crumbling stone wall along its back border, ancient gnarled apple trees, and two rusted cars overgrown with grasses. It also had an eastern-facing view of St. Margaret's Bay, directly across from Peggy's Cove on the other side. From the cottage, it took two minutes to walk to Bayswater Beach, a small crescent moon of white sand covered with piles of seaweed, caches of periwinkles, and the odd shard of perfectly worn sea glass. The possibility of buying it weighed heavily. Since we discovered it on a meandering day trip, before it had even been listed online, didn't that mean it was meant to be?

I believed the real estate agent when she said it would sell quickly, accepting the pressure to make an immediate decision the same way I closed my eyes and swallowed the management speak about synergy. Nevertheless, I had moments of clarity about our relationship. "Things aren't so great between us right now," I said to Mags as she sat on the couch. Through the window, red and white lights from the Macdonald Bridge twinkled behind her. "Do you really think it's a good time for us to be buying property?"

Mags recoiled as if I'd betrayed her by giving voice to the growing distance. Instead of responding, she slumped, glassy-eyed, to gaze at her feet.

So instead of leaning on her to help make the decision, I posted a survey on my new blog with a picture of the cottage. Should we buy this? About a dozen of my library school friends responded. They said yes, no, it depends. If it were the type of big data I was learning about in school, maybe I could have run some rudimentary analytics. But the survey didn't clarify much, and Mags remained passive, ready to go along with whatever I decided. The only problem was I couldn't hear my intuition. My body, knotted all over, didn't know one way or the other, and my head could rationalize either answer equally well. The more I spun from overwork, the more the world around me blurred. I closed my eyes and pretended I couldn't see that the last thing I needed was another project. "Well," I said, "I guess our twenties is a good time to make a big mistake." We bought the cottage.

Now, in addition to school and five jobs, I had a cottage to renovate, pine walls to whitewash, windowsills to paint. I may have been tightly wound but at least, I told myself, I'd found a solid place to land. I worked myself past exhaustion, too busy to worry about anything besides the next task in front of me.

Late summer, Haligonians talked preparations—tape on windows, water, batteries, and canned food on hand—but also reassured me that Hurricane Earl probably wouldn't hit Halifax. Sure, they classified Earl as a category four major hurricane *now*, but he'd most certainly chill out by the time he hit Nova Scotia.

I scoffed at the hurricane's name because it reminded me of the Dixie Chicks' song "Goodbye, Earl" from the late nineties, an infuriatingly catchy song that had irritated me even in high school. So Earl didn't scare me. *Goodbye, Earl.*

Maybe exhaustion had messed with my sense of proportion. I was guaranteed to freak out about finding a blood-sucking tick burrowed into my ankle and the sure development of Lyme Disease, but I couldn't spin myself a single thread of worry about a hurricane. Worst case scenario? I'd step outside and get smacked in the head by a flying two-by-four, then have wacky dreams like Dorothy in the *Wizard of Oz*.

My focus was on how it would be our first-ever weekend at the cottage without a work project in mind. One weekend of rest before school started up and I added homework back onto my long to-do list. I was just looking forward to watching the storm, and what better place to catch the drama of a passing hurricane than a rustic, foundation-less cottage with a view of the ocean?

We pulled into tire ruts in the grassy yard on the Friday night of Labour Day Weekend. Like usual, we brought gluten-free crackers and brie, books, a full bottle of Johnny Walker, and two pairs of tick pliers. We'd even stopped at the hardware store in Hubbards to buy sisal rope because I planned to spend the weekend weaving a welcome mat using knot #2272 from *The Ashley Book of Knots*, a "three-lead by six-bight."

I'd seen similar mats behind display cases at the Maritime Museum of the Atlantic and in tourist shops for $100. "I can make that," I'd said to Mags. I'd recently fallen in love with the book by Mr. Ashley, as thick as a dictionary with almost four thousand careful drawings and divided by category: occupational knots, knob knots, single-loop knots, binding knots, fancy knots. Its idiosyncratic categorization fascinated my librarian brain. He also used descriptive drawings to annotate, or tag, the knots: a wheelbarrow for practical knots, a woman in a corset and top hat for purely decorative knots, and a bready pretzel for knots easy to untie.

Mr. Ashley had the same wisdom as Mags when it came to untangling. Keep the knot open and loose so it unfurls on its own, without trying to force it by tugging on loose ends.

They made it sound so simple.

The next day, while Mags napped inside, I set up a sawhorse in the middle of the untended lawn with a stamp-sized view of St. Margaret's Bay and began wrapping scratchy sisal around nails hammered into plywood. I loved the scratchy feel of sisal. The nails were the crossover points around which to loop the rope.

Over, under, over, under.

The air smelled like dried grass and rotting seaweed, and I lost myself in repetition, wondering if maybe, instead of library school and digital archives and metadata, I should quit now and commit to weaving welcome mats and selling them to tourists full time. But about three-quarters of the way through, I realized I hadn't spaced the nails correctly. I hadn't taken the thickness of the rope into account. In the gathering wind, it draped with oversized holes I couldn't tighten. I was supposed to have been noticing the tension as I went along, like in knitting or spinning. Or life.

My back ached from the sawhorse that stood at the wrong height for over, under, over, under. The wind had picked up, and I needed a break.

"It's taking longer than I thought," I said to Mags.

Mags shrugged and joined me on the stoop for cheese and crackers.

She ate slowly, as if she wasn't really hungry, even though she hadn't eaten all day.

That afternoon I sat in the plaid-upholstered corner chair reading *Bluenose Ghosts*, a classic of Nova Scotian folklore, when silent, heavy air descended. It had been whipping the pine trees not two minutes before. Now the tree tips didn't waiver at all.

I needed to make the downhill trip to the outhouse, but I hesitated to disturb the stillness. "Do you need anything from the car while I'm out there?"

Mags shook her head.

On the short grassy path, my neck prickled. A tick? Panic as I felt the back of my neck. No tick. Just eerie stillness. No birds sang, and I peed in air so humid and suffocating it swallowed the sound. "The air is purple," I reported when I returned, the screen door slamming behind me.

Mags turned on the solar radio we'd stashed for unlikely emergencies, and the broadcast crackled with the information we needed right away. Hurricane Earl had veered inland, heading straight for Nova Scotia's South Shore, making landfall more or less exactly where we sat next to our wood stove on the Aspotogan Peninsula.

Mags and I stared at each other.

"I guess it's too late to drive back," I said. I imagined us racing back to the city and getting blown into the Atlantic, our Toyota Matrix as insubstantial as a Matchbox car. My words seemed to disappear. Had Mags heard me? Did she blame me for getting us trapped in a hurricane, for ignoring the warnings? For deciding to buy this cottage in the first place? She stayed silent. Nothing we could do now but wait it out.

I took a sip of whiskey and savored its burn. I put down the classic of Nova Scotian folklore and picked up my knitting, but I couldn't focus on woolen loops either, when every inch of my skin prickled in awareness of the density around me. But when the heavy stillness broke, instead of spinning into anxiety, I breathed more easily. The howling hurricane-level winds felt lighter than that disturbed underwater silence, even as they gusted underneath us, even as they rippled the floorboards. I thought about the day Mags and I first saw the cottage on our meandering drive. It had looked so adorable resting on its four large, granite boulders. But it turned out that floating plywood and two-by-fours don't add up to an immovable structure to a hurricane.

Maybe the car would have been safer.

The corner of the building lifted underneath me.

My teeth clacked when it dropped again, like driving over a pothole. The more the amber liquid sloshed in my tumbler, the more I stilled. It was a relief, actually, to find myself in the middle of a system so clearly outside of my control. We might blow away but, for once, I found myself the calm eye of the storm. I inspected my house shoes, leather clogs with paint-splattered woven tops, and thought about our wasted effort. What had been the point of all that renovating if Hurricane Earl was just going to blow us away in our freshly painted little shack?

Mags and I made eye contact. She sat just outside of touching distance on the fold-out couch. What did she see when she looked at me? When I looked at her, I saw ratty sneakers and chaotic hair. Cute. But. More disheveled than usual? She still seemed so far away, underwater, eyes wide. I broke the silence. "Maybe if you come over here, we can weigh this corner down?"

Mags stayed where she was, heavy on the couch. "I doubt that would help."

Earl continued to batter the cottage. Lift off the boulder, crash. Take another sip of whiskey.

Lift, crash.

Then as quickly as he'd arrived, Earl whirled away. *Goodbye, Earl.* He made his way back out into the Atlantic Ocean to resume his northerly course, leaving wind in his wake and the cottage still resting on all four granite boulders. I had gotten my storm-watching wish after all.

Mags and I were all good?

EYE-MASKED OUTLAWS

I sat with Sue and Elizabeth at the glass table in the kitchen nook over-looking the rose garden. Sue held Elizabeth on her lap while Elizabeth, now able to sit up, swiped at a cardboard tube empty of paper towels. She shrieked with laughter when it fell over, bouncing on the glass table with its hollow papery trill. We laughed at this deep new belly laugh from a tiny happy person. Elizabeth had a curly top of light brown hair, big brown eyes, and little hands that balled into fists when she laughed. Sue set the paper towel tube on its end again, and the hilarity repeated several times.

When Elizabeth tired of the game, I rolled the tube mindlessly between my palms.

"Her little hands are so cute," I said. The chubby little backs and tiny fingernails. Sue agreed, examining her daughter's hands again like she couldn't get enough. I liked the vibe of her unconditional adoration, one arm clenched around Elizabeth's torso.

My own hands weren't nearly so cute. I'd developed a new self-consciousness about my thumbs after a classmate told me how weird they were. But at that clear glass table in the afterglow of infant hilarity, I let my guard down for a minute. Maybe my hands could be adorable too.

I stuck out a stubby thumb and held it up to Sue, my nail more broad than high. She'd probably noticed my thumbs before but didn't think anything of their slight stubbiness. "Aren't my thumbs funny?"

She looked. "Oh my God!" she said, turning my thumb with her free hand to inspect it from all angles. "What happened?"

"Nothing," I shrugged. "They're just like that." The paper towel tube rolled onto the floor from my moment of inattention. It landed with a deeper trill that prompted no laughter. I hadn't expected the tone of Sue's reaction to match the judgy girl at school.

She looked away. "Well, keep them short and trimmed, and don't draw any attention to them," she said. "That's all you can do."

So they really were freakish, my thumbs? Not the reassurance I'd been hoping for.

Dad didn't like my usual weekend outfit: gray bike shorts and a T-shirt with a cat on it.

"Put on some real shorts," he said. "Then tuck in your shirt and wear a belt."

When I insisted that I did not own a belt—how could he not know that?—he borrowed one from Sue's closet and handed it to me. I took it with caution. Kids my age did not wear belts, and I knew her waist-cinching belt would be too small to reach around the waistband of my low-rise shorts.

"Alyssa's a big girl," I overheard Dad say from all the way upstairs after I told him the belt didn't fit. I could hear his grimace, and my stomach sunk. I knew my dad's opinion of "big" people. I'd stood by his side when he saw a fat man in the grocery store whose stomach drooped over his jeans.

"Shoot me if I ever look like that, okay?" Dad had said. "Promise?"

About a year after Elizabeth was born, Dad and Sue had a family portrait taken, in soft focus like a glamor shot. I know this because I saw it, not because I was in it.

The photo appeared on the built-in shelf in the living room, so freshly developed it still rested in its cardboard frame. Dad and Sue formed the pointy shoulders of an inverse triangle with a smiling, cherubic one-year-old Elizabeth at the tip. Light brown curls atop her head and two front teeth. I stared at it for a long time, seeing the invisible ghosts of me and Zach hovering behind this perfect family trinity.

When had they gotten the portrait done? It must have been on a day when Zach and I had been at Mom's. Surely, they planned to take a second family photo shoot that included us too?

"Cute picture," I said, nervous like I'd been doing something wrong, when Sue caught me staring at it.

As I retreated to my room, I concluded that there would be no second photo shoot. Obviously. My acne and braces and circles around my eyes made me an awkward thirteen. Plus, I was a "big girl," with thumbs that shouldn't be allowed to see the light of day. Why would anyone want to memorialize that?

I snuck Sockie Baby into my room, where she purred on the middle of the bed and blinked at me like she knew and approved of my rule-breaking. We could be outlaws, and dream of escape, together.

ON A MISSION

I needed a dress to wear to the holiday party with my new coworkers, the Army Daves, so I dragged Mags shopping.

Dress. Party. Army. Shopping. Who had I become?

I mean, I was still myself enough to brace for the trip to The Bay in Kingston's Cataraqui Centre. Lights too bright, people too awful, crap for sale too expensive. Malls caused misery no matter what, so our plan was to be as efficient as possible. No distractions. In and out.

Snowflakes landed on my glasses as we marched through the parking lot and melted as we pushed through the glass doors into the gust of hot air. Mags seemed more like herself than she had for months, strutting through the almost empty store, her boots squeaking on the polished linoleum. We tried to march straight to the women's section, but it took some reconnaissance (or, as the Army Daves would have said, "a recce") to find the right one. Military speak had crept into my thoughts, even when trying to identify the appropriate department store section. Why were there so many different women's sections?

Our marching efficiency made it feel like a game. And as I'd recently learned at work, the difference between a game and a mission could be eerily slight. The contractor I worked for on the base was all about video games. Sorry, I mean "simulations." Large-scale simulations to train various defense factions in real-life maneuvers. The Army Daves exclaimed over the graphics of tank models with glee, and I felt like an avatar of myself, there in image only.

And now, here I was, on a mission of my own.

Operation Bay Blitz.

Mall Storm.

Queer Cover-Up.

We'd left Halifax, and my grad school life, abruptly. While I'd expected to turn into a cardigan-wearing children's librarian, I ended up accepting the first job offer to come my way, as a digital archivist on a Canadian army base in Kingston, Ontario.

"Oh, Alyssa," a friend had said. "That's not you at all!"

I hadn't quite understood what the job would entail, but Kingston was an hour away from the farmhouse where Mags had grown up, and I thought if we went back to Ontario, maybe she'd forgive me for moving her away from the timber-framing job she loved in the first place. Maybe if I deposited her near home to find her bearings, the ice of our marriage would melt. The idea of returning to a place that we already knew, where we already had people nearby, felt like what I needed too. I was tired. I wanted to land for good this time.

We left Halifax so abruptly that I missed the notice from Immigration Canada telling me to attend the next oath of citizenship ceremony, a notice I'd spent over two years waiting for.

At first in my new job, I'd had a hard time telling the middle-aged men with buzz cuts and polo shirts apart, and most of them were named Dave. The Army Daves spoke in so many acronyms that I had to learn a whole new language before I could even join the conversation. I spent the majority of the first two months making spreadsheets of acronyms and their definitions. How was I supposed to organize their shit if I didn't even understand what they were taking about?

I struggled with sitting at a desk all day long, which pixelated my body. My brain fogged over a couple hours into the workday, and I infused myself with continuous cups of tea, clinging to the hot water as my only hope of refocusing. And because my legs itched for movement, every day at lunch I walked down to the Saint Lawrence River, where slabs of limestone stacked up against the shoreline like bread on a party platter. I paced the lawn, circling the overgrown patch of blazing Chinese lanterns, trying to recharge. But every evening by the time I got back to our apartment, my muscles ached like I'd just run a marathon, with barely enough energy left to carry me back to the couch.

Despite my frazzling body, I insisted on writing every evening, installing myself at the tiny desk in the corner of the bedroom. It kept me in my head, far away from what was happening on the ground. Mags was

FLOPPY

supposedly looking for work but had started zonking out on the couch before I even got home, retreating so far into herself that I could barely reach her. Alone, I wrote YA stories and drank more of the dry apple cider she had brewed in a glass carboy in the kitchen. Sometimes she still cooked dinner. Sometimes I did my hour of writing to background noise of pot-banging and vegetable chopping, sounds more comforting than dead silence. But one night, I came out of the bedroom to flames on the stovetop. "Oh my God," I said. "Mags!"

She'd fallen asleep on the couch with the burner on high.

"Fire!" I doused the flames with baking soda and moved the pots from their overheated elements, grateful I'd come out of the bedroom when I did. I shook Mags's shoulder to wake her up. "Fire."

Nothing. I confirmed she was still breathing before I scraped off the top layers of unburnt rice and butter chicken into my bowl and sat down at the dining table to eat. But even though my stomach growled, I couldn't force the food down my closed throat. I ran my fingers over the knife marks in the old butcher's table, which we'd dusted off and dragged out from Mags's parents' drive shed.

How could Mags just zonk out like that? Did she have a brain tumor or something?

It didn't make any sense. It was almost like part of my own brain was blocked off and I couldn't pinpoint the problem right in front of me. In any case, I knew I wouldn't be able to run on exhaustion fumes for much longer.

By the time Mags and I had filled our arms with potential dresses, the thrill of our hyper-efficient mission had faded. In the dressing room, the bright lights turned my skin bluish, and the dresses were either too frilly or too exposing. My hair looked weird too. I'd arrived in Kingston with an asymmetrical, queer-chic haircut from a Halifax salon. My recent home trim, however, had turned out like the Army Daves' buzzcuts.

"I'm just trying to fit in," I'd said to Dave the next day at work, who laughed.

Looking at my reflection, I remembered why I almost never wore dresses. I wasn't butch, but I also didn't have the energy for the accessories and makeup required to make dresses look like they were hanging on the right person. If I really wanted to fit in, maybe I shouldn't bother with dresses that didn't suit me. I wondered if the Army Daves would still wear Blundstones and polo shirts to the fancy holiday dinner. My eyes burned in the fluorescent hell. Why did I even bother?

"At least that lady isn't following us anymore," Mags said.

I struggled with a stuck zipper. "What lady?"

"Didn't you notice her following us from rack to rack?"

I shook my head. I mean, I'd noticed a lady but assumed she was shopping for party dresses like us. In her grim smirk, I thought she'd been amused by our mission-like efficiency. She'd been hovering to make sure we didn't swipe anything? I hated that I'd been so oblivious to the insult. I was almost thirty, married, and had secret security clearance on a military base, for God's sake. How much more of a legitimate adult did I have to be? I wanted to leave all the fast fashion in a messy pile on the dressing room floor and storm away from the entire capitalist empire.

Instead, I inspected us in the mirror. Mags's hair made a halo of frizz, and her wrinkled hoodie hung open. The short party dress I wore didn't flatter my pasty white skin or unshaven, scarred legs. Would I always look like a suspicious character with a scruffy wife by my side? I took off my glasses and used my scarf to wipe away the water residue that lingered from the snowflakes. I'd been on my feet for too long. I knew this head-spinning feeling, short on oxygen, like I was so desperate for a place to sit that I'd knock over anyone who got between me and a chair.

I hated video games, I hated war games, and I hated shopping. But I'd spent all day on an army base and all evening at the mall, and the pile of new clothes on the floor smelled like perfume and formaldehyde. So much for spinning a life outside the military-industrial complex. I bought the least unflattering dress from the pile, a royal blue shift dress shaped like a flour sack, with black sequined stripes. I would look like a bumble bee stained with blueberry juice. I also bought new tights so I wouldn't have to shave my legs for the Army Daves.

We marched to the car even faster than we'd marched into the store. It was no longer snowing but the temperature had dropped, and when Mags offered to drive, I took a deep breath of air so cold it pierced my lungs. "You sure?"

She took the keys and swung into the driver's seat. Such a relief, these moments of swaggering return to her old self. Out the passenger window, salt-covered cars glinted in the parking lot. But then, without warning, Mags took an aggressive left into the busy street, ignoring the right turn only sign and blasting over a concrete median. Then she sped up. I'd been riding in the car with her for almost a decade and she'd never driven as if she were playing a video game. I couldn't tell if she was angry or oblivious to the danger.

"Oh my God, Mags!" I yelled. "Stop the car."

Her face was blank as she swerved into the parking lot of an abandoned motel and screeched to a halt. Silence. Our headlights illuminated wide triangles of drifting snow.

"What's *wrong* with you?"

She didn't respond, only stared glassy-eyed into the distance. Where had my confident mission partner gone? "Get out," I said. "I'm driving."

We switched places, squinting as we passed each other in the headlight beams. In the driver's seat, my throat closed shut as my adrenaline rush faded. What was wrong with *me*? I'd yelled at her. My wife could be dying from an undiagnosed brain tumor and I'd shamed her for it. "What's going on, Mags?" I asked. More softly. "You're not acting like yourself at all."

She flinched but remained unreachable, her face expressionless. Did brain tumors click off and on like that? My half-sister, Elizabeth, had died when her cancer spread to her brain, and her trajectory had been downhill fast. Not like these hours with Mags that blinked between her seeming fine and disappearing. But still. I worried that I was about to watch my wife die too.

Operation Sequin Stealth was over. We were back to our new normal.

KUDOS

Ten minutes into choir rehearsal and my hands were already turning purple, which happened if I stood for too long in one place. We lined the perimeter of the small auditorium, me and fifty other eighth and ninth graders, and I eyed the orange upholstered seats, hoping we'd return to our sections soon so I could slip my hands between my thighs to warm them up. Mr. Foster gave his usual speech about how we needed to rehearse as if we were on stage at all times. "Because what does practice make?" he asked.

We finished his sentence in unison. "Permanent." Permanent, not perfect.

"Let's start again from the top," he said. "Everybody ready? Shoulders up and back." I stood military rigid.

"No picking and scratching." I froze in place.

"On the balls of your feet." I stood almost on tiptoe to overcompensate for my very flat feet.

"Breathe into your diaphragm." I puffed out my chest with the deepest breath I knew how to take.

Mr. Foster blew into his metal pitch pipe, and I stretched my sleeves into my palms to minimize the chance of anyone catching a glimpse of my freakish hands while we sang. Singing in choir was a temporary escape from my own awkwardness. All I had to do to belong was memorize my part—second soprano—and blend with the other girls in my section. Just listen and blend. Even though I sometimes felt like I might faint, I was very good at listening and blending. But I still decided to take voice lessons just in case Mr. Foster realized I didn't belong and decided to re-audition me without warning.

My friend's mom gave one-on-one lessons from her pastel living room with a baby grand piano in the corner, and I fidgeted in a chair in the hallway while I waited for my turn, listening to one of the choir's soloists complete her scales. She didn't sound like she needed any help.

Was I even allowed to take voice lessons if I didn't want to be a soloist? I hoped no one would overhear any part of a remedial voice lesson. I could sing on key, but that was it. My friend could probably hear my croaks and breathy scales from her upstairs bedroom, but I wanted more confidence. I didn't want my voice to crack with nerves. And I wanted to feel what Mr. Foster meant when he said, "Breathe into your diaphragm."

What was a diaphragm, even?

Mr. Foster planned self-esteem-boosting activities carefully selected to manipulate us into loving each other. He carried around a copy of the new and popular *Chicken Soup for the Soul*, and the word "kudos" got thrown around a lot.

And I mean a lot.

Those kudos were supposed to tie us together into one big happy knot. Every Friday, he placed the kudos box on stage, where we could write compliments to each other that would be read out loud later. I never left any anonymous kudos, in case someone knew it was me and thought I was weird, and I never got any kudos either. This was fine with me because I did everything I could to avoid being the center of attention. To belong, I knew I needed to remain invisible.

Besides, what would anyone even say about me? All I could think of were anti-kudos: I was too shy to talk; I had braces and two missing teeth; I'd recently trimmed my bangs in the mirror at home, and the results were not flattering.

While I could handle listening to other kids' kudos, the "family time" days made my stomach coil.

"Gather in a circle on the stage," Mr. Foster said. When they held the talking stick, the other kids cried tears of joy at being in concert choir, or they bounced happily at the prospect of an upcoming performance. I sat rigid. When I had to speak, my head spun so fast that my words couldn't keep up and came out jumbled. I cut myself off before I even began.

I passed on the talking stick as if it were a red hot poker that burned my cold purple hands.

A tenor I never spoke to, Logan, paused next to my seat as he got off the school bus one stop before mine. "You should talk more during family time." I smiled, close-lipped, not wanting to show my missing teeth. I didn't know whether to be flattered that he'd noticed or insulted that he'd ordered me to talk without even asking if I wanted to.

Back at my voice lesson in the pastel living room, my voice teacher had me lie on my back on the carpet and breathe into my belly. "Does your stomach go in or out when you take a breath?"

A long pause while I overthought about it. "In."

"Really? Take another one." She put her warm hand on my stomach.

Was I breathing wrong? I blushed on the carpet, hoping the color would be hidden by the several layers of powdered foundation on my face. I took another breath.

"Still in?" she asked.

"Out," I said, the only other answer. Nervous laughter.

She assigned me diaphragm strengthening exercises, fast punches of breath I was supposed to repeat every day as a warm-up. I didn't like this homework or my nebulous diaphragm. How was I supposed to know if it moved in or out? I didn't have that kind of engagement with my body.

I quit voice lessons.

DENIAL BONFIRE

Mags and I sat side by side in a small exam room that had been turned into a waiting area with chairs lining both long walls. Posters advertised flu shots and HPV vaccines. No windows looked out on the dark autumn evening. I believed we could make any hospital glare less depressing just by being together, so I grabbed the metal water bottle from my shoulder bag, which I'd filled with white wine before we left the apartment for Kingston General Hospital. We could at least take the edge off those harsh fluorescent lights while we waited.

"I brought you a surprise!" I said, handing her the water bottle. "White wine."

She shook her head. "No, thanks."

Her hand jittered on her lap, and I pulled back. Her declining drinks was new. Was she really so nervous about being stuck in an MRI tube? "Really? Why not?"

She stayed silent and avoided eye contact.

"It might calm down your nerves," I said, taking a sip.

When we lived in Montreal, it had felt rebellious to sneak drinks in water bottles and flasks, and I'd hoped to recapture some of that thrill. Plus, I needed this moment to be a celebration. After months of worry, we'd finally get some answers. I was sure she had a rare kind of brain tumor, which is why it had taken so long to diagnose. What else caused an otherwise coordinated person to be fine one minute and falling over the next if not for a rare, hard-to-diagnose condition? What else caused those glassy, distant eyes besides some sort of cancer-induced neurological disorder?

When the technician took her away and trapped her in the MRI tube, I stayed in the waiting room drinking warm wine out of the metal water bottle and listening to the symphony of diagnostic machines down the hall. But the wine tasted heavy, not light and celebratory like I'd anticipated. Mags really wasn't herself if she'd stopped drinking completely.

I jumped up when she returned to the waiting room more disheveled than when she'd left. "What'd they say? Did they find anything?"

Mags shrugged. "The doctor has to look at it first."

Her tone didn't invite further questions.

We'd left the car on the other side of City Park to avoid paying for a hospital parking lot, so we crunched over leaves on our way back to the car. Aside from the crisp leaves, the night air stood silent. "I'm just so worried," I said.

Mags didn't respond, and I regretted expressing worry for the millionth time. Was I making things better or worse? The silence weighed heavily. We got back to our ground-floor apartment. "Do you want to rewatch the first season of Downton Abbey?" I heard myself say.

She sighed as if I'd just offered her a million bucks to not talk about her brain tumor. "Oh my God, yes."

In February, Mags stayed at her parents' house for a week to look after their golden retrievers and feed them their afternoon cubes of ice and extra sharp cheddar cheese. I drove out to join her on the weekend, crossing the Lasalle Causeway over the icy Kingston Harbour. In the distance, the Wolfe Island Ferry chugged through the thin channel of the Saint Lawrence River that remained unfrozen. It was the kind of winter day that made the world look filthy and entirely devoid of life. A layer of salt and dirt splattered every car door, blackened piles of snow guarded every driveway, and sumac silhouettes jabbed the gray sky with spikes of red berries, the only living color around.

When I pulled into the gravel driveway of their sandstone farmhouse, icicles hung off the white gingerbread fretwork and smoke billowed from both chimneys. I crunched inside and removed my boots, taking a deep breath of dry air and golden retriever. Mags was sleeping on the couch in the keeping room while the wood stoves creaked. We ate a frozen pizza for dinner and watched the sky glow orange behind the apple orchard. "Let's have a bonfire," I said. "There's some stuff in the drive shed I want to get rid of."

Mags sighed. "It's going to take a while to build it."

"I know," I said. "We can do it tomorrow if you're too tired?"

She flinched. "I'm fine." She opened the screen door to let the golden dogs loose, then followed them outside into the night.

I crunched to the drive shed through snow, the top layer of which had thawed and refrozen into brittle ice, past the big red barn that used to house cows and horses but had recently been transformed into a woodworking studio with cushy standing floor mats. The sound of metal hitting ice reverberated from the field behind the apple orchard, where Mags chipped away at the frozen snow with a shovel to make room for a fire pit.

I wasn't sure where in the drive shed we'd stashed my dozens of spiral-bound notebooks filled with daily stream-of-consciousness writing, my *The Artist's Way* morning pages. I wondered if the mice had already gotten to them. I'd die if anyone read them. I didn't even want to read them. The time seemed right to see them incinerated.

The ladder-like stairs were unfinished and splintering, and I heard scurrying when I pulled the chain that dangled from the bare light bulb. I found the box quickly, surprisingly intact, and wobbled back down the steep stairs with the box against my shoulder, thinking I should have asked for Mags's help with this part too. When I got to her, Mags fed the fledgling bonfire with pieces dragged over from the surplus wood pile. The cold night was the same kind of cold as when I'd slid to school during Montreal winter, one that sliced between muscles and bones, and which no number of layers could block completely. Whiskey required.

"Do you want some?" I asked. I handed her the flask she had bought for me in Montreal, our first Christmas together.

Mags took one small, unenthusiastic sip. She still wasn't herself, even though the MRI test results had come back negative. No brain tumor. The news hadn't seemed to faze her one way or another, and I wanted to shake her. Where had she gone? Why couldn't I reach her? The brittle ice cracked under my feet and my heels sunk into the cold snow. I'd been wasting time at work Googling her bizarre symptoms for potential rare conditions that doctors were likely to overlook. What if her jerking movements and stumbles were caused by Parkinson's? Or MS?

Mags stood still, stoic. The flames crackled, and I flipped through one of my notebooks. My right-leaning scrawl filled the lines with mundanities: the goodness of my morning coffee, to-do lists, moods. I knew they must contain more incriminating things that I wouldn't want anyone to read. But still, I hesitated. Wasn't I meant to go back through and read these at some point? Mine them for ideas? But I didn't have time to read dozens of rambling notebooks, and I wasn't in the mood to dig too deeply into my psyche. Something big sat just below the ice that I couldn't quite see and didn't really want to.

"Fire's ready," said Mags.

I wanted to dump all the notebooks on the fire in quick succession so we could go back inside to the cozy wood stoves, but when I threw on the first notebook, only its cover curled in the flames. The outside pages charred, but the fire couldn't touch the dense internal ones, and my writing remained legible.

"Promise you won't read anything," I said, removing my mittens so I could get a better grip to tear out clumps of pages at a time.

Mags snorted. "I won't."

We tore at the pages. The warmth of the fire kept my fingers safe from frostbite but warm enough to register the pain of the deep cold as I watched my handwriting burn page-by-page, then word-by-word, then penstroke-by-penstroke. The wind scattered crisp black remnants over snow that glowed blue in the moonlight. The stars shone bright and un-attached. What gems had I burned? Did it even matter?

Back in Kingston, I sat on the black leather couch in the tattoo parlor's waiting area on Division Street and jittered my foot.

Daniel had come to visit from Montreal, and he and Mags were get-ting tattoos. Mags had drawn the full moon and tree branch silhouette she wanted inked onto her bicep, and Daniel flipped through my *Ashley Book of Knots* to pick out an illustration for his inner arm. He chose a simple overhand knot with fraying rope ends.

I didn't have any tattoos because I worried I'd end up regretting what-ever I chose. Or that my skin would tear and never heal. I'd been looking forward to Daniel's visit because I wanted him to see what was happen-ing with Mags. I needed validation that I wasn't losing my mind. Why did Mags still wobble and slur her words? My frustration was sinking me. But first I tagged along to the tattoo parlor. My ankles hurt from the walk there on high-impact cement, and the rest of me ached. I wanted to be curled up on the couch at home. Instead, I crossed my arms and legs and looked out the window at filthy spring ice banks and gum-dotted sidewalks. The high-pitched buzzing needles and the chemical smell of the place didn't improve my mood. I drank both of the water bottles I'd stashed in my shoulder bag.

"You and your hydration," Daniel said when he joined me in the waiting area, inked and floating on endorphins.

I clenched my jaw. "Water is good for you." Daniel was in medical school now, back to school in his early thirties. Shouldn't he know that?

That evening, after Mags fell asleep on the couch, I finally got the chance to talk to Daniel about my sickening, months-long worry. I couldn't get the words out fast enough, stuttering over myself, but nothing I said seemed to convey the intensity simmering in my chest. I sputtered out, a fire with no pages left to burn.

"It's good the doctors didn't find anything in the MRI," he said.

But it didn't seem good to me, to have no clear reason for the unraveling I felt. I began to wish that Mags actually did have a brain tumor. At least my anxiety would have something to settle on. Helping my wife through chemotherapy would have been easier to handle than this slippery grasping. We sat silent for a moment after I wrapped up my story about her falls and our inexplicably frayed connection.

"I don't know," he said. "She just seems kind of drunk to me."

Wait, what?

She just seemed kind of drunk to him. Her wobble and jitters. Not from a brain tumor? But Mags had stopped drinking. She'd barely taken a sip in front of me in months. I poked at the little green circles on my duvet cover. My black-and-white cat Vinnie curled up at the foot of the bed while the neighbors thumped overhead. The white walls grew vivid. Daniel's words lifted my denial and allowed me to glimpse the reality right in front of my face. Mags had been drunk and trying to hide it. It hit my chest with a thud that Mags had let me worry myself sick about her "brain tumor" in full knowledge of the connection to my sister. I didn't recognize her anymore, this new version of Mags.

I wanted to shake her, but I wanted to shake myself harder.

How had I missed it?

Where had I even been in my own life?

THE POWER OF NOW

Two weeks into Mags's thirty-day rehab program, I was allowed to come for a weekend visit. I listened to *The Power of Now* on the drive, which one of the Army Daves had recommended. "It really helped me when I was going through my divorce," he'd said.

So I got an audio version from the library, even though Mags and I weren't getting divorced. We just had stuff to work on. While listening to Eckhart Tolle's gravelly voice, I took deep breaths and focused on my hands on the steering wheel in the sun, the lift of my leg on the clutch. Since I was living in the power of now, I'd decided to take the scenic route.

I'd confronted Mags the day after Daniel had left me with clarity about her drinking: "Maybe you should go to rehab or something?"

Mags had looked down at her hands, then at Vinnie sleeping curled on the end of the bed. "Maybe."

I stared at her, waiting for more resistance. But all it had taken for her to acknowledge her drinking was for me to break the spell of denial. Maybe she'd been tired too.

After three hours of driving, I pulled into a gravel driveway in a meditative trance, a Canadian flag waving on a pole in the front yard. The rehab facility was in an old farmhouse similar to Mags's childhood home, only its dormer was Ontario Cottage style instead of Georgian. It had a covered front porch and a long summer kitchen in the back, and outbuildings had been converted into administrative buildings, a dining hall, and a row of motel rooms.

Mags ran toward the car and scooped me into a hug that caught me off guard. I tensed before I let myself fall into it. Her eyes looked clearer than I'd seen them in forever, and as she walked me to the main house for a tour, fresh green maple leaves shimmied against the bright blue spring sky.

Mags was coming back?

Her thirty-day bedroom had deep windowsills, a tiny wooden desk in the corner, and a homemade wedding ring quilt on the bed. "I think you would love my therapist, Sharyn," she said as she plunked herself down on the bed. "She swears like a sailor and tells it like it is."

I leaned against the windowsill and nodded. "When can I come back for a couple's session?" On the website, I'd read that one was included in the rehab program.

"You don't really have to," she said. "I don't want you to have to take the day off work or anything."

I tilted my head. She knew I was miserable at work. "I want to!" If Mags was talking in coherent sentences again, we had a lot to catch up on, like my lingering anger at how she'd let me believe she was dying of a brain tumor for months. But I'd also read a lot about addiction since she'd left, and I wanted to give her the space she needed. I didn't want to be a codependent enabler of her healing process, or whatever.

"I'll ask Sharyn what she thinks," she said, rubbing her fingers over the blue cotton rings on the quilt. She took a deep breath as if working herself up to say something difficult. "One thing I want to change when I get home is I'd like us to eat more salads." She held my gaze. "We have them here with every meal, and I feel great."

I paused, glancing at the journal and pen on her corner desk.

Salads?

We had bigger problems than lack of greens, but I supposed we'd have plenty of time to talk after she got home from rehab, good as new. Maybe she needed me to keep things light, to let us have this pleasant day together where we didn't have to process anything at all. I took a deep breath and summoned the wisdom of Eckhart Tolle. I would focus on the moment right here, right now. Maybe it was true that nothing else mattered. Meditation did help with the tension of anger, which he said was part of the unenlightened emotional "pain body" that the power of now could dissolve. If I grounded deep enough, I could turn that tension into nothing but a warm glow that didn't have to be dealt with at all.

It turned out that relapse is common—expected, even—after rehab, not that I'd been forewarned. As soon as she got home, Mags started disappearing for days at a time, and I hunted for her, finding her on friends' couches, in the hospital, or not at all. She returned home covered in bruises, like she'd been in a fight or a car accident, maybe both. A friend from Perth called to say that Mags was sleeping on their couch for the night. "She says you're getting a divorce?"

My body tensed in a flush of heat despite the power of now. That was news to me.

We still needed to reconnect and process things, but I hadn't mentioned divorce and neither had Mags. Had Mags meant what she'd said or was it a grab for sympathy, to excuse herself for passing out drunk in friends' living rooms? After the call, I threw my phone down onto the bed. Surely, if she wanted a divorce after almost ten years together, she would tell me to my face.

"You're torturing me." I said to her when she returned to our apartment, bedraggled and wobbling. "If you want a divorce, just say it. *To me!*"

Mags made like she couldn't hear me and stumbled to the bed. "I feel like I'm taking crazy pills!" I called after her. If she'd been reachable, the conversation, according to scripted dialogue from *Zoolander*, should have gone like this:

"I'm sorry. I was wack."

"No, *I* was wack."

Laugh. Move on. But in the silence of her non-response, I wondered if Mags really had decided to end our marriage without me. If she wasn't laughing with me over our inside jokes, how would we ever find common ground again? "I feel like I'm taking crazy pills," I said again, to myself. Heartbreak crazy pills.

A few days later, I stumbled upon her on the floor of our bedroom, pulling a half-full vodka bottle from the heating vent. I was impressed both by her secret ingenuity and the opaqueness of my recently discarded blinders. "That's a really good hiding spot," I said, letting out a little laugh at my helplessness.

Mags's eyes clouded over and she didn't respond, only dropped the grate back into the vent with a clang and stared off into the distance as if she weren't clutching a twenty-sixer of vodka with white knuckles.

I left her to it.

I held fast to meditation, still liking the glow that came from paying close attention to my body and my breath, but a weird thing started happening. The more grounded I became, the more I felt the burning in my hands and feet, and the deep ache in my bones. I couldn't brush off the sharp stabs of subluxated joints if I had to pay continual attention to my ever-present body. It turned out the healing powers of dissociation had seen me through a lot of chronic pain. Meditative breathing had lightened emotions, but the more I sunk into the "now," the more physical pain took its place.

We drove to Montreal for a couple's session with Sharyn, her rehab psychotherapist who also had a private practice. I'd insisted that we book a session, and Mags had nodded but avoided eye contact.

Sharyn's office was in a building with no windows above a bank. It didn't feel at all like a picturesque thirty-day retreat in the country. We were back to regular life. But I did like Sharyn. She was older than we were and gave motherly hugs. In her jeans and T-shirts, with her long blonde hair pulled back into a ponytail, she looked more like a friend than a therapist.

First, she met with us individually. I talked about the crazy-making experience of hearing about our "divorce" from our friends.

"Addiction is rooted in avoidance of emotions," Sharyn said. "Mags is highly avoidant, so it's no wonder she's avoiding you."

I talked about the "brain tumor" and how I'd exhausted myself tracking her down to make sure she was safe, and how I hated my job and felt like I was going to snap. I also tried to convince Sharyn that I wasn't being codependent. I took deep breaths and said affirmations that sounded to me like things a therapist would want to hear. "I feel whole without her," I said.

She nodded. "That's really good," she said, tentatively, like I might be missing the point. Then she leaned forward in her chair. "Can you go home for a while, Alyssa? Like, do you feel supported there?"

"Um . . ." I paused. My real home was here with Mags. And what was "a while"?

"I think if you want to stay together, your only hope is to give the relationship some space," she continued. "Mags needs to deal with her own shit."

I liked Sharyn's voice, smooth and balanced. Maybe she was right. Maybe geographic distance was the only thing that could keep me from trying to help. "I guess I've been daydreaming about a few months on the Oregon Coast," I said. "I miss the ocean."

Sharyn nodded and leaned back in her chair. A full-size mirror leaned against the wall behind her chair, presumably to reflect back onto me, but it only reflected the ceiling from where I sat.

"I need to start doing my own sessions too," I said. "Can I use you or should I find someone else?"

"You can use me."

In the couple's session, Mags and I sat at opposite ends of the couch. I sat to the right, close enough to the lamp that I worried about it illuminating my bad skin, broken out from stress.

"I've talked to you both separately," Sharyn said, "and you both say you want to stay together. So what you need to do when you get home is talk to *each other*. Don't just, like, fold the laundry and forget about this."

Mags fiddled with strands of her hair. She crossed and uncrossed her legs, jiggled her foot, didn't look at me. On the drive home I tried to recall the therapy threads that could prompt conversation with *each other*, but anything I said seemed to dangle and fray. Mags stayed silent as we drove past Beaconsfield and Sainte-Anne-de-Bellevue, silent as Highway 20 turned into Highway 401 and we sped through Cornwall and Brockville, silent as we pulled into the driveway of our ground-floor apartment on Bagot Street in Kingston.

The lease on our apartment was up, so I started filling the empty cardboard boxes that I'd ferried home from the liquor store. I wanted Mags's help, especially since I was packing up her stuff too. I needed help with cleaning and making donation runs, and I especially needed help with the moving itself. Mags knew that my wrists snapped from the weight of heavy boxes, that I could dislocate a hip or twist an ankle shoving at furniture, and that I was several times more likely to fall when tired, if I pretended I could do it all myself.

But Mags stayed mostly away, whereabouts unknown. She was falling a lot these days too, but I hoped she'd be able to pull herself together for moving day. She wouldn't leave me to move our whole apartment into her parents' drive shed by myself.

The week before moving day, Mags slept on the couch while I packed books into boxes. I jumped when she spoke, not expecting her consciousness. "I'm like Rapunzel," she said, her voice clear and articulate. "You fall in love with my book collection, then you cut off my hair."

I ran my finger over the sharp edge of a cardboard flap.

It was true that I had fallen in love with her wall of books, flush with the fronts of matching hand-built bookshelves in her apple green, Montreal-perfect bedroom. And it was true that, after we merged our book collections, we gave duplicates away. It was also true that I'd made her leave boxes of books in her parents' drive shed at every cross-country move. But we couldn't move a whole library every two years. Had she been storing up resentment about that since the beginning? "What do you mean?" I wanted to force her to explain herself. It's not like I'd trapped her in a windowless turret.

But she didn't respond, only moaned and put her hand to her head like a tortured Victorian lady on a fainting couch before falling back asleep. When moving day rolled around, she was nowhere to be found, and I made her assessment true. She wouldn't help me move her clothes or her furniture or her precious books, so I left stacks of her luscious locks in the free box along the sidewalk.

When I drove away, I didn't expect my leaving to be permanent. I surfed couches for a couple weeks, including a night with Meli, the ceramicist near Perth we'd befriended a few years before. As I was leaving the next morning, Meli noticed my packed car, which had slipped her attention when I'd arrived. I'd packed it to the hood with boxes, metal IKEA drawers in the hatchback like a portable closet.

Bullfrogs croaked in the distance, and morning dew still sparkled on the wild, grassy field. "Alyssa, are you *driving* back to Oregon?"

I shrugged, eyes focused on the big red barn in the distance. "Yeah. But I'm coming back." I still expected Mags to resurface. I told myself I was just giving us each enough space to align ourselves before figuring out a way to ply our threads back together. This was an opportunity to recharge near the ocean in the constant drizzle that I missed. But I couldn't see myself staying in Oregon for long when my real life was in Canada.

Driving westward, I sliced through the forests of Northern Ontario for two long days, along Lake Superior with its oceanic waves before landing flat in Manitoba, then Saskatchewan, where the old wooden barns leaned at acute angles away from the wind. The Alberta horizon churned mountains out of the soil, which I crested slowly, taking a pit stop at a yarn store amongst the tourist shops in Jasper to buy gray and white merino wool for a cap-sleeved sweater I'd been wanting to knit for months. The moment I hit British Columbia, a gentle rain started to patter on the windshield. A good omen. I took a deep breath, calm in the evergreen air, and turned south, crossing over the US border and down to my retreat of indeterminate length on the Oregon Coast.

FRACTAL

I couldn't wait for the official start of high school. Classes were sure to get more interesting when my grades actually counted. But by the end of ninth grade, I felt certain that every single person in a position of authority was an idiot.

My first high school paper was a ten-page essay on "The Gift of the Magi" for Honors English. The story was about two young lovers, Della and Jim. Della sells her most prized possession, her hair, to buy Jim a chain for his watch; Jim sells his most prized possession, his watch, to buy Della a comb for her hair. Neither of them could make use of the other's sacrifice.

It didn't sound like the sort of trap I'd fall for. I was pretty sure I wouldn't sacrifice anything for some random boy. Nevertheless, I had to write a ten-page paper about the story's theme and plot structure. I wanted to be a writer, and I couldn't wait to channel all I'd learned from reading Strunk and White's *The Elements of Style* over and over while on the toilet.

The week before the paper was due, the teacher had posted the reference style she wanted us to use on the overhead projector. "Copy this down."

I didn't copy it down because I was busy writing a poem in the margins of my notebook. I remember thinking that I would look it up when I got home. I'd done reference styles before. Besides, I knew I could find citation examples in the set of old encyclopedias on my mom's mantle. I'd just use those.

The weekend before the paper was due, I sat down at my desk in my bedroom and wrote the entire first draft in one go, double-spaced on college-ruled notebook paper. While I worked, the whole world reduced to me and that paper, like I'd been drugged on focus. I wrote about how the story was a metaphor for the foolishness of sacrificing yourself for a lover. If both Della and Jim had sacrificed their very selves, they'd have nothing left to give each other going forward, nor could they appreciate the other's sacrifice. Eventually, not only would they lose each other but they would have lost themselves as well.

I omitted needless words until my sentences and paragraphs cinched together, and the next day I typed up my final draft on the boxy new PC Mom had set up in the living room. I floated through the house in the afterglow of knowing that I'd never worked so hard on a school assignment. Things finally mattered, and I liked the way it felt.

The teacher returned the papers a week later. "Why didn't you follow the reference style I put up?"

"I forgot," I said. And by that I meant I'd wanted to figure out how to do it on my own. And I had. Who cared about which style I'd used?

She handed me my paper. "Fix it or you're out of Honors."

I took my paper from her, then stood frozen in place as her eyes returned to her desk and didn't look back up to meet mine. The glasses perched on top of her head had fingerprint smudges on them. That's it? What about my writing and its meticulous adherence to a classic style guide? I returned to my desk and looked at her comments. "I am truly blessed to have a student of your abilities in my class. A+."

Wait, what?

Why did the reference style matter so much, if she'd given me an A+ for the paper? She was blessed to have me in her class but would kick me out for using a different style? Maybe high school wouldn't be different than any of the grades before it. School wasn't about self-directedness and doing the best possible work. It was about following orders. Aside from that, I should save my energy.

I redid the goddamned Works Cited page on my blessed paper.

I'd also lost myself in making a 3D fractal for ninth-grade geometry. I loved the idea of fractals. Self-same geometric patterns that repeated at every scale, representations of chaos. It blew my mind that, mathematically, chaos had a pattern. It's the repetition of an initial condition at every scale until it appears random. A system's building blocks mattered; the slightest change in its initial configuration lead to dramatic changes. Almost everything in nature had a fractal pattern: brains, veins, and heartbeats; snowflakes, Queen Anne's lace, and lichen; seashells, coast-lines, and hurricanes.

For my 3D fractal, I started with a large square cardboard box. On each of the box's six sides, I centered another box, one-third scale, that I'd made out of construction paper by tracing and cutting out a flat box shape with tabs. Trace, cut, fold, glue. And on each of those six boxes' five exposed sides, I centered another construction paper box, one-third scale. Trace, cut, fold, glue.

A total of $1 + 6 + (6 \times 5) + (30 \times 5) = 187$ boxes.

One hundred and eighty-six traced, cut, folded, and glued construction paper boxes. It took me all weekend. At my bedroom desk, silent, I lost myself in replicating the pattern, immersed in right-brain fractal making. My finished fractal was the size of a bar fridge but fragile, as all fractals are. Not a classical geometrical structure, like the triangular trusses used to build bridges. I hung it from my ceiling until Monday so the tiny end boxes didn't get crushed by the harsh carpeted landscape of my suburban bedroom. When our dog saw it, a floppy-eared Dober-man named Ralphie who whined whenever he wasn't being touched, he crouched and growled. Its design was so reflective of nature that his dog brain read it as alive and dangerous. Capable of self-same replication in all directions.

When I stepped onto the school bus, everyone looked up but no one spoke as I slid to the inside of an empty seat, against the window speck-led with rain. The ride to school was longer now, extending eastward to Wy'east Junior High. Wy'east was what the Multnomah people called Mount Hood, even though you couldn't see the mountain from the school itself. Out the window, the field where horses used to stand in the drizzle eating wet grass had been filled in by an apartment complex behind a short brick wall.

The silence in the bus replicated itself as the fractal crouched next to me, higher than my head. Had I crossed an invisible line and shown myself to be an overachiever?

My geometry teacher gave me a B+ on the fractal that had taken me all weekend of tracing, cutting, folding, and gluing. Marks off for slop-piness because tiny globs of glue had seeped out the sides of the fragile construction paper boxes. My alien box fractal was way better than the girl's next me, who got an A+ on a 2D fractal she'd drawn on a sheet of poster board. Chaos is rarely perfect and free of dried glue.

What was the point of school, anyway?

I looked for other ways to entertain myself in classes now. In US History, I completed a worksheet on the Civil War with nonsense answers composed of names of characters from the *X-Files*. The teacher glanced at the worksheet, saw that I'd filled in all the blanks, and gave me 100 percent.

"You always get done first," she'd said with a smile.

Experiment confirmed. The amount of effort I put in had no correlation to grades, and I called bullshit. High school would be pointless too, and I was done overachieving if I could get As for doing absolutely nothing.

With my free after-school time, I ordered college catalogs and lay on my bed daydreaming about the day when everything wouldn't be stupid, maybe at some school on the East Coast, or maybe in Europe, where everyone would be smart and sophisticated. I daydreamed about taking road trips through the Southwest in a pick-up truck with nothing but a 35mm camera and a notebook in the passenger seat.

I bided my time for anywhere but there.

SWEARING TO THE QUEEN

I landed in Manzanita, Oregon, in an above-garage studio apartment with windows that looked onto the rustling tips of hemlocks. The Pacific Ocean roared in the distance. The walls echoed from its sparse semi-furnishing that consisted of an uncomfortable red couch, a desk made of wooden planks built into a nook under the sloped ceiling, and a kitchen table.

I loved it.

The Army Daves had let me take my work on the road, so I still earned a part-time paycheck. I picked away at writing a software manual, but I knew the job would peter out. I could only be so useful to them from the other side of the continent, when I had even doubted my usefulness when I sat there in person.

The best walking route to my PO box—on the tiny town's main drag that T-boned the roaring Pacific Ocean—was to take the hillside trail from my above-garage apartment to the seven-mile long white sand beach, descending through dense salal and blackberry bushes. I still hoped that a couple months of gray mist would charge me back up and I'd go back to Canada refreshed and ready to look for another job, perhaps one in an actual library this time. Or maybe Mags would want to move to British Columbia with me after she got her shit together. We could be close to the ocean there too.

So I walked to the post office through the forest and along the beach, even though it took longer than if I'd walked paved streets, because I wanted to spend as much time as possible next to the healing ocean waves. Also, walking on dirt and sand caused less joint pain with every step than the unyielding slam of pavement. It had rained the night before, and the wet sand shifted like brown sugar underneath my feet. At high tide, the waves chopped in almost as far as the dunes, still talking about last night's full moon and howling storm. White foam blew in billowing chunks along the sand, and a seaweed mound sparkled with sea glass, bottle caps, and a bright orange buoy. A synthetic fishing net draped on driftwood, tangling around a broken lobster pot and a wooden float untied from its ropes. When a piece of billowing foam fluffed against my shins, it disintegrated into filthy water that soaked into my rolled-up cuffs.

I exited the beach at the main street and walked past cedar-shingled businesses housing coffee and donuts, surfboard rentals and beach toys, and the Little Apple Market, which had almost the variety of a full-sized supermarket squeezed into a space the size of a convenience store, but everything cost twice as much as it would have in a grocery store on the other side of the Coastal Range.

When I opened my tiny PO box, my stomach flipped at the sight of the brown envelope forwarded from Mags's parents. I'd used their sandstone farmhouse as a temporary mailing address and left them to deal with the continuation of Mags's post-rehab fallout while I flitted off to my codependence vacation on the other side of the continent, where I worried I'd driven my wife to drink due to my "too-muchness." I didn't know if my in-laws believed me when I'd said that I wasn't abandoning Mags forever, just giving us some space and the chance to come back together later. I had believed it when I said it. But how much longer could I pretend that Mags and I would "work on things" if I couldn't get a sober conversation out of her? Our phone calls ended in my tears of frustration because nothing she said made sense, or she said nothing at all. Or she reassured me that she still loved me and then became unreachable for weeks. I had no clarity, internally or externally.

News of my divorce was coming at me from her parents now too, through the phone lines.

"No," I said. "We haven't even talked about it."

Howie paused, his voice strained with impatience. "I understand if you said something about it in the heat of the moment," he said. "Just let us know the next time you say something like that to her so we're ready to deal with the fallout." He hung up. He didn't believe me.

The undertow of guilt pulled me under. I had left. I wasn't there to deal with the fallout. The bet I'd made, that space would allow us another chance, was not paying off. Maybe my marriage really would end without a single sober conversation, and my leaving hadn't helped anything besides making it easier for Mags not to face me.

I slipped out a white letter stamped URGENT from Citizenship and Immigration Canada, and my stomach flipped again. I tore at the envelope. Yes, finally. My call to attend a citizenship ceremony in Kingston in ten days. I'd completed all the steps, waited for years in between each one, and now I was about to become a Canadian citizen.

I cut back to my apartment the short way, through the paved streets lined with quaint shingled vacation homes. When I got back to my apartment with the birds-eye view of the ocean, I booked my flights.

Mags had just moved out of her parents' house and into a fourth-floor apartment in a yellow brick building off Division Street. The entrance smelled like secondhand smoke and industrial cleaning fluid, and she answered the door in her pajamas, her eyes wide and slippery. My stomach sunk. I knew those eyes. They meant she was fading fast, either from alcohol or the downers her new doctor had given her for anxiety.

She wobbled and pinged around the apartment as if she were gathering her things. "Let me get my bag!" she said, her words sharp and bright. She grabbed the keys to my rental car and held them above her halo frizz. "I'll drive you!"

"You lost your license," I said.

I went into the bathroom, but when I came out Mags had splayed facedown like a starfish on her bed, her hand in a fist on top of my handmade quilt with colorful cotton squares. If she kept the quilt I'd made, did that mean she missed me? I sat on the edge of the bed and looked around. Familiar books sat stacked on the windowsill, and, for a nightstand, she used the pine Tetris shelves she'd built for my studio tour yarn displays years earlier. Her bedroom still sparkled with signs of us.

I put my hands on my hips and felt my pulse speed up. "Are you still coming?" I asked. It was obvious she wouldn't be able to rally herself for my citizenship ceremony. "I have to be there in twenty minutes."

Mags grunted but didn't move. I inspected her crushed profile, but she didn't seem to be in there, and I wanted to kick over those Tetris shelves, swipe the stacks of books onto the floor. I stood up quickly. "I want my quilt back."

"Fine," she said. She rolled off the quilt in a way that seemed to take immense effort. "Take it. I don't care."

I stripped my quilt off her bed and headed for the front door, tripping over her roommate's bicycle repair project spread across the living room and whacking my shin against a serrated plastic pedal. Fuck. I pulled up my pant leg to make sure I hadn't gashed it wide open. The last thing I needed was to sit through a citizenship ceremony with an open wound.

Nothing but a blooming bruise on my shin. A bike chain sat limp on the floor like a rubber band that had lost its elasticity, and I stomped over it on my way out the door.

Near the front of the ceremonial hall in a limestone government building on Clarence Street, I sat in my assigned seat in the middle of a regiment of tightly packed folding chairs with about one hundred other new Canadians. To my right, a woman's thigh pressed tightly against my own, and, to my left, a man splayed his legs into my space but still knocked his knees against the chair in front of him. They couldn't have spaced these chairs out a little?

I held my breath. I was an aisle seat person and avoided middle seats to prevent getting trapped in a crowd when I needed to make a quick exit. I wasn't claustrophobic, exactly, but the longer I sat still and upright the more lightheaded I got, and dizziness could trigger panic. Sometimes I needed to get up and move without warning.

Along the walls of the ceremonial hall, painted portraits hung above the dark wood wainscoting, and a chandelier twinkled above the line-up of local politicians and government officials. Their folding chairs had much more space between them than ours did, and I couldn't concentrate on their speeches welcoming us into Canada's "multicultural mosaic" because I regretted my exchange with Mags at her apartment. Would the last time I ever saw her be the time I swiped the quilt right out from under her? I winced and held back tears that refracted the light from the chandelier, which glared as bright as winter sun on a field of snow.

Mine would be a divorce by freezing out.

My heart squeezed as tightly in my chest as my legs were held in place by strangers' bodies. I had no room left for the patriotic pride the droning speeches were written to invoke. Mercifully, we came to the official bits where I had something to do besides replay the conversation with Mags in my head.

"All rise."

I stood up so quickly that my vision clouded over for the first few lines of our recitation of the Oath of Citizenship.

I swear that I will be faithful and bear true allegiance
to Her Majesty Queen Elizabeth the Second, Queen of Canada . . .

Like a graduation, they called our names one by one to receive our certificates and shake hands with the line of officials. It went so quickly that in my disorientation, I tried to return from the same direction I came, even though I'd had plenty of time to study the choreographed trajectories of the new Canadians ahead of me. A smiling woman blocked me and pointed in the other direction.

We were supposed to loop.

Certificates in hand, we remained seated for—Holy Queen—more speeches. The audience in the pews behind us rustled and coughed. The ceremony finally ended with the whole room singing "O Canada!" in English, then in French, the words of which were printed on the back of my citizenship certificate.

O Canada!
Our home and native land . . .

The deep red maple leaf glowed through the parchment, and my hands shook the paper as I read along and tried not to cry. The process that had taken me almost ten years—from extending my student visa, to the work permit, to permanent residency, to the multiple-choice citizenship exam and hearing to, finally, this years-delayed ceremony—was over.

O Canada, we stand on guard for thee.

The last line repeated three times, after which I was released with the others back onto the limestone streets of Kingston a full-fledged Canadian citizen. During that long, suffocating ceremony, it had finally sunk in that my marriage to Mags, who had been with me from the very first step of the process, was over.

The frosty air crystallized in my lungs as I walked back to my rental car. I was a dual citizen now. My legal right to live in Canada could never be revoked, but whether I lived above or below the forty-ninth parallel, I would have to start over somewhere for reals.

Part III

GENETIC FREAK OF NATURE

Tourists deserted Manzanita in winter, ghosting the residential areas. The houses that lined my street only filled up for the occasional long weekend or holiday before emptying out again. Even the owners of the house to which my above-garage apartment belonged only used the house in August. My brain spun cartwheels in all of my extra time and quiet solitude.

"I just want to be left alone," I said to Sharyn during a phone session.

"Okay, good," she said. "Stay home and lock the fucking doors."

No need to lock the door in a ghost town, but I did it anyway. For work, I fell back on indexing books, my first freelancing skill. Maybe I'd add copyediting after I took a workshop or two. Exhaustion had sunk me too deep to look for another library job, one that would require moving elsewhere and working full-time hours. I wasn't ready for that again. I wondered if I ever would be.

Had all of those years of pushing myself finally caught up to me? And did it even matter? It was autumn of 2012, and I still half expected the apocalypse to come wipe us all out in a month or two.

I snuck down to the beach along the trail lined with salal and blackberry bushes after spending the morning reading about the importance of letting go of ego from Pema Chodron and Thich Nhat Hanh. But in therapy, Sharyn continually reminded me to focus on my own wants and needs instead of other people's.

Confusing. When was my ego important, and when was it not?

My joint pain had increased, and my anxiety along with it. It became harder to leave my little nest of an apartment up in the hemlocks because I didn't want to run into anyone. Walking required more continual focus than it used to, and the presence of other people threw me off. If

I had to talk to people, even a perfunctory hello, what would happen to the awareness I needed to hold myself together?

Of course, crowding is relative. Manzanita Beach never got so crowded that people fought for towel space or umbrella rights. Often the nearest person stood far enough away to be confused with a piece of driftwood. Was that someone in the distance with bad posture and a third leg? Too soon to tell. But if I'd sunk deeply into my own head, as deep as the last person on earth after the apocalypse, even another human who may or may not have been a stump invaded my attention.

The beach was empty, the tide neither fully in nor out, and I had a wide stretch of sand all to myself. But my ankles and knees stabbed with every step, bone grating on bone. I'd always had joint pain. I'd always had to pace myself on long walks. But sand was low-impact: Until now, it had always absorbed some of the pressure my ligaments couldn't. My elbow joints had become looser too; just the swing of my arm could cause them to subluxate, almost but not quite a dislocation. What the hell was happening to me, if I couldn't even handle short walks on the beach?

I recited a grounding meditation I'd just read from Thich Nhat Hanh, each inhale and exhale its own line of three beats. It helped with anxiety and heartache but did nothing for pain. I dragged myself off the sand and wondered what would happen if the pain kept getting worse and prevented me from walking at all.

Was I unraveling for good this time?

After the day of the Maya apocalypse passed without incident, my routine in Manzanita spiraled outwards one step at a time until it started to feel like my actual life, not just a retreat from it. First, I joined a knitting circle that met every other week at the yarn shop on Manzanita's main drag. I made ribbed headbands to see myself through the awkward stage of growing out my hair from buzz cut to ponytail.

The brass bell on the door clanged as Kay walked in carrying a cardboard box. Her short gray hair spiked to one side, and her eyes looked sunken as if she'd been up all night. She wore a wool sweater with a darned hole near the neckline.

"What's in the box?" I asked.

She set it down in the middle of the circle to reveal a days-old baby lamb. "Lambing season," she sighed, plunking herself down into an empty folding chair. "This one was abandoned by its mother." She lifted it from the box, long legs dangling, and held it against her chest. "It only stops quivering when it's held, and it needs to be fed every hour."

My headband looked funny, the ribbed rows no longer matching up, so I brought it closer to my face to inspect the fabric. Had I dropped a stitch? Added one? Had I knit where I was supposed to purl, or purled where I was supposed to knit?

"You look serious," Kay said.

I lowered my arms into my lap and refocused my eyes on her tired face. "I'm trying to figure out where I went wrong," I said.

Kay waved her hand and scoffed. "You just need to embrace it as a design element," she said, handing me the baby lamb and a bottle filled with milk.

The lamb was about the size of a large cat, with black eyes and a coat of coarse white curls. It fascinated me that those curls were the very ones that would get shorn off, carded into rovings, and spun into wool. I could turn this animal's coat into a headband if I wanted to.

So there I was, holding a baby lamb on a winter's evening in a town on the Oregon Coast that I only knew from childhood summers. Besides creating unexpected design elements, what was I even doing here?

"I know you think I'm wrong when I say you need to rest," Sharyn said in a phone session. "You're like 'No, no, I need to go join something!'" She was right. I did think she was wrong. How was I supposed to rest if letting my guard down even a little bit meant probable injury? I could dislocate something by sitting mindlessly, so my brain always had to be on. And now that I was actually starting over, I needed to meet people.

My second social activity, in early spring, was to join a dragon boat team. Sitting in two rows of ten paddlers, we pushed a long wooden boat up and down the Nehalem River. We might look like rowers from the shore, but we sat facing forward and moved our paddles up and down.

"Like pistons!" called the coach, Barb, a smiling woman with short blonde hair. Rain pocked the water's surface, and fog obscured the coastal mountains. She clapped out the rhythm. "Hit! Hit! Hit!"

The tidal river flowed differently at every practice. At low tide, the water sat still and muddy; at high tide, its waves splashed over both banks. One of the reasons I'd joined the team was for low-impact exercise. I was taking fewer long walks on the beach, but I still needed cardio to clear my head.

"Imagine a string tying your arm to the person in front of you," Barb instructed, "all the way down the line."

I thought of dragon boat practice like group meditation, a new mindfulness practice. When the arm of the paddler directly in front of me went up like a piston, my arm went up too. I had no choice but to stay in line with the threads tying us together. The synchronization required tuning out all distractions. It got me out of my own head. To propel the boat forward, I just had to align myself with the world around me.

"Let it run," Barb called. We pulled our paddles out of the water and let the boat coast while we drank from water bottles and watched the wildlife. Elk appeared on the riverbanks, and great blue herons nested on a grassy island. Depending on the day, it smelled like ocean, or fog, or manure from the cattle farm downriver.

Our rows switched sides, from port to starboard, so we wouldn't grow lopsided muscles. "Atten-tion!" Barb shouted. The chatting inside the boat silenced, and we sat alert, paddles across our laps.

"Paddles up!" Barb smiled wide. We raised our paddles perpendicular to the water, waiting for her next call.

"Take it away!" she yelled. We sliced the water, twenty blades in unison. To my right, a sea otter poked up its sleek little head to watch our first pull forward.

Even though my apartment was the quietest place I'd ever lived, my sleep started to tank. I slept curled up on my side, but I woke up at the end of every REM cycle with one hip screaming from the weight of my body, feeling like it might slip right out of its socket. I flipped, and if I could fall back asleep again, I woke up ninety minutes later with the same sharp pain in the other hip. I twirled all night long like a rotisserie on a stick, continually redistributing my weight. My sleep deprivation sunk deeper and deeper. I felt like roadkill lifting myself out of bed in the mornings, assessing the damage of a night's sleep. I worried I wouldn't be able to support myself if pain continued to zap so much of my energy that I struggled to focus on a computer screen.

Another phone session.

"I feel like I have the flu and just got hit by a bus," I said to Sharyn. I sat on the red couch, my back aching, and fiddled with a hair tie I'd found in the cushions. "I literally get back to the apartment in tears because it hurts so much to walk."

"What hurts, exactly?"

"Everything," I said. "My knees, my feet, my back. And I'm shivering like I have a fever." I hesitated. "I know I sound like a drama queen."

"What's wrong with being a drama queen?"

Was that a trick question?

"It's usually only very smart, capable women who get called drama queens," she continued. "What worries me is you've lost your resilience. You're not bouncing back."

I snapped the hair elastic across the room. I wasn't bouncing back.

"I'm just trying to figure out how much of this is physical and how much is psychological," she said.

I was an emotional tangle, obviously. Did that trigger my physical unraveling and glow my whole body with pain? Could grief literally cause a person's body to disintegrate?

The hemlock fronds danced outside my window. It's usually only smart, capable women who get called drama queens.

The morning of dragon boat practice, the Nehalem River at high tide reached almost to the cement sidewalk next to the floating dock. We stood around wearing orange life vests, paddles and water bottles in hand, while we waited to load the boat one row at a time.

I started on the left, portside, and we pushed off the dock. The sunlight refracted through the raindrops to sparkle the trees and grasses along the riverbanks. It was our first practice in full sun, and I wished I'd brought a hat.

"Atten-tion!" Barb shouted. We sat alert and ready.

Barb smiled wide. "Paddles up!" she shouted. With the handle in my right hand, I raised my arm over my head and held the blade of the paddle perpendicular to the water with my left.

"Take it away!" she yelled.

Twenty blades sliced the water in unison on a run toward Wheeler Bay, each stroke jerking the boat forward. Halfway through the five-minute run, however, just when my right shoulder muscles started to burn from the exercise, my elbow bones scraped with a knife-like stab. I grimaced, hesitating to pull out of the water and upset the delicate string running from one paddler to another all the way down the line. But I had to. I pulled in my paddle. The crown of my head radiated warmth as I squeezed my elbow joint with my right hand. It snapped, the good kind of snap, as the joint clicked back into place. The sharp pain subsided and left only a cringing ache. Both water and sky sparkled painfully bright.

"Are you okay, Alyssa?" Barb asked.

I nodded. I wouldn't be a drag on the team's interconnected web, riding the river while they did all the work. We switched sides, and I went from port to starboard, my most difficult side because paddling toward the right twinged my lower back. But I welcomed the rest for my left elbow, which did not appreciate being ordered around like machinery with no will of its own. As a top arm, at least, it could be the piston, unbending.

I refocused on the group rhythm instead of my body. I timed my paddle's slice back into the water with the rest of the team. I focused all of my energy into the meditative trance. My elbow might ache, but if I focused on what was happening right now, aligning myself with the group, everything would be okay. The power of now. But it only took a few strokes for my lower back to snap. A muscle? A vertebrae? A kidney? Who knew. All I knew was sharp pain, a punch and a twist with spiked brass knuckles.

The mountains on the clear horizon wobbled.

"Watch the paddler in front of you!" Barb shouted.

Both Barb and the paddler in front of me seemed to pull farther away. I lifted my paddle out of the water again and put my head between my legs until my vision cleared. The boat jerked forward in regular hits, and I swallowed hard to keep down my breakfast. I took the free ride for the rest of practice, all the way back to the Nehalem dock. I knew emergency breaks were allowed on our ragtag team on the Nehalem River, but feeling faint from pain scared me.

Later that day, my elbow ached, my lower back stabbed, and my neck itched painfully from its first sun hives of the season. I brought out my knitting, the only thing I could concentrate on. Maybe my new, low-impact team sport was having some impact after all.

The reality of the rest of my life was dawning on me. In the private courtyard behind my above-garage apartment, I sat on the steps trimming my toenails and brushed the clippings into the salal bushes below. I wore a skirt to feel the sun on my legs because no one else was around to stare at my crinkled shin scars, the bruising having barely faded over twenty years. Hummingbirds flitted around my head, and the ocean roared on the horizon.

Clip, clip.

I let my mind wander when a thought crept in that froze the hummingbirds in midair: I was tired and in pain because of Ehlers-Danlos syndrome. I'd put the knowledge so far out of my head—because why bother acknowledging it when doctors couldn't do anything to help?—that I froze in a shock of recognition. Of course my rare connective tissue disorder explained why my body pulled apart on the beach, in its sleep, and on the dragon boat. A gust of lavender wafted up from the planter box below where I sat. I'd survived the apocalypse, and I was finally degenerating.

Another phone session with Sharyn. I readjusted the slouching cushions on the red couch, a mug of tea steaming on the windowsill, and planned to mention EDS for the first time. Would Sharyn think me being avoidant for not naming it until now? Addiction was rooted in avoidance, so maybe not having mentioned it suggested that I was one step away from stumbling around all day long like I had a brain tumor. Although I guess denial is rooted in avoidance as well.

"Promise you won't strangle me, okay?"

Sharyn laughed. "That's the beauty of a phone session!" she said. "You don't have to sit right in front of me."

I ran my finger along the piping on the couch cushion. "So I have this medical condition," I said. I explained my falling tendencies, my scars and joint pain, my degenerative future.

"Wait," she said after I'd finished naming EDS. "Promise I won't strangle you about *that*?"

"Yes."

"Okay," she sighed. "I won't." Turns out she didn't think me secretive about my genetic disorder, even though it had taken me almost a full year of therapy to mention it. "What kinds of things can they do to treat it?"

It seemed like such a dumb question. I drummed my fingertips on the windowsill in irritation. "They can't do anything," I said. "I'm just a genetic freak of nature."

Soon thereafter, I quit the dragon boat team. I couldn't keep attuning to an external rhythm over my own. Group mindfulness did not suit my floppy body.

REVOLVING SOUL MATES

Mags and I had to be separated for a year before we could initiate divorce proceedings in Ontario. We agreed to do it the easy way, without a lawyer, splitting assets down the middle and calling it done. With paperwork in hand, which I'd filled and printed from an online form, I met a notary in a coffee shop near the top of Manzanita's main drag, where it hit Highway 101 instead of the Pacific Ocean.

I parked underneath the weathered coastal pines that looked like overgrown bonsai trees and stepped out into salty air mixed with wafting espresso. I'd driven instead of walked to town because I didn't feel like long, reflective beach walks on either end of this definitive administrative ending.

Inside, the paperwork signing took five minutes. I ran the notary's pen over pages of dotted lines like it was no big deal, the signing away of my place in a family to which I had felt like I belonged. I flitted past the barista on my way out the door without buying a coffee, eager to curl back up in my above-garage apartment that had turned into my actual home. After more than a year, my heartbreak had aged. I was already mid-healing by the time I inked those dotted lines. Our marriage ended like it began, with paperwork that seemed overwhelmingly inconsequential compared to the emotions that had come before it.

My above-garage apartment had taken on a different tone once the reality settled in that I lived there for reals, not just temporarily. My bookshelf stood as the clearest reminder of my scorched-earth move. Half empty, it still held only the books that had fit into the single box I had dragged across the continent in the backseat of my car. I had very few artifacts from my old life. None of the battered pine furniture that Mags and I had gathered from her parents and rural antique junkyards, none of my crafting supplies or half-finished projects, none of our cookware or post-apocalyptic survival gear. Despite the heartbreak, it felt clean and sharp, almost refreshing to have lost all of my trappings of adulthood at once.

The wind gusts creeped inside to echo off the empty white walls and exposed beam overhead. Branches glowed in moonlight outside the dark windows. I wasn't lonely there, exactly. I loved the silence and needed the solitude, but something important was missing. Something I could still have. Single or not, it didn't feel right to not have a fuzzy sink of unconditional love in my lap, padding around my space and pouncing on fallen hair elastics.

I needed a cat.

September sun shone on my hour drive up to the animal shelter near Astoria, shadowing the pavement with the lacy silhouettes of hemlock and fir. I crested Neahkanie Mountain and looked out at the navy blue sea, my chest expanding at the sight even though I'd already been taking it in for a year.

I crinkled with excitement as I reached the outskirts of the "big" coastal city, as I drove behind the handful of new box stores, past marshes and cattails lining empty acreage. I crinkled with excitement when I parked, worried I'd be full of indecision in a room full of cats who needed homes. Luckily, the cat room spanned only a few paces. Fewer than a dozen cats lined the walls in stainless steel cages.

On my first step in, a loud tomcat from the top row stuck his paw through the bars and howled to get my attention. On my second step, I glanced past the cage of tumbling kittens, sure of wanting an adult. And on my third step into the cat room, a young tortoiseshell in the middle cage in the middle row locked eyes with me.

I gasped. My crinkling worry of indecision evaporated.

"You," I said. Those beautiful mustard eyes that saw right through me. Caramel patches peeked through her black fur, including a vibrant triangle that wrapped her neck like a statement necklace. Her right paw looked like it had been dipped in a bucket of caramel paint. I signed the adoption papers with no hesitation at all.

I held the cat carrier in my hands like a platter on our walk back to the car, not wanting to induce feline nausea by swinging her like a bag of groceries, and I positioned her to face me from the passenger seat so she could have the drive home to inspect what she was in for. As we drove along, retracing the lacy shadows over the highway, I sang along to the new Neko Case album while my new soul mate examined me and let out only the occasional questioning meow.

When we got back to my apartment, she made a quick tour of the perimeter—noting windows, food bowls, and litter box—before joining me on the couch. She sat one cushion over in loaf position and purred, tracking my every move with her slow-blinking eyes.

I named her Pimm, after the orange liqueur. We were meant for each other.

GIRLS WHO WEAR GLASSES

Dorothy Parker was my first literary crush. I was intrigued by her caustic commentary on heterosexual mating rituals because I was still puzzling out why I wasn't into water fights with neighbor boys like my friends. I watched Leah and Vanessa double over and shriek, their wet shirts clinging to their skin, and wondered at their motivation.

"Come *on*, Alyssa!" only elicited my raised eyebrow in response.

Why did they always let the boys win?

I couldn't summon the energy to shriek at daft boys who wanted to spray us with a hose. Instead, I sat reading on the sidelines, drinking in more refreshment from an intellectual recognition with a writer who'd died fifteen years before I was born—my whole lifetime before I was born—than by cold water on a hot summer's day.

I was not a fun girl.

I wore black in July, and my only concession to teenage girlishness was the concealer I dabbed to cover my pimples and the permanent dark circles around my eyes. The rest was too much work. Even lip gloss made me feel like someone else when I looked in the mirror, someone I wasn't sure I wanted to be. By the tenth grade I could make my friends laugh, but my quiet sarcasm scared away everyone else.

More things than water fights exhausted me. When school started, the long days of classes dragged, leaving me dizzy and fogged over by the afternoon, and I couldn't fathom being like the kids who stayed after school for drama or volleyball or decorating committees. My mom had written a note that got me out of gym class forever, which recouped some of my energy. But otherwise I suffered through, aiming for anonymity and grades that would get me into whatever college I wanted.

Over the ten years of my commutes to various public schools, the evergreen forests out the window of the school bus had fallen one by one to make way for the new Walmart, the new subdivision, the new strip mall. The only thing my high school had going for it was its view of Mount Hood, one hundred miles to the east and dominating the horizon like a snowy jewel.

To and from school, I read continuously, my knees curled into the sticky vinyl seat in front of me. And when I recognized myself in Dorothy Parker's lines *Men seldom make passes / At girls who wear glasses*, I didn't despair. I took a deep breath and let the poem wrap me in a soothing cape of larger patterns at work that had nothing to do with my personal failings. I was simply a girl who wore glasses, and things played out as expected.

The boys all seemed pretty dumb to me anyway.

When I got home—at least on the nights when I stayed at my mom's house in Vancouver rather than commute to my dad's house in Portland—I slung my fleece-lined canvas jacket over my desk chair, let my hiking boots thump onto the floor, and fell into my twin bed to sleep until dinner.

Leah and Vanessa had a surprise for my sixteenth birthday. They picked me up in Leah's red Nissan because she was the only one with a driver's license. She was also the tallest and had the loudest laugh, so she was in charge.

I didn't like surprises, which required not only smiles but also squeals, exclamations, and jumps into rough, extravagant hugs. Such demonstrative pep didn't come naturally. "You have a shell," said Leah. "But you're fun when you come out of it."

Their shell-breaking mission? To make me into the sixteen-year-old girl they knew I was meant to be, one who appreciated butterfly-themed accessories and daydreamed about prom dresses instead of how comforting it might be to wear oversized men's V-neck sweaters. But maybe they were right about me. Maybe I did have the potential to come out of my shell, to do more on weekends than read books in the bathtub while listening to Fiona Apple.

I fidgeted in the backseat of Leah's car, my stomach queasy. I got carsick if I didn't sit in the front—or at least in the middle of the backseat—

but I didn't want them to think me weird for choosing to sit on the hump. Where were they taking me?

"Relax," Vanessa said. "It'll be okay."

She and Leah looked at each other with slight frowns, sensing my unexpected lack of giddiness. "I'll give you a hint," she added. "We're going to the mall."

The mall, the suburban pit of despair. I fought back bigger waves of queasiness. My hotspots at the mall were the benches, but there were never enough of them amongst the dizzying crowds and competing loudspeakers.

If I couldn't be fun, let me at least be serious. Let me at least be ignored.

While I didn't play dumb by letting boys win water fights, I'd adopted my own method: silence, which seemed like the safest way to protect my internal landscape. It was also energy efficient. Why speak and blow my cover, initiating some sort of battle I probably didn't have the resources to win?

But if I could embrace myself as a girl with glasses, maybe other things about me were okay too. I'd begun to share my opinions with a select few. "Alyssa hates making small talk," Vanessa had told her mom.

Vanessa reported her mom's response. "She said 'That's really, really bad. That girl's going to have a hard life.'"

I wondered if she was right, that if I didn't learn to engage in effervescent flattery, my life might be miserable outside of high school too, no matter how cute my glasses or comfortable my sweaters. In any case, Dorothy Parker was still there for me, patting the metaphorical cushion. *If you don't have anything nice to say, come sit by me.*

I prepared myself for worst-case mall scenarios. Maybe they planned to force me to try on fancy dresses I wouldn't otherwise be caught dead in. They'd pick out miniskirts and spaghetti straps that exposed both my padded upper arms and the scars on my shins that I never let anyone see. I prayed they wouldn't pool their funds to buy me an actual dress and make me wear it in public. I knew a disposable Kodak camera nestled into Vanessa's crocheted purse, and I wished for death. A heart attack, a car crash, a mall fire, anything.

Leah parked outside of Nordstrom, and they each took one of my arms to escort me inside, both smiling like they weren't walking me off the plank. When they marched me past the junior's section with baby doll dresses, $100 Silver Jeans, and a grid wall of flickering MTV, I took a deep breath. Maybe this wouldn't be so bad after all. Maybe this surprise really was something good, like going to the food court for Orange Julius. Or one of those giant salted pretzels. But I knew I was deluding myself. They wouldn't have suggested anything that required ingesting extra calories, no matter whose birthday it was.

Before reaching the internal edge of the department store, Leah steered me into the section with glass cases. Uncharted territory, the reeking wilds behind the frontline perfume counters and sample ladies with maniacal smiles.

"Are you ready?" Leah asked.

We stopped in front of a countertop display of lipsticks lined up on gleaming bleachers like high-class spectators. A woman behind the counter smiled like she expected us, and Leah pointed to the padded stool in front of a large round mirror that magnified every pore and pimple and childhood scar from falling on my face.

"Surprise!" Vanessa said. "You're getting a makeover."

FOLD BATHTUB

My above-garage apartment didn't have a bathtub, only a shower stall. I told myself I'd be able to survive without a tub because I loved the apartment otherwise, with its open layout and windows that looked onto the rustling tips of hemlocks. It didn't share any walls, so it was as quiet as I needed it to be. The rain splattered, the crows cawed, and the ocean waves roared in the distance. I was basically living inside a recording of relaxing sleep sounds.

But still.

I sat on the couch pining for water, thinking I'd die happy if only I had a bathtub. My daydreams ached for Epsom salts and lavender essential oil. I needed a plan.

There must be some way to turn a shower stall into a makeshift tub. I considered a large plastic bin, but that would have been too cramped even for me. I could put an inflatable kiddie pool in the living room, but I saw the disaster potential for the pine floors and didn't want to lose my damage deposit. The only friends I'd made in Manzanita so far only had shower stalls too. How had it become okay for landlords to neglect this most important amenity?

Maybe I could rent a motel room. Maybe I could even get a discounted, tub-only rate at a motel if I didn't touch anything else in the room so they'd only have to clean the bathroom. It was off-season in a vacation town, after all. I called around on a weekday afternoon.

"I live in town and really need a bath," I said. "Would you be willing to rent me a tub for an hour?"

The guy on the other end of the line gave me a long pause before he started laughing. It was a while before he caught his breath. "I've been running this place for twenty years and no one's ever asked me that."

Unbelievable to me, that no one else had ever been so desperate for a hot soak that they'd rented a motel room. So many bathtubs just sitting there empty.

"Sure, come on down," he said. "I'll charge you twenty bucks."

So I went on down to soak in a shallow rented tub, but the water tank hadn't fully warmed up, so the water didn't steam as much I liked it to.

Was I lying in a puddle? Was this worth twenty bucks?

I considered working shallow lukewarm tub rentals into my budget but decided against it, mostly because it turned out a bath was much less soothing if I had to get dressed and leave my apartment to take it.

I refocused on my shower stall. A plastic bin would be too small and the kiddie pool was a bad idea, but there must be some solution. Could I build up the open side somehow? If I duct-taped a piece of hard plastic against the opening, would the seal hold?

Again, huge disaster potential.

In a moment of desperation, I searched for portable bathtubs online. Maybe they existed, like for camping or really huge babies? And they did! They existed in China. For $200, I could get a four-foot-long tub made of shiny waterproof fabric attached to a metal frame. It seemed like a lot of money, but it would also be like an endless punch card for steaming hot baths for the price of only ten lukewarm soaks at the motel.

A good deal.

I ordered it.

It took two months to arrive.

When UPS delivered it to my door, the flat crushed box looked exactly like it'd come halfway around the world the slow way. Black scrapes and open corners. I jittered with excitement as I unfolded the tub's metal frame. The shiny, royal blue fabric was covered with yellow-striped angel fish, coral, and undulating seaweed, and the side was printed with Chinese characters and a translation: Fold Bathtub.

It was the best thing I'd ever seen in my life.

Unfortunately, my new Fold Bathtub didn't fit in the shower stall, so I set it up on the balcony, which was encircled by evergreens, for its first use. The houses to either side sat empty. It was private enough. The tub also had flaps that zipped over the top to keep the heat in, which was important because I had to fill Fold Bathtub the old-fashioned way, kettle by kettle. Very slowly. It took an hour, even after I doubled my speed by boiling pots of hot water along with the kettle.

With my steaming cocoon finally—and barely—full, I unzipped its cover and climbed in, pleased with my resourcefulness.

Okay, the tub was a little short. At four feet, it was even shorter than that shallow motel tub. I either had to sit upright, keeping my knees close to my chest, or lie down in the water with my legs straight up in the air. But at least Fold Bathtub was deeper than the motel tub. At least those zippered flaps contained enough heat that I wasn't soaking in a lukewarm puddle.

Fold Bathtub worked its magic. I floated off into daydreams warm and comforted, my painful joints momentarily soothed. So worth it. My happiness prompted me to write my first-ever online review. I rushed to the computer while my skin steamed and my hair dripped dangerously near the keyboard.

"The best purchase I've ever made," I typed into the review box. Five stars.

A few hours after I wrote my enthusiastic online review, I panicked. I never wrote online reviews, and I definitely didn't want the exposure of a review associated with my real name. What an invasion of privacy, if anyone could Google me and see that I'd once been so desperate for a hot soak that I'd bought Fold Bathtub and had it shipped all the way from China.

What a weirdo.

I scrambled to delete it. Anyone looking for a foldable tub would just have to be, like me, willing to risk a review-less product.

After a couple more soaks on the balcony, I streamlined my process, thinking I could do better than my thousand-kettle technique. Plus, what if I needed a bath when the occasional neighbors were around? I needed to find a way to bring Fold Bathtub inside. The question: How could I fit a four-foot-long tub into a three-by-three-foot shower stall? I maneuvered it into the bathroom and considered my options. It tilted too much if I let its extra foot hang off the edge of the stall, so I borrowed a couple of two-by-fours from the landlord's pile of off-cuts in the garage to stack under the end of the metal frame.

Nice and level.

Then I had to figure out how to fill it. I wanted to sit in the tub as it filled so I could adjust the temperature, but I didn't want to sit under hot shower head rain, most of which would hit the walls of the shower stall anyway.

So I bought a hose.

An actual garden hose, which I cut in half with a utility knife and attached to the shower head with a plastic funnel from the kitchen and a bunch of crisscrossed rubber bands. This mostly worked. Sometimes the rubber bands drooped so the funnel spilled over the top. And sometimes a rubber band would snap from being overstretched, a painful sound, and detach the whole contraption. Annoying but workable. I could replace worn rubber bands with fresh ones.

It hadn't even crossed my mind that I could have bought a handheld shower head attachment with an extra-long cord. In any case, I'd figured out how to balance the tub and fill it, but I didn't realize until after my first bath that draining the tub would also be a problem. The tub had a stopper and the shower stall had a drain, but the fabric tub filled with water suctioned against the metal grate so no water could drain at all. I couldn't nudge it out of the way. I had to empty the water from my first soak in the shower stall one bucket of water at a time into the bathroom sink.

I improved the setup yet again.

For my second bath in the shower stall, I fetched an extra two-by-four off-cut from the garage and slid it under the fabric tub before filling it—right next to the drain but not covering it—so the water could flow directly into the drain when it emptied.

In the end, all I needed to have a bath in my above-garage apartment was Fold Bathtub, several two-by-fours, a sawed-off garden hose, and a funnel and rubber bands from the kitchen. From underwater in my soothing tub printed with yellow-striped angel fish, coral, and undulating seaweed—with my unshaven, scarred legs sticking straight up against the shower stall in my quiet apartment—everything was exactly how I needed it to be. I was proud of my resourcefulness, attuned to my body and the fishes in my own little world.

Pimm stood on her hind legs and peeked into the water as if it might attack her. Then she skulked away, annoyed that bath time didn't include her. As I soaked up the Epsom salts and lavender essential oil, the daggers in my joints retracted, the burning in my hands and feet cooled a few degrees, and I let my mind wander. I felt connected to my long-legged family members on my mom's side as I sunk into the steaming water, as I relaxed into that deep shared need for the relief of floating limbs. Regular hot baths was a family tradition I would keep.

I wondered if I really would need more medical help than what I could rig up on my own.

SIBLING RIVALRY

At sixteen, I piggybacked four-year-old Elizabeth around the large yard, her forearm in a chokehold around my neck. I showed her how to make daisy chain crowns out of the blooms we spotted in the lawn. I did math homework at my desk while she jumped on the bed behind me—long curls flying—or settled in with her Beanie Babies and coloring books. Sometimes we even snuck in Sockie Baby, who loved the attention and dozed at the foot of my bed like she owned it.

Four is a very fun age for a little sister to be.

But I did have one moment of sibling rivalry with Elizabeth.

Inside we lounged on the overstuffed chair that faced the long galley kitchen. Sunshine speckled the forest green cushions in the breakfast nook to our left when a flash across the yard made us both turn to look. It was Sockie Baby, prowling the perimeter of the yard. We watched her swoop toward her prey beyond the rose garden before crashing through the hedge where we could no longer see her.

"Socks is *my* cat," Elizabeth said. Her little knees, smooth like she'd never tripped and fallen in her life, were drawn up to her torso.

I paused. First of all, I wanted to say, her name is Sockie Baby. And second of all, she's mine. Who made her all of those red cardboard houses with mailboxes on the side? I could share my beloved masked feline. After all, I was practically an adult compared to Elizabeth. But fundamentally and absolutely? Sockie Baby was mine.

"No," I said. "She's not."

"Yes!" Elizabeth whined in response.

My dad, who happened to be passing through the kitchen, stuck his head in. "What's going on in here?"

"Socks is my cat!" Elizabeth stood up, unfurling her perfect knees and threatening to cry.

Dad stroked her tumbling curls to calm her down.

"She isn't though," I said.

Dad sighed as if this was yet another everyday tiff between siblings that he had to deal with. He looked at me, a warning flashing in his eyes. "She's both of yours, okay?"

The speckled sunlight on the forest green cushions grew more vibrant, and the long galley kitchen stretched out like putty in front of me. He wasn't really asking.

"That's not fair!" Elizabeth said, stomping away and coughing out a sob anyway.

I stomped away in the other direction, headed for my room. I didn't think it was fair either. Did Dad not remember that he'd given Socks to me as an official birthday present before Elizabeth was even born? Or did he just not care?

I let it go with Elizabeth, even though she was cuter and had the advantage of full-time access to Socks, because I liked the role of big sister. I wanted to protect her. Besides, I wanted my kitty to get attention and food even when I wasn't around. But the anger toward my dad remained. Sockie Baby had claimed me completely. He couldn't just take her away to make his afternoon a little easier.

Why did peacemaking always have to come at my expense?

UNTANGLING

I stared at the laminated chart, hating every one of those insufferable little faces always meant to be smiling. I needed to choose one that best represented my day-to-day level of pain. My new primary care provider was waiting.

Did she mean the chronic aching in my bones that waxed and waned, but unpredictably? The yellow face on the verge of losing its grip (five). Did she mean the nerve pain that burned through me in the middle of the night? The orange face with the angry grimace (eight). Or did she mean the acute stabbing after my hips or elbows slipped from their sockets but before I pushed them back into place? The red screaming face (ten).

Where was the face so obscured by unkempt hair that it barely recognized itself as human?

"On average," she prompted when I didn't answer right away.

And relative to what? I couldn't think of any part of my body that never hurt, except maybe my earlobes or the tip of my nose.

"Seven?" I said. Better to underestimate than risk having my pain attributed to anxiety. Although who wouldn't be anxious if their body looked fine but was unraveling at all of its microscopic seams?

She believed me.

She referred me to physical therapy, and she also prescribed opioid pain medications, which worked well once we found the right ones. When my chronic pain lessened, I was able to think more clearly. I was able to work more, sleep better, and take more walks on the beach. My life improved so much that I started to feel like myself again.

But I did not turn into a smiley face of any color.

~~~

I started writing knitting patterns whenever I was too tired to do anything else. I called it a life hack: I listened to my body's need for rest but also filled that downtime with creative productivity. Pimm purred on my lap.

I integrated a lot of spirals into my patterns. Spiral necklace cords, spiral wrist cuffs, spiral slipper socks that looked like soft-serve ice cream. To make a spiral, I only had to modify one stitch per row, then repeat that modification in every row thereafter. That continuous shift in alignment made the spiral.

While my fingers looped the fibers, I could let my brain spin on other things.

⸻

My new physical therapist in Portland, a two-hour drive away over the Coastal Range, specialized in EDS and even had it herself. I inspected her for signs of freakishness. She looked strong, with long blonde hair and a clear voice. "You were diagnosed when you were *ten*, but you've never had physical therapy?" she asked, her fingertips pushing into the exam table.

I shrugged. "I didn't know it was a thing I could do."

"Well," she said. She took notes on my gait as I walked across the room toward her. "There's a lot we can do. And you never got genetic testing for which type you have?"

I shook my head.

"EDS comes in many different forms, depending on which collagen is affected, so it's really important to know." She checked the range of motion in my shoulder, then held my palm in hers to test for finger strength. "You have some of the facial and physical characteristics of the vascular type, so I'd be worried about that possibility for you."

Wait.

The first EDS-expert provider I'd ever had thought I had the *face*? She was *worried*? I knew the vascular type of EDS was most highly associated with spontaneous aortic dissection. Hearts explode. Patients die young. But my parents had always said I didn't have that type.

That night, for the first time in my life, I Googled my condition. The public internet was a newborn when I was ten, and it had never occurred to me later that information would be out there. At least it had never occurred to me until I'd walked into the alternate universe of a physical therapy clinic in which they seemed to have a solution for everything. The amount of information I found online about EDS stunned me. Societies and support groups everywhere I looked. If EDS was such a rare disorder, where did all of those people come from?

Turns out pretending something doesn't exist can keep a lot of information hidden right under your nose.

The vascular type is caused by a mutation in type III collagen, an abnormality that weakens the structure of blood vessels and intestinal walls in particular. And the clinical characteristics? Yes, I had been born premature, and yes, you could see blue veins scrambling across my chest. I had the yellowish circles around my eyes and the wrinkly hands and feet. I had the chest pain and cigarette-paper thin scars on my shins.

Now that I'd reached my limits of denial and sought support, my practitioners needed to know what I was working with. Knowing my EDS type had finally become very, very important. Would I be lucky to see forty, or would I get to keep doing physical therapy to keep my body aligned for decades?

⎯⎯∿∾⎯⎯

I accidentally twisted the stitches in a cowl I was knitting, but I couldn't see my mistake until a few rows later. It turned out I was knitting a Mobius cowl. A Mobius plane is a non-orientable one, a flat plane that loops back in on itself with a built-in twist. It looks like the recycling symbol. I didn't really want a Mobius cowl, but I didn't want to waste my time by unraveling it and starting all over again.

So I finished and wore it. One simple change affected the final pattern so fundamentally. I started researching other stitch patterns based on mathematical theory. What unexpected structures could I make if I stitched a repeat "mistake" intentionally?

⎯⎯∿∾⎯⎯

My mom sent me my 1992 medical records from OHSU, a PDF of several typed pages in Courier font, the pages scanned slightly askew.

My chart notes said that I either had classical EDS or vascular EDS, but that only genetic testing could confirm which one. The diagnosis: Ehlers-Danlos syndrome, type unknown. The recommendation: get genetic testing and come back for a follow-up.

I stared at my laptop screen for a while.

They had intended to follow up. But the genetic testing hadn't happened, and neither had the follow-up.

The wood grain on the built-in desk wavered.

It was true? I might have the vascular type after all? My parents had learned I had a rare medical condition, potentially one that could end my life decades early, but they didn't follow the doctor's recommendation for genetic testing. What's more, they told me I didn't have to worry about it. I watched myself reread the chart notes. I was not imagining this.

The EDS types have big differences. Both classical and vascular types have higher risk of arterial dissection, but the risk is much, much higher with the vascular type. Eighty percent of people with vascular EDS experience a significant medical complication, such as an arterial dissection, by age forty. I was thirty-four when I finally saw those childhood records.

Tick-tock.

I made the next available appointment with a geneticist in Seattle who specialized in Marfan syndrome and other connective tissue disorders. The wait time was two years. Adult geneticists were few and far between.

⁓⌁⌁⁓

More options for mathematical knitting:

I could represent fractals by placing stripes according to the Fibonacci sequence, found throughout nature, from tree branches to seashells. Or I could knit a geometrical representation of chaos theory through the Lorenz manifold, continuous looping planes that look like ocean waves.

⁓⌁⌁⁓

"Most people have loose muscles and tight ligaments," my physical therapist explained. She waved her hand over her thigh. "But with EDS, you have tight muscles and loose ligaments, because your muscles have to overcompensate to hold you together."

Tight muscles hurt, but they can also clench in weird ways that throw your bones out of whack. So first I had to release the tight muscles, then strengthen them, so they had more hope of holding me in proper alignment. And I needed to wake up the supporting muscles around the tight ones to spread out the extra load.

I learned the word proprioception, which refers to awareness of how the body is aligned and moving through space. EDS patients often have poor proprioception because their bodies don't send warnings to their brains when they fall out of alignment. "There's no such thing as a sprained ankle for us," my physical therapist said. "We just pick right back up and feel it later."

Which was true. I could make any angle work, at least for a while. I had a built-in obliviousness, which it turned out was not a strength. My goal in physical therapy was not to become more flexible but to tighten my proprioceptive range. Athletic mindfulness training. She called it "the head, shoulders, knees, and toes" game.

I started relearning how to walk, untwisting my pigeon toes and engaging my glutes. I learned how to keep my core engaged—strong and breathable—not the desperate contraction of "sucking it in."

I learned that when I stood on the balls of my feet, which I'd always thought had indicated good posture—up and alert so my voice didn't sing as flat as my feet—my body turned up its fight-or-flight response. I needed to stop standing as if I were getting ready to race a tiger; I needed to sink back down onto my heels, unlock my knees, and resettle my pelvis directly over my hips so I didn't stick my bum out behind me like an old-fashioned bustle.

I learned how to roll my shoulders back—in between military rigid and helpless slump—and which back muscles to strengthen to keep them there. I took home promotional pens with grips as wide as toddler crayons for relearning how to hold a pen without hyperextending my fingertips. I learned that pain and cold contracts, causing collagen and nerve endings to retract instead of integrate and align with each other. In cold weather, I literally had fewer fibers holding me together.

I made every movement conscious, adjusted myself, and then repeated that adjustment until it became unconscious again. I was rewiring my brain to my body.

Practice made permanent.

Or for me, practice made semi-permanent, given that my joints could still dislocate even with perfect proprioceptive awareness at every moment. Physical therapy would be continual, cycling through my body and realigning as often as necessary.

My dad eventually mailed me a paper copy of the same medical records my mom had sent digitally. His copy had a list attached in blocky, all-caps handwriting. He'd taken notes during that long visit with the geneticists who had first diagnosed me with EDS. At first, his notes were descriptive.

- Connective tissue
- Surgery risk
- Childbirth risk
- Skin
- Small joints

Then his blocky all-caps handwriting began a to-do list:

- Physical therapy: strengthening
- Protection
- Shoes
- Genetic testing
- EDS: classical or vascular?
- Mild murmur—echocardiogram
- Marfan: 50/50. See doctor, world expert
- Marfan I or II
- Zach: Marfan risk

He'd written the list on a strip of paper the width of a receipt. I stared at its bent corners browning with age. I ran my fingers over the top perforated edge without feeling its sharpness. My breathing was shallow, like I'd been winded by a thud to the solar plexus. An even more concrete list proving that, even if that long genetics appointment had been complex and overwhelming, my parents had been given the next steps for how to move forward. The only item checked off, in a different color pen, was "protection." Those massive shin guards I'd worn to softball practice.

Pimm jumped onto my lap, taking my stillness as an invitation. I ruffled her head and scratched behind her ears. She flopped onto her side and stretched out her limbs. When I stared into space, she raised her head to glare at me for my lack of attention.

I looked back at the emphasized words on his list. "Physical therapy" was circled, starred, and underlined, undoubtedly emphasized by the doctors. The few sessions I'd already had at my new physical therapy clinic had been so helpful in terms of reducing the sharp pain of dislocations. In improving my gait so I could walk longer before pain caught up to me. That too I could have started twenty-five years ago, a fact known to my parents but forgotten by ten-year-old me.

"Marfan syndrome" was highlighted in orange, the connective tissue disorder that affected half the people on my mom's side of the family. Instead of affecting collagen, Marfan affects fibrillin, which is also essential for elasticity in connective tissue. People typically have one disorder or the other but, given my family history, it was important to rule it out.

"See doctor—world expert" highlighted in orange. This was the same doctor with whom I had already booked a genetics appointment two years out.

It was clear that, at least during that genetics appointment when I was ten years old, nothing had yet been ruled out and, even then, I'd had a ticket to specialists who could help. So how had I learned that the only thing I could do was "be careful"? I paced, the anger building in a way I wasn't sure I could contain. What would my life have been like if I'd started physical therapy and learned to move with less pain and fewer falls from the beginning?

⌇⌇⌇⌇

I was breaking out in sun hives like crazy that summer, so I wrote a pattern for a knit sunhat with a hyperbolic surface for its brim. A hyperbolic surface is one with a constant negative curve; in theory, the sunhat's brim would scrunch up into itself so tightly that its dense ruffles, like a stiff tutu or the wrinkles of a coral reef, would block out the sun.

〰〰〰

I went into physical therapy with a shoulder injury from the night before. It had slipped out of its socket while I slept, caused only by gravity, and it still pinched even though I'd easily slid it back into place.

The physical therapist didn't skip a beat. She nodded. "Sleep injuries are the most common injuries I see in my practice."

I replayed that sentence in my head. Sleep injuries. A real thing. The most common injuries a totally legit health care professional saw in her practice.

"Our bodies mold themselves to the mattress," she explained. Without support, knees and elbows can hyperextend backward. A rib cage can lose its shape so much that individual ribs pinch, or puncture, internal organs instead of protect them. A shoulder can slip away.

Was there a way to train my body to be proprioceptive during sleep? No. I had to embrace the absurdity and pile my bed with pillows to support my limbs on all sides—shoulders and hips and knees—so that my body cinched in place no matter which position it flopped into. Pimm liked to sleep on me at night, sometimes my shoulder and sometimes my hip, which I loved but which added another challenge to whatever joint she landed on during my nights of constant rotation.

But once an army of support pillows crowded my bed, I woke up in pain much less often.

I asked my mom about the content of my medical records and the lack of follow-up.

"They told us you probably didn't have the vascular type," she said.

"But that's not what my medical records say. The only way to be sure is to get genetic testing."

The ocean grumbled in the distance, and I caught my poor-postured reflection in the glass-paneled front door. I straightened my back and shoulders. My records glowed on the computer right in front of me.

"And Marfan syndrome? The records say I needed to be tested for that too."

"You were tested by the researchers," she said, referring to the ones researching our family's particular mutation. "I got a phone call saying we didn't have it."

"But it's nowhere in my medical records." Even the chart notes from my pediatrician showed that he tried repeatedly to follow-up about the Marfan test results but was never able to get them. "How could that be?"

Mom didn't know.

The only clarity was that several links were missing. My test results had gotten lost, maybe, or the researchers didn't share the results with my actual doctors. Or I'd never been tested in the first place. But without the results in my record, I couldn't be sure. And I couldn't get further into treatment, the cyclone of waitlists and paperwork, without clear test results, about which doctors always asked first. Maybe it was a safe assumption that I didn't have Marfan syndrome, given that neither me nor my mom had the tall, thin body type. But I needed those genetic test results in my record so I could access appropriate care.

⁓⁓⁓

My first—and unfinished—hyperbolic sunhat failed.

To scrunch the hyperbolic folds as tightly as I'd envisioned, I'd had to cast more than two thousand stitches onto circular needles, then decrease by half that number on every subsequent round.

I kept losing count.

The idea might have worked if I'd had more patience, but I didn't, so I modified the pattern to make a brim of less dense, and less hyperbolic, folds.

⁓⁓⁓

In physical therapy, I learned the importance of alignment and strengthening, but I was also integrating how having EDS meant a lot more than

FLOPPY

loose joints and dislocations. The human body is 30 percent protein, and the most abundant protein in the human body is collagen. Because collagen is in every cell, genetic tangles affect every system in the body, from the autonomic nervous system to digestion to immune response.

That's the simplest explanation for why EDS is but one diagnosis in a cluster of related disorders, an EDS trifecta that also includes postural orthostatic tachycardia syndrome (POTS) and mast cell activation syndrome (MCAS). POTS is a type of dysautonomia, an autonomic nervous system that doesn't always do its job automatically. POTS explained my lightheadedness after standing in one place, my dizziness if I stood up too fast, my extreme and persistent thirst, and my purpling hands. Mast cells are immune cells, so MCAS explained why I was allergic to everything, why I ran a raging autoimmune response almost all the time, one that could be triggered by stress, sunlight, or even noise.

I would need to get myself treated for those conditions as well, but the physical therapy clinic gave me the first steps. "You just thought this is life, feeling like you might faint every time you stand up?"

That's exactly what I thought. "Doctors didn't have any suggestions when I was a kid, so I never expected there to be any," I said.

She shook her head and suggested drinking four liters of salt water per day to increase my blood volume.

"I already drink a lot of water," I raised my water bottle in hand and gave it a little shake. "And I'm still always thirsty."

"But you have to put electrolytes in the water," she said. "Otherwise you're washing salt out of your already leaky cells and making it worse."

My eye caught an extra flash from the gleaming metal of the paper towel dispenser. Every glass of water I'd drunk in desperate thirst had only made me thirstier. I welcomed the simplicity of this solution, but my stomach knotted at the thought of how much easier my life could have been if I had known earlier.

I threw myself into DIY management of these new conditions, which were not yet officially diagnosed, even though they would be once I found the right specialists. And once again, I tangled into a familiar pattern: spinning myself into a little cyclone of doing too much at once.

196

My dad, when I asked him about the lack of follow-up: "Your mom dealt with all that stuff."

I paused, gaining fury over his dismissal of any parental responsibility for "all that stuff." They had both been given information about next steps and the kinds of support they needed to line up, and they had both disregarded it.

"That's not an excuse," I said.

"And we *did* follow up," he said. "We got you those shin guards, remember?"

I remembered the gargantuan shin guards that would supposedly keep me from adding more scars to my already torn-up shins. As long as things look good on the surface, everything was fine. But protection from scars is not the same as preventing falls in the first place.

"They also recommended physical therapy," I said. "You wrote it on a list and underlined it." The grief at how much unnecessary daily pain I'd lived with stretched open.

He changed tactics. "I was always so worried about you," he said. "Don't you know how much I love you?"

Like usual with my dad, any conversation about me shifted quickly away. I ended the conversation, still angry but learning to conserve my energy for where I could use it.

―⁓⁓⁓―

I'd knit the hyperbolic sunhat loosely, with linen yarn instead of wool. It was for summer, after all. I didn't want it to be too hot to wear.

Unfortunately, I hadn't taken the properties of the linen into account. I'd expected it to act like wool, which has some bounce. But linen only droops. It looked more like a tutu of dripping wet cotton than bouncing tulle. It wilted like a piece of old lettuce.

I owned my design element and wore the semi-hyperbolic sunhat even as I considered the redesign.

―⁓⁓⁓―

My collection of compression garments grew. Knee-high compression socks in all the colors. Compression sleeves for feet and ankles and knees and hips and wrists and elbows and shoulders and core. I didn't squeeze into all of these garments every day but chose based on what hurt each morning. I even went so far as to try finger compression sleeves that looked like ten miniature sweatbands. They turned out to be more annoying than wearable, but at least I'd been thorough. The extra constriction helped with both POTS and EDS. It kept my blood flowing and also offered a little extra snugness to activate my proprioceptive aliveness, preventing falls on days when chronic pain reduced my ability to pay attention to every joint every second.

Several times a day, when exhaustion crept up to suck the air from my brain, I elevated my feet to recirculate the blood from its backwater pools. Integrating a million small compensations for what my body had a hard time doing automatically made a huge difference. I felt better than I'd ever felt in my life, my veins cinched up to help keep the necessary workings somewhat in place.

In terms of what I needed now, what my parents did or did not do didn't really matter. If my reality was important enough to me, I could get my own answers. I could summon the energy emanating from my freshly stabilized core and redirect it to where I needed it. Even if the medical system was difficult to navigate, I would see it through, slowly expanding my network in all directions until I got the help I needed.

⌁〜〜⌁

I doubled back to unravel the pattern of what I thought I knew, and I went from there. No matter where the thread had gone awry, it was now on me to follow it.

WAITING FOR THE BUS IN LYON

After watching the city bus continue toward Lyon without having let me on, I vowed to buy less conspicuously American shoes as soon as possible. I looked over my shoulders to make sure no one had seen the bus roll away, six inches from my face, even though I knew the only thing behind me was the leafy canopy of a hillside drop off. The plane trees with the puzzled bark didn't care one way or another.

I stumbled back to the bench, my leg throbbing.

Had I missed some critical component of French bus-catching? Maybe I was only allowed on buses if I got swept in by a crowd of real live French teenagers. Or maybe I'd just experienced one of those cross-cultural misunderstandings everyone had been going on about during my exchange student orientation.

Merde. The first French curse I didn't have to look up.

I considered walking back to tell my host mom, Pascale, that I'd missed the bus, trying to make a joke about the absurdity of my incompetence.

"It's your job to bring up any problems," they'd said over and over at the orientation. Communication, or lack thereof, was on me. And it had sounded easy enough in that hotel conference room, sitting around lacquered tables with hundreds of other sixteen-year-olds about to fly abroad. But when it came down it, I didn't actually know how to go back to that walled-in house only a half block away to discuss my failure at catching the bus. Was this problem even worth figuring out how to communicate? I doubted Pascale would've laughed and given me easy advice about navigating the city. I'd already sensed her frustration. Nothing had gone as planned in my first week.

"*Bon courage,*" Pascale had said as I left the house, all but rushing me out the front door.

The little brass bell on the wrought iron gate clanged behind me as I left their gravel courtyard. A definitive sound. So I decided to just wait for the next bus, and I used the time to retrace my steps from the beginning.

Where had I gone wrong?

I'd sat on a wooden stool in my mom's kitchen, eating pasta on one of the pullout cutting boards we used as retractable tables.

"You're so miserable," Mom had said, unprompted. "Maybe you should go be an exchange student or something."

The kitchen brightened, almost overwhelming in its matching mustard refrigerator and countertops. I'd been daydreaming about all the different ways to leave home but hadn't expected the opportunity to come so easily, and before I'd graduated high school. What if I skipped my junior year to spend it in another country, maybe somewhere a bookish girl would fit right in? "Are you serious?"

Mom had shrugged. "Something to think about."

Eight months later, I flew out of Portland, expecting my year in France to turn me into a whole new person. I'd become less awkward, more sophisticated. I'd wear all black, obviously, and also learn to emanate an unaffected world-weariness that would make me immune to all that was insufferable about American high school. Unfortunately, I boarded the plane with an extra liability.

My friends Leah and Vanessa had handed me a glittery gift bag that, while thoughtful, did not scream sophistication. They'd covered a journal in black fabric printed with lime green aliens. The gift bag also included a set of pastel gel pens, a sheet of alien head stickers, and two paperweight-sized rocks onto which they'd painted their cartoon faces.

I inspected their loving pen strokes on rock, filled in with glossy nail polish.

Would a sophisticated European write with pastel gel pens? Doubtful. And what would a sophisticated European do with alien head stickers? Maybe die of embarrassment to be seen with them. My friends had always interpreted my love of the *X-Files* as an obsession with aliens when, really, I was infatuated with Gillian Anderson as Special Agent Dana Scully. I'd never quite figured out how to communicate that to them.

Maybe if I'd been truly dedicated to increasing my sophistication, I would have left the gel pens and the alien head stickers on the plane, but I didn't. My first misstep.

After three days of travel and orientation, I was corralled onto a tour bus with all the other students who would be dropped off along the route running down to the southeast of France.

I slouched into my seat and rested my forehead against the window, disappointed to see billboards along the highway, not because of their content but because of their existence. Just like in the United States, they were everywhere. I noted the orange tiled roofs on the houses we passed, but I did not feel as if their novelty was shifting my consciousness in any way.

We stopped in Dijon, like the mustard. Part of me had expected the houses and cobblestones to have a yellowish tinge to them. I watched a fellow American *fait les bises* with his host family, kissing both cheeks twice, four kisses of greeting.

"You have to kiss four times?" I asked the student sitting next to me, a girl with short blonde hair and dozens of lip balms in different flavors. "I thought it was only two."

"It's regional," she said, applying the papaya.

I wondered how many kisses were required in Lyon. How many times would I have to kiss each of the six members of my new host family? Four seemed excessive, but maybe making twenty-four smooching sounds would distract them from the fact that I understood very little beyond *bonjour*.

"Did you hear that Sarah went home already?" she asked, smacking her papaya-flavored lips.

No. I hadn't heard. "What happened?"

"Homesick."

My stomach sunk at the thought of returning home after only three days, not having acquired any world-weary sophistication at all. Even though I was so exhausted from traveling that heavy rocks had stacked up inside my skull, I vowed to push through the full year no matter what.

We pulled away from Dijon, the city with a grayish tinge just like that of any other. The architectural details had changed but, so far, reality in France weighed more or less the same. How bad could culture shock actually be?

I kissed my new host family members twice, once on each cheek, and was jolted away from the air-conditioned tour bus in their dented and dusty blue Peugeot minivan.

I unpacked my suitcase—alien head stickers, gel pens, and cartoon paper weights and all—into the closet shelf that had been cleared for me. The basement bedroom I'd be sharing with my thirteen-year-old host sister had particleboard floors that smelled like sawdust and glue, and I slept on my new bottom bunk for a solid sixteen hours. I told myself I'd start cross-culturally communicating after my nap.

Pascale stared at me wide-eyed as I sat on the concrete steps that descended into the entrance to the hillside funicular, like she couldn't quite grasp how a quick commute demonstration could go so wrong so quickly. We'd made it to Lycée Jean Moulin in the fifth arrondissement, where I would start school the following week, and touched its wrought iron door before turning around to trace the commute in reverse.

But still. There we were. My ankle had twisted and I'd had nowhere to go but down.

Ahu, an exchange student from Turkey who'd been placed with a host family down the street and who'd be attending the same school, handed me my French–English dictionary, which had tumbled down the stairs ahead of me. "*Tiens.*"

My hand tremored as I took it back.

I hadn't followed their conversation during the practice commute. And I'd been leaning on the dictionary instead of the handrail when I'd fallen. I flipped through its pages but looking up single words at a time was futile.

Pascale recovered her shock. "*Ça va, Alyssa?*"

"*Oui*," I said, pulling myself back up, shaking it off.

I was okay. Maybe I could ignore the injury this time. New country, new rules. I was transforming into a whole new person and whatever physical limitations I'd had in the United States no longer applied. My head was too full taking in the European splendor, the cobblestone streets and Roman arches, to process an injury as well.

But my knees didn't hold, so I sat right back down.

I'd thought my falls were behind me, childhood relics. But two days in France and I'd fallen already? Why hadn't I been more careful? No sophisticated person would fall down the stairs while catching a hillside funicular. Reluctantly I pulled up my bootcut jeans to see my split shin dribbling blood into my very American sneaker.

There'd be no pretending this wasn't happening.

How would I explain that this was more than a simple cut? A bandage wouldn't fix it. And if I didn't get stitches, it would take months to heal. I wanted to hurl my French–English dictionary at the cobblestones and leave it there, useless.

I nearly tore its pages finding the one I needed.

L'hôpital.

Like I'd even needed to look that one up.

A nurse in a traditional white uniform ushered me into a treatment room with stone walls, chilled like a wine cellar. No equipment beeped. No paper curtains or hand sanitizer or condescending informational posters on the walls.

The doctor arrived wearing a pressed suit.

I tried to explain that I needed her to stretch the flap of skin and sew it back together because otherwise it wouldn't close. Ahu had arrived from Turkey already fluent in French, and since she spoke some English too, she did her best to translate.

To no avail. No entry for "Ehlers-Danlos syndrome" or "genetic connective tissue disorder" in my dictionary. All I could communicate was panic. But I'd found the words for stitches. *"Les points de suture."*

The kindly doctor shook her head. *"Ce n'est pas nécessaire."*

I watched, powerless, as she cut off the flap of stretchy, fragile skin with tiny scissors, taped a bandage over the wound the size of a child's fist, and sent us on our way.

Back to that bus stop, my first week in a French high school. After the city bus rolled away without me, six inches from my face, I elevated my throbbing leg on the bench. I waited, sinking into the peace of not having to decipher any rolling French phrases for a while. In addition to the injury, I hadn't been sleeping well because my four-year-old host brother screamed for hours every night, and the wet toilet paper earplugs I'd made for myself out of desperation could only block out so much. I missed my actual four-year-old sister. At least she slept through the night.

I gazed at the plane trees with their puzzled bark. All the houses along that suburban street hid behind privacy gates and walls, so there wasn't much else to look at. Only the smell of lavender escaped from hidden courtyards. French people liked their privacy from the prying eyes of limping foreign exchange students.

That first week, I'd fixated on the wooden shutters that framed every window of every house. Each one clacked shut at night, and I loved the ritual of it, the slap of wood against the house at dusk and the whoosh of opening in the morning to signal the definitive lines between night and day. Daily life in France glowed vivid in its orderliness. Why did we only have fake shutters in the United States?

I brushed designs in the red gravel with my Skechers. Most of the girls in my *classe de seconde* wore lace-up leather boots, not bright blue sneakers with thick grabby soles. I was waiting for the bus to come, for French to congeal, and for my leg to stop throbbing. Soon all the daily rules and fashions would become clear.

A boy about my age joined me at the bus stop. We avoided eye contact, but when the next bus rolled around the corner and stopped at the curb, I watched as he strutted up to the side door in his leather lace-up boots and pushed the flashing button about the size of a hockey puck.

The bus flung open its doors.

I almost laughed out loud at how I hadn't seen the flashing red button right in front of my face, but I choked it back. Laughing to oneself in public did not suit orderly French composure.

I limped onto the bus to finish the first leg of my commute to Lycée Jean Moulin.

THE MARFAN SPECIALIST

"Did you know there's a research paper written about your family?" the Marfan specialist asked when the day of my genetics appointment finally arrived.

I did not know. I'd never seen it.

He plopped the article from an early nineties medical journal onto the exam table. It was about a novel familial mutation of Marfan syndrome. "This is your family," he said, pointing to a genetics family tree. "The filled circles indicate those who have Marfan syndrome, and this circle here must be your mom."

It took me a second to understand what I was looking at. The unfilled circle meant to indicate my mom without Marfan syndrome. But there should have been five siblings in that row. One was missing. "But that one could also be my aunt?" I said. Like my mom, my aunt also had two children, a boy and girl.

"Oh," he shrugged. "It's pretty common for them to combine subjects for the sake of analysis."

The exam table paper crinkled as I fidgeted. It still seemed possible that they had never tested me or my mom at all. But if this doctor didn't think I needed to worry about Marfan syndrome either, I told myself not to.

"I was pretty upset when I saw my childhood medical records and saw that my parents didn't follow up with genetic testing," I said.

The doctor shrugged. "Some people just don't want to know."

I didn't respond. I understood why someone would choose not to know. But my parents had assumed that they *did* know even when they didn't. In any case, knowing more meant treatment options, which was why I sat in that triple-sized exam room decades after my initial diagnosis trying to piece together the whole story.

The doctor ordered the blood work that would determine whether I had classical or vascular EDS.

In the three months waiting for those results, my unease about the unknown grew. By then I had already waited two years for the genetics appointment, but I felt a new urgency now that an answer was right around the corner.

Something my mom had said when I was younger rattled deep in my subconscious. "Don't write a book until after I'm dead," she'd said, probably in response to some snarky teenage observation. I think she meant it as a joke, at least partially, but on some level I had internalized that constraint. I still wrote fiction for practice, but I rarely shared it. I wrote about anything but myself.

But now, if I had the vascular type of EDS, outliving my parents was not a given. And even the classical type carried some risk of fragile arteries and dissection. Nothing was guaranteed. While I waited to be seen in that genetics clinic, for the first time since elementary school, I started writing about my own life.

WAITING FOR GODOT

A whole new school in a whole new country in a whole new language I didn't yet speak. The possibilities were wide open. I could become anyone I wanted. I limped around the courtyard until I found my name on one of the lists taped to the Roman arches. I was in a *classe de seconde*, the equivalent of a sophomore. My stomach sunk. I'd basically flown halfway across the world to repeat a grade? I wondered if I'd even get credit for the year when I returned home.

After we filed into the classroom, I watched as each student placed a leather planner and a pencil bag on their desk. Everyone wore perfectly pressed clothing, with creases in their jeans. Even though my host mom, too, delivered flat piles of ironed laundry to my bottom bunk—including socks and underwear—I did not feel nearly as put together as they looked. The girl next to me, who wore thick round glasses and a low ponytail, introduced herself as Emilie. She took a fountain pen out of her pencil bag and lined it up with the rest of her supplies.

A fountain pen? Like for calligraphy?

The professor read out the semester's schedule, which I didn't understand but which other students recorded in careful looping script in their sleek planners. When Emilie made a mistake, she erased the ink with a striped correction stick, the clear fluid squeaking like a tiny highlighter. Then she underlined the days of the week with a ruler and brightly colored gel pens. I envied her focus, but I also cringed at the mockery I'd have invited if I underlined headings with a ruler back home, where I sometimes felt self-conscious for taking any class notes at all. I looked around. Everyone had their little rulers, their tight focus.

What was with all this attention to detail?

I wanted to hide the planner my host mom had picked out for me at the grocery store Carrefour. Its white paper cover was printed with a waifish cartoon girl in a mini skirt and go-go boots. I hated it. I wouldn't have been caught dead with a flower power-themed accessory back home, not that I would have carried a day planner at all. Compared to the French students, I was unrefined, even slovenly. I doodled in the margins of my humiliating planner with a disposable Bic pen, both my head and leg injury throbbing.

"*C'est un drôle de cahier*," Emilie said, pointing to my planner.

I wondered if she meant funny as in comical or funny as in weird. "*Je ne l'aime pas.*" I don't like it. I placed an alien head sticker over the cartoon girl's pouty-lipped, vacant stare, which made little difference to its overall effect.

The principal summoned me to his office. Due to my lack of fluency in French, he wanted to demote me to a class of twelve-year-olds.

I sat up straighter. "*Non.*"

Did he think fluency in French and intelligence were the same thing? I knew I'd still struggle to understand the assignments in a classroom full of twelve-year-olds, and that would have been even worse. Luckily, he didn't insist. He sighed and handed me a printed schedule so I'd know which classrooms to show up to and when. With a heavy fountain pen, he crossed out the blocks of time allotted to chemistry and physics.

"*Trop difficile*," he said.

I was insulted that he thought I couldn't handle science, but I liked the look of my new, lightened course load. Maybe I'd have time to wander around the city between classes. But I saw one more subject that needed crossing off.

"*Pas du sport*," I said.

He looked at me with renewed interest. "*Pourquoi?*"

I couldn't explain why gym was a bad idea, but I insisted. "*Je ne peux pas.*"

He sighed again and slashed a large X through gym class. My schedule lightened up even further. If I said no firmly enough, no one pushed me to explain myself.

"*Bon chance*," he said.

I limped away from his office through the wide hallway, passing windows that overlooked a red gravel courtyard with two symmetrical rows of plane trees. Maybe the year would be manageable after all.

In the third-floor hallway, waiting to file into the classroom, I leaned on the radiator to warm my hands and gazed out the window at Lyon's most iconic cathedral, Notre-Dame de Fourvière, towering only two blocks away. Adjacent to the school, a handful of people wandered the ruins of a Roman amphitheater with deep stone seating.

I was in France! I was looking at Roman ruins! I was touching an old-fashioned radiator that clanked! Halfway sophisticated already, even though I still wore bootcut jeans instead of tight black pants. I eavesdropped on the pre-class conversations.

"As-tu une cartouche?"

Instead of asking about weekend or after-school plans, my classmates made sure they had full ink cartridges in their fountain pens.

My host mom also bought me a three-ring binder covered in a sepia-toned print of a false-fronted wooden shack, in front of which a cowboy sat gazing at tumbleweeds. Maybe she thought it would make me less homesick, but it didn't work. My school supplies reflected American stereotypes that hadn't even formed conscious parts of my identity. Flower power on my planner and the lawless grit of the Wild West on my three-ring binder? The symbolism was clear: a silly American with bad taste, possibly deranged with individualism. Worst of all, I couldn't counterbalance that image by cracking sarcastic comments about the absurdity of, like, everything.

I just had to sit in class, gaze at the Roman ruins out the window and wait for my personality to return.

After I figured out how to decipher her calligraphic cursive, Emilie let me copy her lecture notes. But the harder I tried to stay on top them, the deeper I seemed to sink. French immersion gave me a headache.

I failed my first quiz in English class, for example. "Interesting," the *prof d'Anglais* had said when she slapped it down on my desk. In conjugating verbs—I go, I went, I had gone—I'd put the tenses in the wrong order and lost marks for incorrect usage of British English. I'd gotten it all wrong; I mean, I'd *got* it all wrong. Even math equations, I mean *maths* equations, which I'd expected to be language-free, were incomprehensible to me in French. Math was easy for me at home, but they laid out algebraic factoring in culturally specific ways that included a bazillion inscrutable steps. While I could arrive at the answer, I didn't follow the French process, so I passed absolutely nothing.

My favorite class was French literature. Mme Ramozzi wore black leather pants and heavy pendant necklaces, and talked about the wall-to-wall bookshelves in her downtown apartment. She spoke loudly and used her full body to express her enthusiasm for Charlie Chaplin, Émile Zola, Telemachus, and Jean-Jacques Rousseau.

"Stay cool," she said, emphasis on the "L," after she'd asked me a question I didn't understand and I'd only offered wide-eyed muteness in response. I had more time to figure out what the hell was going on when both students and professors ignored me, but that wasn't always possible.

It was clear that I had no chance of getting by in a French lycée with the minimal effort and engagement I'd honed in my American high school. It was novel to try my best and still be the worst student in class. Surely, a moment would come when French would click and life would be easy again? I'd need to excavate my childhood love for school supplies and buy a fountain pen and ink cartridges to go with it. Maybe I could reclaim some aspects of my perfectionism in public. Eventually, I might even understand the subtleties of conversations I was part of.

"Stay cool," she repeated, emphasis on the "L."

My classmates laughed.

English slang was universal, even if school supplies were not.

On Wednesday afternoon, the midweek break, I went to the internet café in downtown Lyon. In 1998, the best way to stay in touch with family and friends back home was to pay for fifteen minutes of internet access at a time. While I'd already spent my early teens with the novelty of being able to look up inane jokes and message friends in chat rooms, none of my French peers had email addresses.

I sat on a stool in front of a computer screen embedded into the wall, intending to write about fountain pens and Roman ruins, but I mostly ended up complaining about French keyboards, which are not

QWERTY and ASDF but AZERTY and QSDF. Close enough to be workable but different enough to infuriate.

I'd taken a typing class in the eighth grade in which looking at the keyboard was a grave mistake, and I prided myself on my words-per-minute rate. But under my internet café time crunch, typos become yet another thing to practice being okay with.

School became easier as I watched and followed the daily rituals. Upon arrival to the courtyard each morning, framed on three sides by the Roman arches of a covered walkway and filled with evenly spaced plane trees, I *fait les bises*, kissing each classmate on both cheeks. These kissing rounds took up the bulk of the time before the first bell because the arrival of each classmate paused the conversation for a new round. When I was still learning their names, I came to tell them apart by the texture and warmth of their morning cheek skin: Fanny, warm and dry; Berangère, cool and ruddy; Maude, hot and smooth.

I bought a fountain pen—a black *stylo plume* with silver flowers and a silver cap—and equipped myself with ink cartridges, correction sticks, and a leather pencil case to carry them in. Nevertheless, I couldn't get the fountain pen ink to flow properly. My nib scratched the paper, inkless, and ink dripped all over my fingers instead.

Just when the routine of school started to make sense, class would be canceled for reasons unknown to me. I showed up to French class to find a few students milling around but no professor. Instead of going back to my host family and spending the day on the bottom bunk in my basement bedroom that smelled like sawdust and glue, I went to see if any other exchange students were checking their email at the internet café.

They were.

We sat in the common area, slightly removed from the futuristic screens built into the wall, and got drunk on the beer they served even to sixteen-year-old foreign exchange students.

The second time class was canceled for what seemed like no reason, I ran into Emilie in the hallway in her oversized sweater with three thick horizontal stripes of white, tan, and brown. I pointed to the word in my French–English dictionary that I thought I'd overheard.

Grave, adj. Serious.

Could she please explain to me what was so serious? Emilie laughed. She flipped the page of my dictionary and pointed to *la grève,* n. Strike. The students had gone on strike. I didn't know what, exactly, they were striking against, but I added this important word to my French vocabulary.

And then, of course, I was still healing from my fall the first week. Whenever I'd split open my shin when I was little, my mom slipped a modified plastic grocery bag over my calf like a crinkly leg warmer, cinching both ends with rubber bands so I could lay in the bath water with one leg splayed over the edge of the tub, the stitches protected from drips and splashes.

In France, however, I had no access to the bathtub for soaking, not that I had any stitches to keep dry. My four-year-old host brother's toys filled the tub to the brim. Besides, before I'd arrived, my host mom had been forewarned about what were likely to be my water-wasting American ways. She'd spread her arms wide and brought her palms close together to illustrate the difference in hot water availability.

"*Tu prends les douches très courts,*" she ordered. Short showers only.

And so I turned the water off and on again several times during a shower just like them. Off to lather up, on to rinse, and much maneuvering with the handheld shower head. A hot bath for the sake of pain relief was out of the question.

My host mom laughed when I asked to change my bandages myself. A silly request in a country where doctors made house calls. Every other evening for weeks, I squinted under the bright lights of the kitchen, with my well-scarred and freshly injured leg up on a second chair, while a doctor changed my bandages for me.

When I got lonely, I flipped through the journal my friends had made for me. The picture of the Oregon Coast looked tropical now, a totally different world than a large European city. I gazed at these pictures and tried to situate myself. Which parts of me were American, and which parts were just me? Which parts did I stick with, and which parts did I let go of for the purpose of cross-cultural integration?

Maybe culture shock breaks you down in sort of the same way they say that basic military training breaks you down, so that you become pliable enough to be remade however they want you. But I had no drill sergeants screaming in my face, only French people who doubted my intelligence, spoke louder than necessary, and limited my access to hot water. I would have to figure out my own way to build myself back up.

The world got colder. The heater in my basement bedroom broke and didn't get fixed for months, so all day at school, in between classes, I clung to those radiators underneath the windows overlooking the Roman ruins.

My heart twisted when I arrived at the courtyard, ready to *fais les bises*, and saw that the evenly spaced plane trees had been mutilated. Instead of the last of the colorful autumn leaves, every leaf-dangling branch had been sawn off, exposing a gnarly knot at the top of each trunk. I'd never seen, or noticed, pollarding before and thought a landscaping crew had made some very ugly mistakes over the weekend. Would those trees ever come back to life?

Bus drivers went on strike too. After class ended at 18h00, I called Pascale from a pay phone to see if Christian, my host dad, could pick me up.

Pascale laughed. "*Il travail.*" He's at work.

But surely he'd finish soon? I could wait for him to come get me. I lingered on the phone.

"*Bon chance,*" she added.

Good luck. I was on my own. She really did expect me to limp the two hours home, in the dark, with a leg that still throbbed with every step. As I walked through the cobblestoned city and along busy commuter roads, I re-evaluated my situation. Was school attendance really so critical to learning French? If my host family didn't care one way or another how I got home, *when* I got home didn't seem so important either.

I could set my own rules.

I could take my own strikes.

By winter, my limp was gone and the precedent had been set. As long as I appeared to be making an effort in class, no professor asked questions if I didn't do the assignments or even show up regularly. I could hold the comforting illusion of inconspicuousness by going through the motions of sitting at a desk and writing on Clairefontaine paper, even though I more often wrote letters to friends back home or studied French vocabulary instead of taking lecture notes.

If standards and rules shifted so much from place to place, what was the point of following any of them? Even when my French got good enough to understand the rules, it was more convenient to pretend I didn't. "You're good at playing the French student game," the English teacher said.

I fell into my old pattern of going through the motions of school. I was no longer a good student who thought school was a joke, however. Instead, I admired the French academic rigor but didn't worry about meeting it. I preferred to direct my attention elsewhere, like passing for a French teenager when making small talk with strangers in public, complete with colloquialisms.

C'est cool, quoi.

I usually attended French literature with Mme Ramozzi. Midway through the year, she gave a lecture on etymology. "*Quelle est le base du mot rationalité?*"

She stared at our blank faces and repeated her question more slowly. "What. Is. The. Root. Of. The. Word. Rationality?" Still nothing.

For the first time, I knew the answer when no one else in my *classe de seconde* did. I'd been picking apart French for months, waiting for the pieces to come together. *T'as raison* = You are correct, i.e., rational. I looked over my shoulder before speaking as if someone might stop me. "*Raison?*"

Mme Ramozzi exhaled. "*Oui.*"

To my classmates' surprise, *l'Américaine* who didn't speak French had just proved she'd been learning something after all. They applauded, and I wondered if I were dreaming, to be applauded for saying something smart. But I was awake. I'd lost the illusion of inconspicuousness, and French had begun to click.

I did not, however, start doing homework. In a culture more regimented than my own, I'd found the space to do whatever I wanted.

In the spring, after the snow melted and the knotted stumps of the plane trees exploded with twigs, Mme Ramozzi sometimes held class in the ruins of the adjacent Roman amphitheater. We sat on the deep stone steps and read scenes from Samuel Beckett's existentialist play *En Attendant Godot*. Madame Ramozzi stood on the stage in her black outfit, with long wild hair and heavy bejeweled necklaces, and assigned us parts. *"Alyssa, tu lis Vladimir."*

I shuffled forward on the stone warmed by the spring sun, and read my first line as Vladimir, in response to Estragon's struggle to take off his boot while waiting for someone who would never arrive. I understood waiting and existential struggle. Waiting for the bus, waiting for French to click, waiting for someone else to swoop in and identify all the invisible cultural expectations I wasn't quite meeting. Waiting for perfect balance between the desire to fit in and the need to stand by my most important idiosyncrasies.

Some of the sophistication I was waiting for had arrived. I was, after all, wearing French lace-up boots and reading Beckett in French in a Roman amphitheater. But maybe I'd acquired a sliver of true worldliness as well. If no one person or place could define absolute rules, then striving for perfection was absurd. To do so would trap myself in a single rigid world, not a real, dynamic one.

I'd need to find my own balance between brain and body and place. Keyboard or fountain pen, the tools didn't matter so much. I was beginning to realize that the only person who had a reasonable chance of making perfect sense of my experiences was me.

THE LAVENDER MENACE

I wished I had a better story to go with fracturing my right elbow, like a DIY project gone wrong or that I'd rescued someone's enthusiastic golden retriever from getting hit by a car. But the real story was I'd just arrived at the Sou'wester Lodge, a mossy, Airstream-filled resort in southwest Washington where I'd come as a board member of the local Q center for a weekend retreat. My body hurt, and my brain felt more foggy than usual, so I took a quick walk on the beach before the first meeting to try to clear my head. At the end of that walk, just as I returned to the street from the sand, I twisted my ankle and landed on the pavement, my extended palm bracing the fall. The moment of fracture sounded like one hard knock, bones in direct collision, and my locked elbow shattered.

I stood, brushing off the tiny pieces of gravel embedded in my palm. Fine one moment and broken the next. I scowled, squinting at oncoming car headlights that shone in my face as I walked back to the lodge, holding my right arm tight to my chest.

Too fucking bright.

I could do as much physical therapy as I wanted, but my ankle twisting for no reason was a harsh reminder of my endless fragility. And I didn't need a reminder. I already knew. With two days of strategic planning ahead of me, I took the pain meds I'd brought with me and told myself it was only a sprain. Nothing to do but wait it out. The slightest move sent daggers down my arm, so I turned my scarf into a sling for stabilization. It was often difficult to pinpoint which pain could be fixed and which I needed to learn to live with. Only after twenty-four hours did I finally go to the hospital, where they confirmed the fracture and splinted my right arm.

"You're tough," another board member said, despite having seen me sobbing on my return to the lodge. "I can't believe you waited a whole day to go the hospital with a broken arm."

I functioned at half speed for over a month, using thrice the energy for every task and wobbling more than usual without two extended arms for balance. No driving myself anywhere in my stick-shift car. No freelance editing, which required both typing and scribbling temporary style sheets, because it would have taken me four times as long and I was paid by the job, not the hour. Not even knitting. I could read books and microwave gluten-free frozen dinners for easy, one-armed meals. Luckily, November was slow season with my new Airbnb rental, so I had several days between each guest to clean the space one-handed.

When Thanksgiving rolled around, I was still exhausted. But a visible injury was a better excuse for avoiding holiday stress than invisible chronic pain. Everyone could see that I wore a splint. In any case, because of my freelance schedule and made worse after I'd turned my second bedroom into short-term lodging, days of the week—and even major holidays—were indistinguishable. I was always on call.

My mom and brother Zach made a last-minute Thanksgiving plan for me. They drove the two hours over the Coast Range from Portland to my house in Astoria. "A day trip," my mom had said. "Just for a few hours."

While I sat in my armchair waiting for them to arrive, Zach called. "We're stopping for coffee. What do you want?"

"Extra hot vanilla latte with coconut milk," I said. My standing order.

I was glad to see them when they arrived, Zach in a hoodie and day-old stubble holding a tray of coffees. Mom had straightened her gray-white hair, which hung to the neckline of her mock-neck fleece. She carried a plastic bag of the essential groceries I'd requested too—apples, red wine, and toilet paper—plus unexpectedly, a single tray of grocery store sushi. I liked sushi. Maybe this visit wouldn't be so bad. Zach handed me my latte, which had a green stick in the mouth of its lid.

"What's the stick for? I don't have to stir in a flavor, do I?" I pinched it between my thumb and forefinger, and braced myself. Nutmeg sprinkles? Pumpkin spice?

Zach squinted at me. "What's it *for*? It's a stopper so it doesn't spill in the car."

"Oh," I said. "I always thought these were stir sticks."

Mom and Zach exchanged a look and started laughing. "That's exactly what Mom said."

I moved the stick up and down, its plastic grating against the mouth of the lid. How irritating, that my mom and I had both been oblivious to the same thing. "Anyway," I said. "No stirring required."

"I got you one with almond milk instead because I remembered you like almond milk too," said Mom.

Thankfulness, I reminded myself. Family, Thanksgiving, and a latte and toilet paper delivery. But I hated almond milk in lattes. Too sweet and chalky. Why'd she even have Zach call for my order if she was just going to change it? "Thanks."

I sat down at my kitchen table to devour a few pieces of grocery store Thanksgiving sushi, awkwardly, with my unfractured left arm.

Six months before, I'd had a carpenter put up a wall to create a hallway and door to separate the front part of my house from the second bathroom and a loft-like bedroom. Guests let themselves in through the back door, so I didn't usually see or speak to them, which meant I didn't have to waste energy changing out of my sweatpants unless I actually planned to leave the house.

The stairs to the loft bedroom were so steep that I put four warnings about them in my online blurb. Hard to miss, even for prospective guests who skimmed. I didn't want someone with a bad knee to get here and find the ladder-like stairs unmanageable. In fact, their steepness was part of the reason I'd decided to turn that part of my house into an Airbnb in the first place. I knew if I had to descend those treacherous stairs every time I needed to pee in the middle of the night, sooner or later I'd fall for sure. So I let the able-bodied tourists do the midnight climbs and little falls down every steep step.

I'd painted the bedroom walls purple and named the rental The Lilac Loft, also because it overlooked a lilac bush in the yard. I considered calling it The Lavender Menace because the reference to iconic lesbian history would have been funnier, but I decided the word "menace" might scare away prospective guests and few would appreciate the reference.

I just called it that in my head.

The upstairs windows overlooked ivy-girdled fir trees, overgrown English laurel, and rhododendron bushes overrun with cane-thick blackberry suckers. Zach hadn't been to my house since I'd set it all up, and we had about half an hour before the guest check-in window, so I took them up there. He sat on the freshly made bed, which I'd fluffed earlier with my one good arm.

"Don't mess it up!" I said. "It has to be hotel-like."

He ignored me and leaned back on the pillows. "Do you make them breakfast?"

"No. I leave them coffee and granola bars."

"Turndown service?"

I scoffed. "No."

"Really? No chocolate on the pillow?" Zach put his hands behind his head.

"No way."

"Seems like that would be a nice thing."

I brushed a tiny speck of dust off the nightstand. "Who wants chocolate right after they've brushed their teeth?"

"The first time I stayed in a hotel that offered turndown service," my mom said, "I thought someone had broken into my room."

Zach and I both turned to her. We needed more details.

"I'd only ever stayed in places like Motel 6," she said. "So . . . you know."

"What'd you do?" my brother asked.

"I went to the front desk and reported it!"

We laughed at her, but I agreed with my mom on the invasiveness. After I've checked into a private room, I don't want to think about someone waiting until I leave to sneak in, fold down my sheets, and leave confection on my pillow. How do they even know when I've left? Are the chocolate-leavers like suspicious characters in bars waiting for my trip to the bathroom to slip something in my drink? And if I don't leave the hotel room, do they sneak in while I'm soaking in the bathtub? Which other of my activities are hotel staff monitoring?

"It's creepy," I said. "Like they're stalking your every move."

My mom rolled her eyes. "They just do it when you go to dinner."

"Did you eat the chocolate at least?" I asked.

"It was a mint."

Since I wasn't at risk of leaving myself a bad review for not polishing the water drop residue off the shower faucet, or tucking the duvet perfectly into the corners of its cover, my part of the house didn't get cleaned nearly as often. My bed never looked crisp either, due to my U-shaped pregnancy pillow that took up half the bed. I needed it to prevent sleep injuries, to contain and support as many joints as possible while I slept.

Mom walked through my bedroom on her way to the bathroom. "Do you think you have enough pillows on your bed?"

"Not quite," I said. I would build a fort of pillows if I had to.

The three of us returned to the wood stove in my living room, which I'd kept stoked for coziness despite my fractured right elbow.

"Are your guests loud?" my brother asked.

More than anyone, he knew about my noise sensitivity. As teenagers, he'd tried to listen to the radio while falling asleep, but our bedrooms shared a wall and I always barged in to tell him to turn it down.

"Yes," I said. "But I turn up my white noise machine really loud."

He laughed. "Remember how you used to sing to me when I was falling asleep?"

I shook my head.

"You wouldn't let me listen to music," he said, "so I asked you to sing your choir songs from your room. You had such a pretty voice."

From our late teenage years, I remembered my anger when he stole the French cigarettes hidden at the back of my desk drawer, but I didn't remember singing him to sleep as a compromise.

My mom added her hypothesis. "I think your eardrums are too loose and vibrate at every little thing."

Why did people stay in my Airbnb? Some came to Astoria for the seafood and breweries; some for its proximity to beaches; some for the *Goonies* house, taking selfies where the 1985 movie was filmed, infuriating both the current residents and their neighbors.

Astoria felt to me the way Portland had felt twenty years earlier, before it lost most of its grittiness in the decades after I left home. Astoria also felt like the big city after living three years down the coast in a tiny tourist town. It used to be known as Little San Francisco, and, like San

Francisco, Astoria is perched on a peninsula with dramatic views of water and bridges. *The* view, however, is north-facing, toward the four-mile-long Astoria–Megler Bridge and the partially buzzed-cut forests of Pacific County. Houses on that side of the hill overlook cargo ships in the Columbia River, waiting their turn to be released into the giant sandbar at the river's mouth known as the Graveyard of the Pacific.

Also like San Francisco, the houses on the other side of the hill have views of water and bridges too, but these views don't count as much with the locals. My house sat on this south-facing slope, and if I ever hired someone to trim the tree-height English laurel hedge, my guests would have had views of Old Youngs Bay Bridge and its bay. But I did without this view because I liked nestling into overgrown foliage, which allowed me to retain at least some privacy, even when strangers continually let themselves in and out of the back door.

When my guest for the night showed up in late afternoon, Zach, Mom, and I still sat around the wood stove in my living room, which had no windows onto the driveway, where guests park. I'd emailed a lockbox code in advance and didn't expect to see or meet her, but Zach was curious. He went to my bedroom to peek onto the driveway, and I worried my guest would see him and get creeped out.

"Make sure the lights are off so she doesn't see you," I called after him.

My mom closed her eyes and leaned back in the chair. "I'm sure he knows how to spy on someone."

Zach reported back to the living room shortly. "She looks nice," he said. "Like someone you'd be friends with."

"Did she see you?"

"No. But she's wearing a knit hat. You should go talk to her."

I stayed put but slumped a little into my chair. Should I be making more of an effort to befriend every hand-knit hat-wearing solo traveler? In my Airbnb blurb, I did my best to manage expectations. In addition to the ladder-like stairs, my house was old: light switches in odd places, awkward bathroom layout, and permanent stains from decades of water deposits on the porcelain tub. The cups and glasses I provided didn't always match and definitely didn't come plastic-wrapped. My guests should prefer cozy eccentricity to anonymous hotel rooms.

I also did my best to manage expectations about how I, as the host, wouldn't be offering any entertainment value. I hoped to dissuade any guests who'd feel cheated if I didn't attend to them every second, sneaking into their room as soon as they stepped in the shower to fold down their sheets and leave chocolate—or a mint—on their pillows. I tried to make it clear that I offered a clean and quiet space cozily nestled into the shrubbery, and that was it. "Interaction with guests will be minimal," I wrote.

If I had to make conversation with all of my guests too, in addition to battling the stairs to clean it and being on call, the energy costs would've been too high. So I guess you could say I was inclined toward DIY hospitality. My favorite guests were those most like myself: travelers who just wanted to be left alone. I filled a binder with local maps and brochures to cover touristy logistics and let them be.

By the time guests pulled into the driveway, my work was mostly done. When they knocked on my front door to say hello, which few did, I summoned the energy to be friendly and welcoming and to answer their questions about restaurants or hikes or the real estate market. I didn't mind doing this occasionally; sometimes, I even enjoyed it. But the truth was that if I'd had to pretend on a daily basis that I cared about strangers' weekend trips, or interest in the Columbia River Maritime Museum, or surprise and/or disappointment at seeing sunshine in a place known for its drizzle, it would have slowly but surely drained me of all will to live.

Welcome to The Lavender Menace, and have a nice stay.

ESCAPE BABIES

People called me brave for becoming an exchange student to France at sixteen. I was a quiet girl, after all. No one expected adventurousness. Maybe I was brave, or maybe I felt like the best place to grow into myself was in a time zone nine hours away. But I didn't want four-year-old Elizabeth to forget about me, so I sent her letters filled with stickers and doodles in which I described my host family's pets and the magical snow in Lyon, more than we ever got in Portland. Dad reported that she wanted my letters read to her every night before bed. One of the things I most looked forward to about coming home after a year was seeing her again.

On my flight back to Portland, and at the decompression weekend hosted by the exchange program, we heard lectures on reverse culture shock. They told us coming home would be difficult too. Still, I pictured my return as joyful, back to a family where I belonged at least more than I did to the one in France. Jet-lagged at the Portland airport, threads pulled taut behind my eyeballs, I couldn't wait to reclaim my own bedroom(s), to lie down and spread out in spaces I didn't have to share with anyone. They waited for me at the baggage carousel, my mom with Zach and my friend Sara. My dad stood with them, only without Sue and my half-siblings, who I'd thought would also be there.
    "Where are they?" I asked.
    Dad didn't respond, and his face seemed to be holding back intense emotion. Happiness, presumably. Since he hadn't seen me in a year. But he looked less clean-shaven than I remembered him. Older even.
    "I need to talk to you," he said.
    He took me aside, a few steps away from where everyone else crowded the luggage carousel. I expected him to make a joke or to say something lighthearted, something welcoming.

"What?" I said. "It looks like you're about to crack up."

He eyed me sharply. "It's not funny at all," he said. "Elizabeth has cancer."

Luggage started rumbling down the chute, landing with thuds that made it hard for me to think straight. I needed some time to put his words together. Elizabeth can't have cancer. She's five. She likes stickers.

There were no benches anywhere, and I wished I had my big suitcase to sit on for a second. "Is she going to be okay?"

"We don't know yet."

They thought leukemia at first, and she was still in the hospital after the first round of diagnostic tests. I could go visit her the next day.

I went back to my mom's house that night. In the car, driving the span of I-205 that crossed the Columbia River into Vancouver, I sat in the backseat crying between Zach and Sara.

"I can't believe I thought it was a big deal for me to be home when Elizabeth has *cancer*."

No one said anything.

The streaming raindrops on the window glowed red from taillights. I was home.

Later, when I went to my dad's house, Socks had disappeared. It felt like a weird time to ask about my beloved cat when Elizabeth had cancer, so I didn't.

I had one more year at my large suburban high school in Vancouver, Washington before I could leave again. I couldn't wait. The idea of prom made me want to scratch my eyes out, and the teachers threatened no graduation with even a single unexcused absence. Attendance fascists compared to the freedom I'd had in France.

Different sorts of etymology lessons too. The mustachioed psychology teacher with the beer belly assigned us worksheets on personality type, and he played educational videos on the TV/VHS cart almost every day.

I became interested in his class for the first time when he put in a video about lucid dreams. After seeing it, I wanted to do more research. I wanted to learn how to consciously navigate trippy dream worlds, to fight unconscious demons in my sleep. It sounded more worthwhile than high school.

After the video, however, he positioned himself on a stool in front of the class and gave a brief interpretation of the video that snuffed out my budding interest. "You know where the word 'lucid' comes from, don't you?" He smirked at the class, recognizing our blank stares as proof of our unworthiness as recipients of his wisdom. "It's from Lucifer, the devil. It means 'bad.'"

I sought eye contact with anyone, hoping for validation that someone else had heard the wrongness of what he'd just said. Hoping I wasn't the only eighteen-year-old who knew the word "lucid" comes from the Latin prefix *luc-*, which meant light. Which meant lucid dreams were about clarity and illumination, the opposite of the big, bad devil. But no. I was back in the United States. No one studied Latin etymology.

I wanted to slam my head against the desk.

What's the root of high school teachers who think they're hot shit even when they're idiots?

The bell rang. Bad dream over.

Of course, life was a bad dream too.

Elizabeth didn't have leukemia. She had alveolar rhabdomyosarcoma. Rare.

"We wish she had leukemia," my dad had said.

Between her rounds of chemo, I babysat Elizabeth and Ben on Tuesdays and Thursdays after school. I held Elizabeth's arms down on the floor of her bedroom and distracted her with Beanie Babies while Sue changed the gauze around her chest tube.

During her days-long trips to the Doernbecher Children's Hospital for chemo "camping trips," as Sue called them, I babysat two-year-old Ben after school and drove him to the hospital for afternoon visits. The expansive eastward view from the children's oncology wing overlooked the city with a gleaming backdrop of a snow-covered Mount Hood. I liked to gaze out that window while Elizabeth slept. The cartoon wallpaper couldn't mask the smell of iodoform and gauze.

When she had energy, we sat on rolling chairs from the nurse's station and bounced a basketball back and forth in the hallway. The ball echoed even louder than Elizabeth's squeals, but the nurses smiled benevolently and no one told us to stop. We all ate as much Jell-O and vanilla ice cream from the snack room as we wanted.

Elizabeth's private kindergarten teacher came to the house three days a week. While I did physics homework at the kitchen table in the next room, her teacher yelled out a question.

"Alyssa, do you know how to spell 'dessert'?"

"With two s's," I said. "Because you always want two scoops of ice cream for dessert instead of one."

"Oh! That's a good one."

I overheard the awe in Elizabeth's words to her teacher. "My sister is really smart," she said. "She even speaks French."

I liked being idolized.

That night, Elizabeth lounged with me on my bed while I watched the *X-Files*, fast-forwarding through the scary parts for her benefit. She drew me stick figure and smiley-face renditions of Mulder and Scully.

The weirdest moment at Doernbecher's that year was when I went not for Elizabeth but for myself. I took the same elevator as when I went to visit her but got off on a different floor, pediatric cardiology. The view was similar, if a little lower in the sky. I worried that, at any moment, an official-looking person in scrubs might ask me to explain my presence as a patient. Did I deserve all that attention? But I'd been having chest pains, so my mom had made an appointment at this clinic tucked back in the winding West Hills.

"We wouldn't worry about most teenage girls complaining of chest pain," the doctor had said before running an MRI. "But you're a special case."

The last time a doctor had mentioned my EDS was when I'd been fitted for those overwrought calf guards, so it was strange to have it light up again as something that mattered. It had been a few years since I'd had any emergency room visits for stitches, aside from that fall in France the year before that hadn't included any stitches at all. The technician handed me headphones tuned to a country radio station—which I would never have chosen—before sliding me into the MRI tube that stretched the length of my body. Stillness and twangy torture, but my test results were immediate. My hair elastic had slipped out during the scan, so I stood disheveled in my hospital gown while the doctor showed us the recording of my beating heart valves.

No problems.

I got dressed. The doctor told me to come back if the pain got worse.

The summer after I graduated high school, Elizabeth was in remission, but the hospital camping trips and chemical warfare had taken their emotional toll. She didn't want to be alone with other kids yet, so I went with her to a Spanish language day camp for six-year-olds at an elementary school in Beaverton. She wore her favorite purple bandana with little white flowers, and she walked on tip-toes due to leg muscles that hadn't yet recovered their strength.

"Everybody get in a circle," the teacher called, clapping her hands together. "We start with numbers!"

Elizabeth looked up at me with wide brown eyes, and I nodded. This was doable. I took her hand as we joined the circle. Leading the circle counterclockwise, the teacher started at *uno* in a whisper, then climbed numbers and volume with every step until we all screamed *diez!* and threw up our hands. Elizabeth laughed at every screamed *diez!*, her face turning pink and our joint fists raised in the air. But she lagged behind when the teacher herded us outside into the hot sunshine. "Do you want to play basketball with everyone else?" I asked.

She shook her head. "I'm tired."

I could relate. That circle was dizzy-making.

So we walked over to the bleachers, which had no railings, and climbed to a middle bench—her tip-toeing and me slightly wobbly—leaning on each other so we didn't fall. On the bench below, we lined up our almost-matching sneakers side by side, hers with purple wavy lines and mine blue. An unplanned serendipity. I'd chosen mine with my mom, and she'd chosen hers with hers.

The kids screeched around the basketball court with the low hoops while the teacher tallied up the score in Spanish. Where'd they get all that energy? "Too bad we don't have rolling chairs out here," I said, reminding her of our hospital game.

She grinned. I handed her a juice box and some gummy bears.

I was leaving for Montreal in a few weeks. McGill University was almost as far away as I could get without crossing any oceans, but I felt waves of relief to be leaving Elizabeth in remission.

REALITY CHECK

At the EDS conference, a dozen gray cubicle dividers sectioned off a private area in which attendees could lie down on cots but still listen to the presentations. The nap area stayed full all day long.

I had found my people.

My new physical therapist had organized the conference and encouraged her patients to attend. When I found out it would be held at OHSU, I imagined walking into a building tucked into the hillside with an eastern view over the city and of Mount Hood, a view that reminded me of spending all that time in the hospital with my half-sister, Elizabeth. But the conference was being held at the new waterfront campus along the Willamette River, connected to the hill by an aerial tram that had become Portland-iconic during the twelve years I'd lived in Canada. I walked into an unfamiliar modern building with a glassy central atrium.

EDS awareness had increased exponentially over the previous twenty-five years, and with it, research and diagnosis rates. It turned out that while some types of EDS are rare, some are common. Like the hypermobile type of EDS that a significant subset of dancers have. They pay for all of those studied overextensions later, but when they're young, they glide around superhuman. I was at the conference to learn as much as I could about management and prevention, to keep tightening what I could of my body's unraveling.

At the check-in desk, I recognized several physical therapists from the clinic. They directed attendees, both patients and practitioners, to the main hall and the swag room, where we could buy raffle tickets to win zebra-themed baskets of black-and-white striped makeup bags, notebooks, and rice pillows. The zebra is the EDS mascot because of a common saying in allopathic medical school: "When you hear the sound of hooves, think horses, not zebras." In other words, doctors are explicitly taught that when a young, healthy-looking woman comes in complaining of severe pain, fatigue, fainting, and/or allergies to everything, a whole grab bag of seemingly disconnected complaints, assume the "common" thing—say, anxiety, depression, or hypochondria—rather than a rare genetic disorder.

But zebras are real animals.

I took a seat. Many attendees walked with a cane, used a wheelchair, or wore visible braces. Several had elevated their feet on second chairs. I inspected their profiles out of the corner of my eye. Aside from the physical therapist, I'd never knowingly met another person with EDS and now, here I was, surrounded by them. No one blinked an eye about using two chairs instead of one. I'd fallen deep into a parallel universe in which everyone was floppy like me.

What if my genetic freakishness wasn't so freakish after all?

While I waited for the first presentation to start, I brought out my knitting, a scarf with wavy rows. I kept track of the stitch count since I planned to sell the pattern online, in PDF form, after I finished writing it. (I would keep the scarf I knit from the pattern, however. I no longer sold my handmade creations for next to nothing.) In any case, I wanted to have something to do with my hands, something to show for sitting in a conference all day long. The large room contained many more knitters per capita than average.

First, a presentation about the whys of POTS. How is it possible for collagen to royally screw up the autonomic nervous system, which controls things like breathing and heart rate and blood pressure? A diagram of a human circulatory system lit up the slide on the front wall. Faulty collagen in blood vessel walls stretches them out, causing blood to pool in lower extremities. Not only does this cause lightheadedness and a lack of circulation, but stretchy veins send garbled messages back to the body's automatic processing center.

If it gets the message that you're hemorrhaging blood volume all of a sudden, the autonomic nervous system presses the panic button.

So my extra stretchy blood vessels made it harder for blood to circulate when I stood up. First, I got dizzy. Then my heart panicked and my fight-or-flight system clicked on to work double-time on getting the blood flowing. Which is why just standing around spiked my heart rate and blood pressure to dangerous levels.

No wonder I didn't like standing around in crowds, insisted on fidgeting or walking away. Maybe it wasn't the crowds so much as the fact that my brain was suffocating from lack of blood flow.

The autonomic nervous system also regulates body temperature, which means people with POTS are extra sensitive to hot and cold. We have to regulate our body temperature manually and often. No wonder Montreal winter was so hard to handle. No wonder I had a life-long obsession with hot baths.

The cardiologist who specialized in EDS/POTS also discussed medications and symptom management. I took notes on all the things I could do for my stretchy blood vessels, many of which I'd already learned in physical therapy, such as wear as many compression garments as possible and drink liters of salt water every day. And never stand still in one place.

They were pretty simple, these life-changing adaptations. I looped wool around my needles and instead of feeling gratitude for having integrated them, I felt grief for all the life lost to fatigue. I thought about the times in my twenties when I'd stayed home instead of going out because I knew exhaustion would overwhelm me. I'd missed out on a lot for want of electrolytes and compression socks.

The cardiologist emphasized one point over and over. "You are *not* chronically ill," she said. "You have a *condition* that can be *managed.*"

She said this in many different ways: "I don't let any of my patients say they have a chronic illness," and "There's always something more you can do to treat your symptoms."

I heard her insistence, but I didn't quite see what was so earth-shattering about her point. I mean, I understood the idea of not limiting myself. I didn't want to be defined solely by EDS. I was still living a full life. But EDS also defined the structure of every system in my body and, thus, how I experienced every aspect of the world. What was so wrong with accepting how a chronic disorder affected my identity?

So, whatever. I didn't have a chronic illness, I had a "condition to be managed." Either way, I needed to add several more things to my daily to-do list, to my awareness of what was happening in my body at any given moment. But if I spent my whole day attending to my body's "automatic" processes, I started to wonder how I'd find the time to live my actual life.

Chronic illness or chronic management. Did the semantics really matter?

I thought about the last time I'd attended a conference. I signed up to volunteer for the Canadian Library Association in Halifax just after I'd gotten my master's degree, just when I started to crash from overwork. My body had reached its limit. I ended up backing out of my volunteer shifts in favor of a job interview for a job I didn't get. Then I berated myself for laziness, telling myself that, in not volunteering, I was sabotaging every chance I'd ever have of getting a real job.

I'd barely been able to drag myself to that downtown conference center in the salty air of the Halifax peninsula, let alone stand around talking to people I would never see again about metadata. I only went to a couple conference sessions before I left. No way I could level back up to networking enthusiasm, which I'd only faked my way through for two years with great strain. I had the degree, but I was so tired it seemed as if I were no longer tethered to my body or the words coming out of my mouth.

I no longer cared where I landed after library school, as long as it was paid employment. Certainly all of that over-volunteering and over-achieving and working three too many jobs would pay off in the end. It was like I'd shut down, and my input as to direction was no longer required.

My physical therapist gave multiple presentations. She had perfect posture, high energy, and a loud laugh. She looked normal to me. Then again, would anyone see the genetic disorder if they looked at me from a distance? They would have to feel my skin and bend my joints and identify the characteristic gait patterns and postures of the over-flexible. It was a mind-fuck to feel so different from how I appeared.

"I like to play a guessing game with people," she said. "Guess how many braces and orthotics I'm wearing right now." She waved her hands up and down her body like a beauty queen.

I paused my knitting to look for telltale straps or bulges, but I only saw the sterling silver finger splints that wrapped her knuckles like armor. "People never guess right," she said. "I'm wearing thirteen! And it's a relatively light day."

I tried to picture strapping myself together with thirteen braces on a day when I was too tired to get dressed. Then she said something I would process for days afterward, even though it seemed so simple. "You just have to learn how to say, 'Look, I have a chronic illness, and I can't take on this, this, and this.'"

I loosened my grip on my ergonomic note-taking pen. She had not echoed the cardiologist's insistence that it was only a "condition to be managed."

According to someone living and thriving with EDS, the answer was to do less, not more. It was a valid *excuse*?

In the room full of knitters with feet elevated on second chairs, no one else seemed to freeze in the crystallized clarity of her statement. Nobody in the nap section peeked around the cubicle dividers in wide-eyed awe. In slow motion, I picked up my needles to knit one loop, then another. Her words had led me to the edge of an invisible chasm, the vast difference between working within physical limitations and pretending you can manage them away, no matter their severity. The idea of accepting the reality of EDS as a chronic illness, with all of its design constraints, rushed through my veins like the buoyant relief of drinking a liter of electrolyte water, increasing my blood volume and lifting my brain fog.

Her statement resonated with kindness. It reclaimed reality for what it was. I just had to own my EDS, and all of its comorbidities, as something to structure my life around.

I thought back to grad school again. I hadn't accepted EDS as a chronic illness then. I'd accepted it as this weird thing about me that I didn't like to talk about. I'd accepted it as a factoid, relevant only as an explanation for why my shins were covered with scars.

But a chronic illness? No.

I thought about how hard I'd pushed myself, how the more exhausted I got, the faster I spun. Self-care had been right at the bottom of my to-do list, just below reorganizing the sock drawer. And I'd gotten to the sock drawer. Maybe I would have been more focused, less oblivious to my body and relationships, if I'd been able to say, "Look, I have a chronic illness, and I can't take on this, this, and this." Maybe if I'd kept closer tabs on my crazed autonomic nervous system and chronic pain as if they mattered, I wouldn't have spun out at all.

Instead, I'd run myself into the ground and then tried to manage away the exhaustion with an extra self-prescribed supplement, or twenty. Not only was it unkind but it didn't work. Denial had turned my life into a never-ending spin. When I pretended I did not have a chronic illness, I made that illness worse.

Despite growing awareness, I also learned that the most common trajectory for people—especially female-identified people—to finally get diagnosed with EDS is to first spend decades being gaslit by medical practitioners. They're put on antidepressants, dismissed as hypochondriacs, are told to lose weight regardless of the problem. But if they're lucky enough to finally earn a referral to a geneticist, they're at least primed and ready to carry that diagnosis back into the medical system to find appropriate care. If they haven't given up on the medical system entirely by then, they might even hold out hope for treatments that alleviate their symptoms.

I'd always thought I'd been lucky to have taken that particular fall at ten years old, to have had a random emergency room doctor recognize my fragile skin and hyperextended joints as indicative of EDS. But the randomness of that catch put my trip to the children's genetics clinic at OHSU on a thwarted trajectory. Instead of hoping to find information about how to address particular chronic symptoms, the whole experience felt like information gathering for the sake of information. Never mind that the information gathered was exquisitely incomplete. Aside from the scars on my shins, we weren't there to address specific symptoms, so I didn't ride my early diagnosis into the hands of medical specialists. I'd taken the information from that team of doctors in white coasts as the pinnacle of medical help.

I'd understood that no cure meant no treatment.

When I made a rare trip to the doctor in my twenties, they didn't usually treat me like a hypochondriac. I could at least point to the diagnosis.

But my assumption was that if a doctor couldn't pronounce Ehlers-Danlos syndrome (which was most of them), they'd be unlikely to know how to treat it. I never mentioned any EDS-related problems, extrapolating from my meager experience with doctors that, for me, they had nothing. I never mentioned the falls or the pain or the dizziness or the fatigue or the allergies to everything. I just closed my eyes and pretended these symptoms didn't exist.

So I didn't spend decades weathering dismissiveness from ill-informed general practitioners. Instead of being gaslit by the medical system, I'd internalized the dismissal of my every symptom as something I just had to live with, floppy freak of nature that I was. Not until the pain had become debilitating did I even seek out a primary care doctor at all. I'd never even considered requesting referrals to specialists.

It seemed like EDS patients either had to run an internal or external gaslighting gauntlet.

Of course, the third option was to be fortunate enough to find specialists who actually helped from the beginning. From where I sat, the fact of their existence glowed like divine revelation. My most important realization was this: Maybe EDS and all of its comorbidities only spin themselves into full-blown disabilities when they are ignored.

An allergist gave a presentation on MCAS, the third in the well-known EDS trifecta. On the recommendation of my physical therapist, I had already seen an allergist and tested positive from a twenty-four-hour urine test that showed elevated levels of n-methyl histamine. But I didn't yet have a strong grasp on what that meant.

Mast cells are part of the immune system. They activate in response to stimuli they perceive as potentially harmful, releasing histamine and other mediators. With EDS, connective tissue in the extracellular matrix is wonky enough to affect change in mast cell behavior. They become overeager to activate and mediate, triggered by both the more common environmental triggers like grasses and certain foods, but also by overexertion and stress. With MCAS, they can even be activated by sunlight, noise, and temperature.

When histamine flooded my system, it felt like seasonal allergies but the season never ended. It felt like having the flu, flushed and feverish and weak. It felt like my head was drowning in a spin cycle, catching every activity with its centrifugal force, desperate for still more. But getting caught up in the spin only made the mast cell activation more severe. No wonder it was so hard to keep my head from spinning once it started. No wonder my body triggered overwork in response to stress. An abundance of histamine can foster type A personality traits, someone for whom spinning is the default.

I was in free fall in the parallel universe now, a parallel universe in which every one of my extremely weird symptoms, even personality traits, had not only an explanation but also known treatments. Medication could stabilize my trigger-happy mast cells. I did not have to spend the majority of my days feeling on the verge of the flu.

But back to my physical therapist with her thirteen splints and braces. How did she both embrace her chronic illness and live a full life, one that included a career and family and public speaking? How did she find the energy to organize an entire conference? What gives?

Why wasn't she doing less?

She talked about pacing.

"You basically have to be self-employed," she said. "I see patients in the mornings and then I spend the afternoons in my chair with my feet up doing paperwork."

I recognized myself in her daily flow. Maybe I no longer had to feel as if I were getting away with something every time I sank into my chair in the middle of the afternoon. Maybe the schedule I'd lined up for myself was both workable and medically necessary.

The cardiologist had it backward.

My condition could be managed, but only after I had accepted its reality as chronically fundamental. My reality was that no mind-over-matter mantra would change the fact that one-third of the protein in my body—including the matrix in which bones and muscles and organs are suspended—was made out of misaligned and loosely connected knots.

No amount of management, or like, yoga, would fix my genetic disorder. That's why they called it a chronic illness. If I acted as if the problem wasn't built into the fibers of my everyday existence, then where was the motivation to prioritize the endless work of symptom management?

Items on a long to-do list can always be shuffled off until tomorrow. Pretending I had control over every misaligned cell spun the story of self-blame disguised as wisdom. If my problem was structural, however, a wobbly foundation that could never be permanently stabilized, I could build around it with important limitations in mind.

"I think there's an EDS personality," my physical therapist continued. "We tend to be overachievers. We tend to overwork and take on what would be too much even for a healthy person."

I wrote that one down so I would remember to let it sink in later. Did I have an EDS personality? Had I overachieved myself into a pile of unsupported fluff? Someone else's cane fell to the floor with a clack. Was it common for the audience of a specialized medical conference to be half-filled with patients?

I guess we often ended up having to DIY our own health care.

"I think of it like this," she said. "My brain is a bulldozer and my body is a delicate flower, and I have to keep the machinery of my brain from crushing the petals." She insisted on a mindful bulldozer operator, one well-trained to work within certain limits.

"You can still have a life," she said. "I mean, I'm here! I'm presenting at this conference." She looked at the audience and paused. "I'm going to need a nap later, but I'm here."

Embracing my limitations—acknowledging my chronic illness as such—was key to my good health. I needed to prevent spin-outs before they happened. Yes, I still had to integrate a million little supports to make my life more manageable, but I also needed to remove external obligations from my to-do lists, not add more.

Creative energy thrives on limitations; it amps up when it is circumscribed. The more I accepted my physical limitations as real, the more I could focus my creative energy within them. And the more I embraced my personal design constraints, the more my accomplishments aligned with my goals. If I only had four hours of energy and focus per day, I would make sure I did what was most important to me within those four hours.

I could have wisdom without the self-blame.

It was possible to redirect that bulldozer's power to protect, rather than destroy, the delicate flower. I just had to prioritize projects and pick away at them one stitch at a time. I couldn't make plans as if I might have loads more energy tomorrow.

Maybe I could spend every afternoon in a chair with my feet up and still be a creative powerhouse.

UNFAIR

As the final exam period of my first semester at McGill approached, I wasn't doing well. Montreal I loved, but I hadn't been able to fully land, hovering somewhere between the cold city and the rainy one. I'd already made one quick flight back to Portland to visit Elizabeth, whose health, not long after I'd left for school, had tanked. Remission over. The cancer had returned. I wavered on whether to delay my exams and go home for the holidays early. Did she want me there? Did she need me?

Another call from my Dad. "I think you'd better come home to say goodbye," he said.

Her doctor emailed me the note I needed, saying these were her last days and they could do no more. She was home from the hospital now, and she was dying.

When I got to my dad's house, my dad having driven me from the airport, the family huddled in the basement on the L-shaped couch watching *The Parent Trap*, the one with Lindsay Lohan instead of Hayley Mills, one of Elizabeth's favorites. Ben ran toward me, his top-heavy curls pouffing with each stomp, and I scooped him into my arms.

"How's my boy?" I asked, ruffling his hair. "I missed you."

Then hugs to Elizabeth, Sue, Zach on the couch. Zach's presence was notable, as he usually spent as much time as possible out with his friends. Elizabeth's skin had grown yellow and the bones of her face more pronounced. She wore her favorite purple bandana with little white flowers. I joined them on the couch, followed by Ben, who crawled into my lap. This is how it is, I thought. I leaned on Zach's shoulder. We sit together on the couch in the middle of a December afternoon and watch a kids' movie while Elizabeth slowly fades away.

The day when I otherwise would have been taking my final exam for Introduction to Psychology, I sat with Elizabeth on the forest green couch in the living room. Behind us, a shrub-sized jade plant caught soft winter sunlight among its thick leaves. The room smelled of wood smoke and the heady needles of a fir Christmas tree, one of whose tips had reached beyond the high ceiling and been clipped off.

We sat side by side in silence, listening to the fire crackle, when she turned to me. Even the yellowing whites of her eyes didn't diminish the glow of her big brown irises.

"Am I going to be okay, Lyssa?"

I felt my heart catch. Sue had been reading her picture books about death, which she pushed away on the pages she didn't like. But maybe she still needed her death spelled out for her in non-storybook form. She was asking me for clarity. Confirmation, maybe, of what she already knew. I couldn't betray my emaciated six-year-old sister with a comforting lie. I couldn't say yes.

"I hope so, Elly."

I hope so, and I'm afraid you won't be.

Elizabeth moaned with understanding. She drooped heavy over my lap, and I rubbed her back as my eyes burned and we rocked in the lucid, painful truth, though it may have been more like shaking than rocking. Life and death were unfair. Things were not likely to turn out the way we hoped.

A week after Christmas and a decision needed to be made again. Elizabeth was still alive but still dying. Should I return to McGill for winter semester? If I went back, I'd be flying home soon for her funeral. If I stayed, months of grieving with nothing else to distract me. What would I even do at home when my new life was elsewhere? It felt unnatural to ask my brain to make a practical decision when my body already flooded with anticipatory grief.

A phone call with Daniel as I wavered. "I guess if I stay I won't have to deal with Montreal winter for another year."

"Yeah," he said. "It's really not that bad."

"Maybe not," I said. "But it wouldn't be the real reason anyway."

"I know."

No matter how many weeks of limbo, death comes as a shock. The finality of it. The vast silence and space left behind after Elizabeth vanished. And when the avalanche of grief toppled me, my decision was made. No way I could fly back to Montreal for winter semester without first having the time and space to regain my breath. My brain had no room for classes.

I held Ben on my hip when a pastor came to our house to talk to Dad and Sue about the funeral. The front door creaked open, shuddering at the swing that broke its peaceful silence.

"Hi, Ben!" the pastor said, giving a gentle shake to his dangling foot. He looked at her blankly. When she made eye contact with me, she paused.

"I'm Alyssa," I said.

Her eyes didn't register the name.

"Elizabeth's sister?"

The pastor's eyes grew wide, and she placed her hand over her heart. "Oh!" she said. "I didn't realize there were other children."

I needed the time that a semester off would allow, but Dad and Sue's grief filled the house with a heavy stillness. The emptiness of Elizabeth's room seeped out from under the threshold of her closed door. Mid-January, after the funeral, my presence at home became jarring to me. I had already left home for college, so how had I ended up back in my childhood?

If Elizabeth was no longer there, I didn't need to be either. I decided to hit the road. Both Mom and Dad murmured briefly about the safety of an eighteen-year-old traveling alone, but I insisted. At sixteen, I'd navigated public transit in France before I even spoke French, so I could definitely handle driving in my own country.

I planned my most quintessential road trip around youth hostel locations. In Klamath, California, I walked through redwood trees as big as houses, and when Highway 101 veered inland, I stayed right on Highway 1 to hug the sheer cliffs over the Pacific Ocean. I sat in an internet café in Santa Cruz and sipped a latte while I checked my email, gazing out the window at palm trees instead of living through my first

Montreal winter as expected. I stayed at a hot springs hostel in Truth or Consequences, New Mexico, where I ate gingery stew in the communal trailer with dusty twenty-somethings with whom I later soaked in a corrugated metal tub under a full moon. In Camp Verde, Arizona, I went to Montezuma Castle and gazed up at the cliff dwellings embedded into a limestone cavern, daydreaming about perfect tiny cozy living spaces. And I went for a short circular hike on a deserted trail through faded hieroglyphic rocks and found myself squatting in the red dust and clutching at my chest ripped apart by grief.

My back ached from long stretches in the car, and my joints stabbed when hikes went too long, but health was relative. I might have an extremely weird body, with wrinkles and scars and stub thumbs, but at least I was still alive. My floppiness wasn't as bad as cancer that killed a six-year-old. By comparison, I was healthy. I'd lived to adulthood. Might as well keep on living my life without dwelling on any genetic weirdness. I had no more faith in doctors anyway, useless as they seemed to be with illnesses both chronic and acute.

I carried grief with me back to Quebec but also relief. This time I'd start classes without having to worry about Elizabeth's health, without having to fly home early to watch her suffer. On the other side of the continent, my grief could evolve alongside my new life. Not long after I got back from the road trip, I escaped eastward, back to Montreal for what I expected to be for good.

CAULIFLOWER FRACTAL

I had another conversation with my mom about what happened after I got my clinical diagnosis of EDS at ten years old. She brought up the time she took me to the Vancouver Public Library to find information. "I just thought it was really important that you understood what was happening," she said.

I remembered the helpful librarian. The leafy logo of the JSTOR database. A heavy stack of medical articles spit out on a dot matrix printer, the pages perforated end to end. I'd understood the gist. Pictures of bodies bent in freakish ways. Statistics about life expectancy. Risks associated with childbirth. Stuff I couldn't fully process at ten. I understood those articles as proof that something disastrous would happen to me sooner or later.

"If you had known your type earlier, would you have done anything differently?" Mom asked.

I shrugged, not sure if she was trying to make light of the importance of genetic confirmation. Whatever my genetic type, I was glad I'd had the freedom to travel, pick up degrees across the continent, and spin myself into piles of overachieving fluff. Yes, I wanted to know my relative likelihood of dying young. But at the very least, having genetic confirmation would have saved me years of legwork as an adult, legwork that delayed the medical care I'd needed immediately. And I could have prevented so many tumbles down stairs if I'd started physical therapy as a child rather than a thirty-something. A big chunk of the pain I'd lived with every day had been preventable, and I wished the pattern of listening to my body's symptoms had been set early, that when my body wasn't well, I had known I could do more than suffer through it. "Be careful" from those geneticists was never meant to be the final word.

The most abundant protein in the human body is type I collagen. Its three-ply rods provide the structural support for both bones and soft tissues. Gram for gram, type I collagen has more tensile strength, the ability to stretch without breaking, than steel.

Stronger than *steel*.

But type I collagen doesn't function in isolation; type V collagen tells it what to do, how to form into those stronger-than-steel rods.

Twenty-five years after my first diagnosis of EDS, I got my genetic test results. I had a missense substitution in type V collagen, the regulator of fibril diameter and structure, an adenine (A) where a guanine (G) was supposed to be. An A for a G, and again and again and again at every scale throughout the body.

I had classical, not vascular, EDS.

A heavy sigh of relief.

More specifically, my mutation regulated how collagen fibrils align side by side. Healthy collagen fibrils are made up of striated connections, staggered like stairs, but my regulatory type V collagen ordered type I collagen to fold into other types of three-dimensional structures. Instead of orderly stacking, it advised them toward knots and chaos. Even my little regulator collagens had issues with stairs.

Under the microscope, I'm a special kind of fractal. My skin looks like cauliflower, loosely packed fibrils that look smoother the more you zoom out. They're basically unaligned, like wool that's been spun without first being carded. At the microscopic level, I just look like I could use a comb.

Even though I didn't have vascular EDS, my genetic mutation still put me at some risk of arterial dissection. But with a rare mutation of a rare disorder, the statistics weren't clear. It's difficult to get a representative sample of people with just my type of floppy, but just because a pattern isn't fully understood doesn't mean it isn't there.

I let my parents know about the test results, but my having the genetic marker for classical EDS just confirmed what they already thought they knew. More importantly, shouldering my way back into the medical system had changed my relationship with myself. To find the information

I needed, I'd had to keep digging. I'd had to fight for myself and put in the time.

I talked about this during the phone sessions I still had with Sharyn, my therapist all the way across the continent in Montreal. My internal monologue had changed since my divorce. I no longer second guessed my symptoms as imaginary. I listened to my sensitivities as if they had something important to say. I didn't dismiss the necessary attention to a living—and genetically floppy—body as high maintenance. And if I didn't always do perfect job of said maintenance, I let myself off the hook for that too. Perfection was an illusion, the stress of which I wanted nothing to do with.

Pimm splayed across my lap as I scratched one side of her head, then the other. Her deep purr vibrated us both. "Sometimes," I said to Sharyn as I watched spittle of happiness bead around Pimm's jaw, "I even talk to myself like I'm talking to Pimm."

It had become clear to me that the process of seeing a geneticist had three distinct steps. Step one: the clinical exam. Step two: the blood work. Step three: the relay of taking your genetic confirmation out into the world of specialists. Step three is the point. Step three is where I would find treatment and prevention.

Treatment for aortic dissection is mostly preventative, and now that I had my genetic test results, I had easier access to that prevention. I needed regular echocardiograms to monitor my heart valves; I needed to keep my POTS and MCAS in check; I needed to avoid stress.

Avoid stress. The adult equivalent of "be careful, Alyssa."

So maybe I didn't have the kind of physical strength that made carrying boxes of books down a flight of stairs a great idea. But I was getting better at knowing how to function within the unexpected architecture of my body. I paid close attention to when I started to unravel or spin, to when I tried to force a head of tangled cauliflower to act like a rod of steel.

My strength would come from listening to my physical limitations, the patterns threaded throughout my own body, as if my life depended on it.

Which it did.

There's no such thing as being too sensitive. I could work within any design constraints, as long as I knew what they were.

BEACHCOMBER

I thought it would be easy, walking with a cane. Give me a third leg for balance and watch me never fall again. But the ease wasn't automatic, especially since I didn't want to leave my living room until I could run my new gait without missteps. Five steps across the room and five steps back. I tripped over the area rug and I tripped over Pimm until I was ready to take my third leg to the beach for a practice walk. Sand is much more forgiving of falls than pavement.

I drove the hour down Highway 101 to Manzanita's seven-mile beach, arriving to an expansive low tide that would give me plenty of space to set my new rhythm. I wove through dune grasses to emerge on the hot sand that massaged my feet with every step. When I reached the flat packed sand, I turned right toward Neahkahnie Mountain to walk parallel to the waves, midway between pavement and surf.

I imagined myself an avoidant little hermit crab, scuttling one direction, then another, to keep as much distance as possible between me and the other people who filled the beach. From a distance, I'd be unrecognizable to anyone I used to know when I lived here. Gaits are unique as fingerprints, and I now left different tracks in the sand. My footprints used to point in instead of out. I used to twist my hips with each step so my feet landed in a straight line as if I were on a balance beam. Now they fell from side to side on parallel tracks. Less twisting. Better balance. Not to mention the cane divots. If my improved proprioceptive balance obscured my gait identity, then adding the cane was like burning my fingertips on a car cigarette lighter to avoid police identification. Another layer of incognito.

I relaxed into my disguise, pulling into myself to focus on setting a new rhythm. But I kept getting distracted. I kept trying, and failing, to anticipate the trajectory of a man in the distance with two small dogs.

The three of them engaged in an elaborate game of hopscotch, zig-zagging back and forth at random. As soon as I shifted my angle, they shifted too. I jabbed my cane more forcefully into the sand, deepening the divots that looked like air holes for gigantic razor clams just beneath the surface.

My avoidance strategy wasn't working.

I not only had to avoid the zig-zagging man and his dogs but also shake my followers. Just behind me, three gray-haired straight couples walked in a line, advancing like Columbia Sportswear-clad riot police out of the corner of my eye. Only instead of stoic, polycarbonate-shielded silence, their laughs hit my ears as squeals and barks that grated up the back of my neck, like the sound of a plastic box of pins spilling all over a hardwood floor.

I was learning to walk! I needed to concentrate. I counted my breaths, four seconds in and six seconds out, to summon homecoming to my body. The smattering of dead moon jellyfish quivered lifeless, stripped of their flowing tendrils. I stopped walking and paused my counting to let the row of barking tourists pass me, poking bull kelp with my cane as I waited.

Did it work better to swing my cane in my right hand or my left? The right, opposite my bad hip. A crow paced me for a while, warning me not to disturb her friend that pecked around an abandoned fire pit a few yards off.

"Are you keeping an eye on my old apartment for me?" I asked.

Caw, caw.

I walked toward a large flock of seagulls who squawked away, leaving the sand spotted with white dots. For a moment, I thought they'd gathered amongst a hoard of perfect baby sand dollars, and I almost bent to retrieve one. But no. Round shit circles, not sand dollars.

The erratic man with the little dogs approached, avoiding eye contact. His dogs ran ahead of him to dance around my feet, half-excited as if they wanted to warn me about something, and half-hesitant as if they saw my cane's weapon potential.

"Yip, yip!" Their paws and tiny black noses sparkled with sand.

The wind blew biting sand at my ankles and soon I reached one of the seasonal freshwater streams that fanned out like a fractal as it meandered

ward the ocean. It looked like a miniature river or a subsection of the
man circulatory system, with half-submerged sand islands tapered at
her end, shapeshifter stepping stones. My cane also worked as a depth-
ter. I took a moment to consider my crossing strategy, then rolled up my
ns to keep them dry, exposing the scars on my shins I didn't like anyone
see.

Forget about the people, Alyssa.

splashed into the shallow freshwater veins.

I leapfrogged from island to island with more lightness than I would
have risked without the cane for balance, and halfway across I paused to
sink my feet into the sand and let the cold water rise to thrill my ankles.
By the time my rolled hems soaked through, I no longer cared about
getting wet.

And then, in the middle of that freshwater stream, taking a pause after
hopping from sand bar to sand bar, I realized how I might look to someone in the distance, someone trying their best to avoid other people at all
costs. Who's the person with the third leg and no discernible trajectory,
clawing back and forth at random?

Too difficult to predict where she'll scuttle to next.

Avoidance impossible.

I laughed at myself, something between a squeal and a bark, for acting
exactly like the erratic man and his two small dogs. The sound of my
voice might have been insufferable to anyone within hearing distance
lost in their own thoughts, but who cared? I exaggerated a couple of
splashes just for the sake of taking up space. Let them hear me laughing
to myself and see my erratic hopping and think whatever they wanted.
Maybe I was only irritated by people to the degree that I hid from them.
I had just as much right to flail around as the rest of them.

I looked up from my splashing at the forested Neahkahnie Mountain.
It's part of Oswald West State Park now, but two hundred years ago the
mountain had been cleared for pasture and dotted with sheep. I no longer had sheep-farming daydreams about carding and spinning and felt-
ing wool from my own flock. Breathtaking how landscapes can change.
Despite a clear-cut, Neahkahnie's lush forest had grown back.

After I'd had my fill of splashing, I turned ninety degrees and walked
to the edge of the surf to let my toes and shins say a full freezing hello

to the Pacific. I walked across wet sand crisscrossed with meandering lines carved by ghost shrimp, and I stepped through stretches of shallow pools shaped like human vertebrae gone askew. A line of navy blue ocean stopped the sky on the horizon. I looked down at my faded scars that tingled loudly in response to the ocean breeze, and I felt more kindness for my body's trajectories than shame. Yes, I was at perennial risk of falling, but it wasn't end of the world.

The strong relief at finally having an answer to my genetics question floated me above the waves.

As I started back toward the dunes, stepping backward with my eyes still on the horizon and my cane plugging the sand, I crossed a real smattering of whole, unbroken sand dollars. The minus tide undertow had eased up enough to leave them there, ocean-washed and sun-bleached. I picked one up and rubbed off the wet sand, considering whether to gather the whole constellation. Maybe I could line them up on a windowsill and never feel like the world lacked meaning again. But I only pocketed a few of the right size and symmetry for the day. I didn't want to use up their magic by hoarding them.

My legs wanted to carry me back up the familiar secret forest trail, lined with salal and blackberries and chanterelles, to my old cedar-infused above-garage apartment where I'd watched the talkative crows rustle the hemlocks. Instead, I corrected course and walked my three-legged gait back to my car. I drove north with sandy toes, the highway hugging the coastline through towering evergreens, gnarled pines, and peeks at the sparkling ocean. I'd taken the space I needed to find my balance.

When I got back to my little house in Astoria, I wiped my feet on the woven welcome mat, and my cat greeted me with chirps and whirs of complaint about her hours-long abandonment. She flopped belly-up at my feet.

Don't worry, Pimm Pimmity.

I am home.

AFTERWORD

I'd always thought it would be my heart that exploded, an aortic dissection that left a very slim chance of survival even if I rushed myself to the emergency room without hesitation. But in summer 2020, three years after this book's last scene and a few months into the COVID-19 pandemic, my head exploded instead.

I was thirty-eight when my left intracranial vertebral artery dissected. A layer in the artery wall tore open, and blood rushed in between the layers, where it got trapped and inflated the artery like a balloon. This blocked blood flow to my brain and caused a series of ischemic strokes. Each time, it felt like an invisible force on my left pulled my head to the ground. As that first week went on, my blood balloon inflated and deflated according to its own logic, exacerbated by me sitting or standing instead of lying down. Each time it inflated, it re-blocked blood flow to trigger another stroke and seizure-like jerking.

I would like to say that the second I felt the most intense thunderclap of head pain in my life, I rushed to the hospital. I would like to say that I had unlearned all the cultural conditioning that would make me second guess the severity of my symptoms even as I lay seizing on the floor. But I hadn't. I spent an entire week throwing up from pain and with periodic paralysis, thinking I was just having a really bad migraine, one that got worse as the week went on.

It wasn't until after my partner—who had been away—witnessed me having an episode in which I slumped right off a park bench and onto the dirt that we went to the hospital. There I spent three days immobilized in the ICU, unable to move without triggering another episode. When I was released, stabilized but far from recovered, they gave me blood thinners to prevent a blood clot and told me not to sit up, work, or move my neck. Healing crept along for over a year.

I was very lucky to be alive.

In the years before the dissection of my left vertebral artery, I'd found a dream EDS specialist, a naturopathic doctor in a pain management clinic who not only knew way more than I did but also cared about putting together the pieces of my complex symptoms. She helped tremendously in decreasing my chronic pain and increasing my energy. I still worked from home with my feet up, but the relief of finally finding a doctor who could help with the big picture was immense.

Help was out there, even for me.

Immediately after the dissection, she ordered more genetic testing. "When they tested you in Seattle," she said, "they only tested for three specific genes, and I think we need to run the full panel for connective tissue disorders. You're at higher risk of dissection with classical EDS, but it's not common. We need to make sure there's not something else going on as well."

Only a few weeks later, we had our answer. In addition to classical EDS, I had a variant of the *FBN1* gene. Marfan syndrome. The syndrome that ran on my mom's side of the family. The syndrome associated with tall, thin bodies and high risk of aortic dissection. An *FBN1* mutation disrupts fibrillin, a glycoprotein that makes up the structural scaffolding of connective tissue. This mutation weakens medium and large arteries, and it also causes joint pain and chronic fatigue, but its biggest risk—like with vascular EDS (the type I'd been relieved to learn I did not have)—is spontaneous aortic or neurovascular dissection. Explosions of the head and heart.

"But I saw the Marfan expert!" I said to the best doctor I'd ever had. Everyone on my mom's side of the family who was tall and thin had also seen this same expert. How could I have put in all of those years and thousands of dollars to reconstruct the missing legwork of my childhood and still not have gotten all the answers I needed? "Is it because I'm not tall and thin that everyone assumed I didn't have it?"

My best doctor paused before answering. "It shows a real lack of . . . curiosity."

My medical history tangled like a riddle in my vertiginous and slowly regenerating brain. They are differential diagnoses, EDS and Marfan syndrome, one or the other. Not both. Usually. How many geneticists does a young woman with a connective tissue disorder have to see before earning the test to rule out the rare condition that runs in her very own family?

"I'll be honest," she continued, "you're up against some extremely shitty genetics. Like, some of the worst I've ever seen. The chances that you have mutations in both the *COL5A2* and *FBN1* genes . . . well, you're probably the only one in the US."

Did a doctor really just tell me I had extremely shitty genetics? I liked her even more for her honesty, despite this not being great news for my longevity.

After my head exploded, I spent days watching—and delighting in—the summer sunlight as it shifted along my bedroom walls, surprised at my peaceful mindset when I couldn't even make it the ten steps to the bathroom without falling over from vertigo. So yes, I have joy and gratitude for my life. I'm grateful that my head is knitting itself back together, for a loving partner in a little house in a rainy town near the ocean, for an abundance of pens. But I can't bring myself to preach toxic positivity or joy-taking in the little things. We cannot joy and gratitude our way back to health or access. I think the more important question is, where do we find our resilience?

The disabled and chronically ill have a resilience advantage in that we have always had to develop self-awareness and creativity. When systems are not built for us, creative problem solving becomes necessary for staying alive. No one is going to figure it out for us. We must be continually aware of our essential physical needs, then build worlds around us that meet those needs. That adaptability we develop for survival builds our resilience from day one. But also, the creativity we develop for survival helps us to navigate our unique paths toward meaning in our lives. And it's that meaning, whether a sense of purpose or alignment with something that we love, that grows a resilience so strong it can handle the weight of anything.

We need to focus on the big things, not the little things.

So being told to build resilience by focusing on the little things feels like wearing a wrist brace to keep my ankle from dislocating. It won't actually support me when I need it. Sometimes I even feel like it's a ploy to keep me small. Just because a person lives with a chronic illness or disability doesn't mean they have to live a small life in which their only possible joy is watching a zippy sunset. I don't have access to joy in the little things unless I'm already channeling my energy into something larger than myself. Once we align with self-defined meaning, the whole world becomes precious, even an idiosyncratic body with an absurd number of health challenges. We necessarily become more resilient; joy and gratitude flow naturally. When we know what we're living for, the motivation to bounce back is built into our very fibers.

However, what we really need are systems that don't require us to be resilient at all. Before the pandemic, many disabled people (whether disabled by a chronic illness or not), were already in quarantine-like isolation. But imagine a COVID-19 quarantine without regular Zoom social events, when everyone besides you is going about their non-homebound lives. Imagine a quarantine without access to virtual doctor appointments, where you are required to put your health at risk to get medical care, even if your biggest risk isn't viral but the loss of a full week's energy from traveling to a long-distance specialist. Imagine having few pick-up and delivery options from local stores, and definitely no preset shopping hours for vulnerable populations. And imagine a quarantine in which it is rare to be allowed to work from home, unless of course you choose to become your own boss and take on a freelance career with variable income, no benefits, and a never-ending hustle.

According to the CDC, in 2018, 26 percent of the US population had some type of functional disability. That's one-quarter of the US population living at least some aspect of the life I just described, including myself. But before the pandemic, people just told me I was lucky for getting to stay home so much.

There are more ways to think about disability than something that happens to individuals, who are then fixed (or not) by the medical system. Social and political models of disability define a body as disabled when societal barriers prohibit that body from accessing what it needs. A lack of ramps is what defines a disability, for example, rather than that a person uses a wheelchair. During the pandemic, because able-bodied people needed a platter of accommodations all at once (virtual social events, curbside pick-up, virtual medical appointments, the option to work from home), the disabled got them too. In other words, during the pandemic, much of that 26 percent of the population—those that had been previously disabled by lack of access—became able-bodied.

Homebound and horizontal, I was less isolated while recovering from a brain injury than I had been before the pandemic, when I'd only had my humdrum daily limitations. Collectively, many of us in that 26 percent spent 2021 holding our breaths. Will these accommodations be taken away once able-bodied people no longer need them? Even after the speed and ease with which we saw them implemented, do we matter enough to keep them in place?

Ten to thirty percent of the approximate thirty million people who have tested positive for COVID-19 in the US also experience long COVID symptoms similar to dysautonomia—dysregulation of the autonomic nervous system—and those symptoms look somewhat like a cross between POTS and ME/CFS. Until now, it has been easy for primary care physicians to dismiss chronic conditions—including EDS—as stemming from neurotic anxiety. Specialists (if you could find one) were out there, but it had not yet been a requirement of primary care physicians everywhere to accept these conditions as real and worthy of treatment. Long COVID patients, on the other hand, are part of a cohort that shoves the myth of individuality out the window. You can't blame this illness on individuals when it's clearly a societal issue. And if long COVID is real, then maybe what patients say about other chronic conditions is true too.

So the hope and opportunity—for people who had chronic illnesses before this pandemic, for people who survived COVID-19 only to be left with long COVID, and for people who are currently healthy but will someday become sick or disabled (read: everyone)—is that the research and knowledge about long COVID will be bidirectional with all of these other chronic conditions. Perhaps even general practitioners will learn to tell one from the others. To do so, they will have to see the reality of systemic illnesses, and we can all hope that universal acceptance and better treatment will come out of that capacity.

So you could be up against obliviousness or denial or blame from yourself or your family or your world. You could be up against misogyny or racism or fat phobia in the exam room. You could be up against deep, underlying ableism everywhere you go. But whether activities of daily life dislocate you into a human pretzel, you can't stand up without a spin that falls you back down, or your arteries threaten to explode, hold tight to your tangled body. Awareness around connective tissue disorders and chronic illnesses—with all of their variations and comorbidities—has increased and will continue to increase. It's worth it to keep looking until you find the answers you need. Practitioners with both expertise and curiosity are out there.

—August 2021

ACKNOWLEDGMENTS

I am elated to be part of such a vibrant literary community. First off, thank you to Kate Gale and Tobi Harper for their editorial enthusiasm, as well as the rest of the skilled crew at Red Hen Press, including Mark E. Cull, Natasha McClellan, Rebeccah Sanhueza, and Monica Fernandez.

Heartfelt thanks to my editor Ariel Gore for her badass feedback that helped me to refine an early version of this manuscript into its current shape. I also couldn't have done it without support, feedback, and encouragement from the amazing writing community that congregates in the Literary Kitchen, including but not limited to Ana June, Dot Hearn, Meg Weber, Barbara Robidoux, Nicole Phoenix, Emily Skelding, Nina Packebush, China Martens, Sara Schultz, Rebecca Dunn-Krahn, Susan Koenig, Ky Delaney, Abby Braithwaite, Karin Spirn, and Naomi Luce.

Thank you to Jenny Forrester of *Mountain Bluebird Magazine* for her relentless support, and for facilitating Zoom readings and study halls that kept us connected all throughout the pandemic.

A special thank you to Megan Moodie-Brasoveanu, Alyssa Alarcón Santo, Rebecca Fish Ewan, Laraine Herring, and Chloé Bedmonk for knowing what it is to be sick and to write about it.

Love and thanks to those close to me who provided beta reads and/or much-needed encouragement along the way: Lindsay Hobbs, Jason McDevitt, Jennifer Macdonald, Naomi Balla-Boudreau, Beth Gomez, Karyn Robertson, Rhonda Alderman, Vanessa Mortinson, and Rachel Nelson.

Thank you to Missy Ladygo and Kacy McKinney not only for their creative support but also for lingering bedside after my head exploded. And to Sharyn Hedbloom, Jill Mulholland, Becky Tonkin, Kaisa Saavalainen, and Suzanne Myers Harold for providing food and other necessities from the outside world during my long recovery.

An immense thank you to the writers and cartoonists whose workshops throughout this process sustained my creative momentum and connected me to so many people I am grateful to know: Michelle Tea's Magical Writing workshop at the Corporeal Center, Lynda Barry's Writing the Unthinkable tour, Martha Grover and July Westhale's at the Sou'wester Lodge, Kane Lynch at the Independent Publishing Resource Center, and Tillie Walden at the Center for Cartoon Studies.

For local, on-the-ground support, thank you to Dinah Urell of *Hipfish Monthly*, Ryan Hume of *Rain Magazine*, Marianne Monson of the Astoria Writer's Guild, and the late writing group Write Astoria, including Kate Deeks, Ann Ornie, Angela Stephen, Abby Card, and Diana Kirk.

Thank you to my family, including my two brothers, for their continual support.

Last but not least, a huge loop of gratitude to Melinda Nickels for always being willing to act as my sounding board and for her unwavering belief in my creative work. And for doing all the grocery shopping.

BIOGRAPHICAL NOTE

Alyssa Graybeal is a queer writer and cartoonist whose work focuses on the emotional landscape of living with chronic illness and disability, in particular the connective tissue disorder Ehlers-Danlos syndrome. *Floppy: Tales of a Genetic Freak of Nature at the End of the World* is her first memoir, and it won the 2020 Red Hen Press Nonfiction Book Award. She has a BA from McGill University and an MLIS from Dalhousie University, and she works as an editor and writing coach. You can find her online at www.alyssagraybeal.com. She lives in Astoria, Oregon.